T.

After spending ten y̲ ̲ ̲ ̲ ̲ ̲ ̲ ̲ ̲ ̲ ̲ ̲ ̲ ,000 interviews and collecting no less than 4,000 literary quotations, sociologist John Alan Lee has come to some fascinating conclusions on the subject of love.

He likens lovestyles to colours – there are the primaries and the secondaries. Through his research he has discovered that many people mix or combine the basic tendencies in a whole variety of lovestyles. And the more recurring patterns he discovered, the more he began to see just how and why some lovestyles simply do not mix.

The most important thing is to find out which is *your* favourite lovestyle. To help you decide, the author has provided two highly revealing tests that you can answer yourself – and then get your partner (or partners!) to fill in. The results of these, together with the descriptions, chapter by chapter, of the whole 'spectrum' of lovestyles, should give you more than enough to map out your path in love.

John Alan Lee

LOVESTYLES

First published in Canada by New Press 1973
under the title
Colours of Love: An Exploration of the Ways of Loving

First published in Great Britain by J. M. Dent & Sons Ltd
in a substantially revised and amended edition 1976
ABACUS edition published in 1978
by Sphere Books Ltd
Copyright © John Alan Lee 1973, 1976

Set in Intertype Times

*Printed in Great Britain by Cox & Wyman Ltd
London, Reading and Fakenham*

Acknowledgments

So many people have been involved in the ten years of study leading to the theory of lovestyles that I can mention only a few, and must hope that the rest will know that I am no less grateful to them. Professor Zevedai Barbu of the University of Sussex was my mentor and friend throughout the early years of work. Professor Fernando Henriques, Roy Bowles, Alistair Chalmers and Ralph Beals provided valuable assistance. I am grateful to Professors S. D. Clark and Bernard Blishen for their support, and to the Canada Council for financing the initial research.

The Canadian edition involved many valued helpers: Raymond Norman, Roy Macskimming, Ruth Brouwer and Peter Maher – to name only a few. I am also indebted to Carol Tavris at *Psychology Today*, and especially to Michael Werthman, who helped me to revise an academic work into a popular idiom.

Finally, I cherish and appreciate those experiences of love revealed to me by many anonymous respondents, and – most of all – the revelations to those dear ones who have undertaken the difficult task of loving me!

J.A.L.

to my beloved children, Ruth and Peter

Contents

1 Looking at Lovestyles   9

2 Eros – Love of Ideal Beauty   22

3 Ludus – Love as a Game   46

4 Storge – Love as Friendship   69

5 The Love-Spectrum   82

6 Mania – Obsessive Love   86

7 Ludic Eros – Pluralistic Love   107

8 Pragma and Storgic Ludus – Realistic Love   125

9 Agape and Storgic Eros – Dutiful Love   141

10 The 'Tertiary' Lovestyles   154

11 Which is Your Favourite Lovestyle?   166

12 Mixing and Matching Lovestyles   194

13 The 'Love-Story' Influence   214

14 Loving and Living   239

    Appendix   244

    Bibliography   273

One

Looking at Lovestyles

Tell me who you love and I will tell you who you are, and more especially, who you want to be.

Theodor Reik

If you have ever loved, been loved, or wanted to be in love, you have had to face a frustrating fact: different people can mean quite different things by that deceptively simple phrase 'I love you'. Most people avoid saying these words until they think they are sure of their feelings and ready to commit themselves. But when they are spoken what do they mean?

Does truly loving someone mean being faithful to that person alone? Is a true lover a jealous lover? Should you expect your partner to be loving, even when he or she doesn't feel like it? Or would you prefer honesty to kindness in love?

The lover facing questions like these won't get much help from the experts. They've always disagreed about the nature of love. For instance, which expert would you agree with, in each of the following pairs of contradictory statements?

1a The lover who is not jealous is not a true lover. (Capellanus)
 b Jealousy is not a barometer by which depth of love can be read; it merely records the degree of the lover's insecurity. (Margaret Mead)
2a It is good to love in moderate degree but foolish to love to distraction. (Plautus)
 b When one does not love too much, one does not love enough. (Pascal)
3a True love ripens slowly out of friendship; it does not happen suddenly or dramatically. (Proudhon)
 b It is wrong to think that love comes from long companionship. Love is the offspring of spiritual affinity, and unless that affinity is created in a moment, it will

not be created in years or even generations. (Kahlil Gibran)

Perhaps you don't agree with either expert in some cases. On the question of jealousy, for example, you might believe that every normal person feels jealous sometimes, but that a mature lover learns how to control jealousy and not be overly possessive. After all, these six opinions take into account only three factors involved in defining love: jealousy, intensity of feeling and the time it takes for love to develop. There are many other aspects to consider: honesty, fidelity, compatibility, equality of the two sexes in love, homosexual love, unrequited love – to mention only a few. When we see the conflicts between various experts in their statements about each of these aspects of love, we begin to wonder if they are talking about the same thing.

Some authors have attempted to resolve these conflicts by defining several different kinds of love. Four kinds seems to be the favourite choice, but unfortunately no two authors seem to come up with the same four! In 1621 Robert Burton, one of the first authors since ancient times to analyse love systematically, indicated four kinds: animal attraction, attraction to beauty, rational love and compassion. Stendhal's list in 1820 overlaps Burton's by including sensual attraction and sympathy, but suggests passion and gallantry as the other two. The familiar twentieth-century analysis by C. S. Lewis in *The Four Loves* includes Burton's attraction to beauty and compassion (labelled eros and agape by Lewis) but suggests affection and friendship as the other two kinds. In his recent *Love and Will*, Rollo May also agrees there are 'four kinds of love in Western tradition' but alas, his list varies again: lust, eros, friendship and charity.

Most of the authors who have identified several different kinds of love are not far removed from those who argue that there is only one kind of love, because in their schemes there is always one kind which is superior to the others. C. S. Lewis, for example, prefers charity, and considers that his other three loves are *really* love only to the extent that they resemble charity.

Of course many authors have recognised different kinds of love in terms of the *object* of loving – love of children, love of God, love of a pet, and so forth. We are not concerned with this distinction. This book deals only with the adult intimate relationship we usually associate with marriage, or with such phrases as 'romance' or 'falling in love', or 'a love affair'. I call this 'affiliative love' to distinguish it from love of God or kin or other things, but most of the time the term 'affiliative' will be assumed, and I will refer simply to love.

Part of our problem in identifying different kinds of love is that our language contains only one word for love. Terms such as affection, fondness, passion and desire are not the same as love, but part of the way love is expressed. Because there is only one word for love, we tend to think of love as having only one true or real nature.

The ancient Greeks and Romans took a more pluralistic view of love. Their languages contained several terms for different loves which were equally valid, just as their temples contained altars to a variety of equally important gods. Individuals were free to choose their favourite god and their favourite kind of loving. This tolerance was destroyed by early Christianity, which insisted on one true God and one true definition of love.

Modern society is now recovering the permissive tolerance and pluralism of ancient Rome, though of course not everyone approves. We are prepared to accept each individual's right to his own religion. Indeed, modern pluralism has gone far beyond religion, to include politics, the arts, different systems of education, and (in principle at least) equality of all races and of both sexes. But we still have a problem accepting the right of individuals to hold different definitions of love.

We think our own idea of love is the real thing, and disparage other notions by calling them 'infatuation', 'only an affair', or 'just a sexual thing'. Consider the problem of John and Mary, who have recently fallen in love. (Of course we could as readily discuss John and James or Mary and Jane, for what I have to say about different kinds of loving applies as much to homosexual as to heterosexual love.)

Scene One
John: I saw you talking to Tom, the guy you used to go out with. Are you still in love with him?

11

Mary: Yes, I suppose I am, but I think I love you more than him.

John: Well you'd better make up your mind. You can't have both of us. I won't have you cheating on me.

Mary: It's not cheating, John. I feel differently about you than I do about Tom, but I love you both.

John: I don't see what you mean. Maybe you still like Tom but how can you really love me if you love him too?

Scene Two (some weeks later)

Mary: By the way, I've stopped seeing Tom. You were right. I love you a lot more than him.

John: I'm awfully glad to hear you say that, Mary, but did you ever really love him? Wasn't it just an infatuation?

Mary: Oh no, it was love all right, but different from my love for you. More . . . well . . . more physical.

John: You mean it was just a sexual thing then, not really love?

Mary: Oh it was love all right. He still turns me on when we meet in the street – but we don't go out any more.

John: I don't think you really love me yet, Mary.

Scene Three (a few weeks later)

John: Do you really love me, Mary?

Mary: Yes, I've never loved anyone the way I love you.

John: What about Tom then?

Mary: Oh that wasn't true love. You were right. Now I know what true love is. Tom was just a mistake. I thought I loved him.

John: I'm awfully glad. We're going to be very happy together.

Mary's instincts told her there are different but equally valid kinds of love, but she found no adequate way of expressing this idea. She didn't have different *names* for these kinds of love, so eventually she gave in to John's insistence that her other experience was not really love at all. Even if we restore some Greek and Latin names for love, it won't help those in Mary's predicament unless we have an effective method for identifying the various ways of loving. How do we develop such a method?

In the past, authors writing about love have usually gathered ideas from previous authors and combined them with insights from their own personal experiences. There is nothing wrong with studying love in this way, and the results have often been useful. The insights of Stendhal, for

12

example, and of the modern Spanish philosopher Ortega y Gasset, have contributed to contemporary theories of love. The works of Gustave Flaubert, Somerset Maugham, D. H. Lawrence and even Erich Segal have each found audiences who recognise their own experiences and could agree 'love *is* like that'.

The difficulty is that the kinds of love these authors describe can be starkly different. It isn't just a case of blind men grabbing hold of different parts of the same elephant; there are systematic differences which should enable us to distinguish several separate *species* of love.

Another method of describing love is that of the psychologist or marriage counsellor, who relies on case histories to construct a theory of love. Again the result can be useful, as in the case of Erich Fromm's *Art of Loving*. But isn't the sample rather biased? How many happy, lazy, or pedestrian love affairs come to the attention of the therapist?

Occasionally sociologists have studied the problem of love, though less than one might expect, considering the importance of love to many people. A few theories have emerged, such as Robert Winch's theory of complementary needs. But almost every sociological study begins with a definition of love which automatically excludes large portions of human experience. The most flagrant examples are those which define love as an attraction between opposite sexes – as if homosexuals could never love. Others exclude what the author chooses to label 'infatuation'. Still others develop two definitions of love, one called 'romantic' and the other 'realistic', and there is never any doubt which one the author considers real and which one counterfeit.

I have tried, in contrast, to take a more comprehensive approach, and have included in my analysis any intimate adult affiliation which was *believed* to be an experience of love – whether it was heterosexual or homosexual, short-lived or lasting, happy or unhappy, 'normal' or tinged with sado-masochism. There must be accounting of all such human experience in an adequate theory of loving.

This approach will necessarily cause the reader to react to some of the experiences I discuss with the feeling 'That's not really love!' Yet someone else believed it was. What I propose to demonstrate is that affiliative love can be divided into different species, each of which has as much right to be called love as red, blue and yellow are equally colours. Everyone has his favourite colour, but this does not make it better, or more truly a colour, than the others.

How many kinds of love are there? As with colour, this is entirely a matter of useful distinction. For most of us it is sufficient to distinguish, for example, brown from green or yellow; but the artist or decorator must be more precise. 'Shades of brown' is not accurate enough as a way of describing sepia, auburn or umber. Of course, there is an astronomical number of possible distinctions between ideas of love. Suppose, for example, that you and a friend each indicated your preferences among the three pairs of opinions on page 1. You may have selected 1a, 2b and 3b, while your friend chose 1b, 2b and 3a. These are already two different ways of thinking about love, and only three aspects have been considered. The number of possible combinations of just these three pairs is eight. Clearly, then, my first problem in studying love was to develop a method that would organise the thousands of conflicting definitions into a few distinctive types.

I began sorting ideas about love into types by collecting over 4,000 statements from the fictional and non-fictional literature of love, including Plato and the Bible, Doris Lessing and D. H. Lawrence, romantic Lord Byron and cynical La Rochefoucauld. All of the statements were then cross-classified according to such topics as jealousy, altruism and physical beauty.

Some common themes began to emerge. Some authors, such as St Paul and the American psychoanalyst Erich Fromm, spoke of love as a universal altruistic quality rather than as an attraction to one person. Certain ideas seemed to accompany this theme, such as the notion that love is not demanding or jealous. Another theme was quite different. It included ideas from Capellanus and Stendhal, of a love that is jealous, possessive and attracted to a single person.

By weeding out duplications I was able to boil down the thousands of statements to just over one hundred. With the help of professional friends in literature, sociology, psychology and philosophy, the statements were eventually reduced to only thirty, which described six basic themes or kinds of loving. I devised a questionnaire from these thirty statements, to see which kinds of love people agreed with most.

This didn't work very well at all. People agreed with some quite contradictory notions about love. For example, the same individual might argue both that a shipboard romance was possible – in which two people truly love each other for a few days, yet never meet again – *and* that the only way to know whether love is real, is the test of a long period of time! Some people explained these apparent contradictions by suggesting that 'it depends on which kind of love you're talking about'. When asked to define different kinds, however, they were at a loss. There aren't even names for these different kinds, yet many people instinctively realise that they exist.

To identify the different kinds of love, it was necessary to get behind people's general opinions and sort out the specific aspects of their actual love experiences. This required a refinement of my testing procedures. I also wanted to avoid relying on the most easily accessible and therefore most overused subjects of previous studies of love: the college student and the therapist's client. So I constructed an interview method in which a complete stranger recruited on the street could tell me, in an organised and pre-coded way, what happened when he or she was in a relationship defined as love.

The new test covers a wide range of events in the person's life and the various steps in the love relationship. Questions begin with recollections of childhood, and move to feelings about work, close friends, self-esteem and life in general at the start of the love affair. They probe one's expectations of love, the ideal sought for, if any, and how the partner was met. The person being tested reports his or her thoughts and behaviour while away from the beloved, the nature and timing of their sexual intimacy, experiences of jealousy, and the number and nature of arguments. There is room for variations such as breakups and reunions, love triangles, homosexual love, serial love affairs, simultaneous involvements, and so on. The result is that all sorts of people, with widely varying experiences in life and love, can generate a coherent picture of their distinctive styles of loving.

This is, of course, a very brief summary of my methods in studying love. In the Appendix, the interested reader will find a detailed report of my procedures, the characteristics of the people tested, and an account of the techniques used in processing the data. Most readers, however, will be more immediately concerned with the results of my research: what kinds of love did I find?

Three really basic kinds of love emerged, each of which is quite different from the other two. All other kinds of loving seem to be variations on these three themes. It was at this point that I noticed a striking similarity between love and colour. There are only three basic hues: red, yellow and blue. All other hues can be produced by varying combinations of these three 'primary' colours. So I called the three basic kinds of love 'primary loves'. The combinations became 'secondary loves', just as orange and green are secondary colours. There are even some tertiary loves, like the tertiary colour, brown.

In love as in colour, 'secondary' does not mean inferior; it simply refers to basic structure. Just as orange is no less a colour than red, and no less worthy, so there is no one true love among my types. Nowhere in this book do I define love itself. Countless authors have failed in their efforts to provide an adequate definition of love, because, like colour, it can only be understood by an awareness of its various kinds.

The basic kinds of loving are called *lovestyles*. There are three primary lovestyles: *eros*, *ludus* and *storge*. The most important secondary lovestyles are *mania*, *pragma*, *agape* and *ludic eros*. Each of these lovestyles is discussed in detail in the following chapters. We shall also discuss some other common lovestyles, such as *storgic ludus, storgic eros* and *manic eros*. Simply to introduce the new names, here is a brief description of the common lovestyles:

EROS

This is the ancient Greek term for a love fascinated by ideal images of beauty. This lovestyle is the search for the one perfect beloved.

LUDUS

This is the Latin word for play or game. It was first used by the Roman poet Ovid in the year AD 1 to describe a love that would rather be playful than serious. Any number can play.

STORGE (STOR-GAY)

The ancient Greeks used this word for the natural affection that develops between close brothers and sisters or childhood friends. This is an affectionate, companionate style of loving.

MANIA

The Greek philosophers believed that some lovers were seized by a madness from the gods, which made them act foolishly. Mania is my term for obsessive, jealous, apparently irrational love.

AGAPE (AGA-PAY)

When St Paul wanted to explain gentle, unselfish, dutiful love to the Corinthians, he used the Greek word agape.

PRAGMA

This is the Greek root for our word 'pragmatic'. I use it for the style of loving which emphasises compatibility and common sense. In former times, this lovestyle was often called arranged marriage. Nowadays it can be arranged by computer matching services.

LUDIC EROS

A hybrid mixture of ludus and eros in a playful pursuit of beauty. It's less fussy and serious than eros.

It is important to remember that this book is about love-*styles*. Just as a person can change his lifestyle – from a suburban family life to the jet-set, for instance – so too, a lover can change his or her lovestyle. It is even possible to apply different lovestyles to different partners one day after the next. A relationship with the same partner can gradually change from one lovestyle to another. When I refer to an erotic lover, for example, I do not mean a person who always was and always will be typical of the eros lovestyle, any more than a hippie or a swinger must always act according to those lifestyles.

One swallow does not a summer make, and neither does one manic experience confirm you as a lifelong obsessive lover. One playful affair in which you wandered from the straight and narrow of a storgic marriage, does not make you henceforth a ludic lover. A person's preference in love arises from a general, overall pattern of experience. Like a favourite colour, this preference may change over the years, as a result of your experience of love. These changes will be discussed in Chapter twelve.

One immediate benefit you should enjoy from an awareness of the different kinds of loving, is a re-evaluation of your own experiences. Many lovers go on thinking that only one person can be truly loved in a lifetime, or, at best, only one at a time. In order to believe that your present relationship is 'real love', your previous relationships must be defined as mistakes, or at best something short of the real love you now enjoy. But if you accept the existence of different, equally real kinds of love, then it is possible to regard your past experiences as valid, instead of discrediting them. By comparing the varying aspects of these experiences, you can clarify the precise lovestyle you are looking for, or decide more confidently whether you have now found it.

Another likely outcome of awareness of love's various forms will, I hope, be a greater acceptance of the validity of other people's experiences of love, even if they don't conform to your preference. Rather than accusing someone you are involved with by saying 'You don't love me as much as I love you', you may instead find yourself considering how your partner's love differs from yours – while accepting that your partner's love is valid for him or her.

In fact, a sensitivity to the many 'colours' or kinds of love will probably lead you to measure love less by amounts. When love is viewed in black-and-white, then there is only more or less of it. 'Chris loves me *more than* you do.' 'Do you love me *as much as* I love you?' 'Why can't you show *more* love for me than you do?' When love is seen 'in colour', then we pay attention to differences of kind as well as of quantity – 'My love for you is more jealous than your love for me', and so on. This is a more specific observation, and more likely to lead to useful discussion of each other's approach to love.

Lovers can then discover which aspects of love are most important to them, where they agree, and where they differ. One may emphasise possessiveness as a proof of love, the other, unquestioning trust; one honesty, the other, kindness. A simple test of some of the aspects of love will be found on page 171. It indicates which of eight, readily distinguishable

18

lovestyles comes closest to your experience in any particular relationship.

Although not everyone will view it as a benefit, another result of an awareness of different styles of loving can be the enjoyment of serial or even simultaneous love affairs. The decorator who is really hooked on colours will not be content to appoint all furnishings in one favourite hue, but will want to know what colour combinations work best. Some lovers will want to experience a variety of lovestyles – if only to find out that there are some combinations which work better than others.

As long as love is considered to be of one kind, with but one word to describe it, we are likely to act as if love comes in a limited amount. Thus, if I promise to love you, and then give some of my love to another person, I am 'cheating' you by that amount. We do not take this attitude when comparing love of different objects. For example, a husband who loves his children is not thereby cheating on the love of his wife. Likewise, a lover who appreciates the difference between two kinds of loving may enjoy relationships of each kind without feeling that one of them 'cheats' the other.

Of course, one of the difficulties of modern lovers is that we have so much choice. We are like children in a candy shop with only pennies to spend. Daily encounters in the city streets remind us that there are more beautiful and more interesting people than the one we are presently in love with or married to. Advertising encourages us to be dissatisfied with what we have, and to search for something newer and better: if only each of us could find the perfect lover, someone with this person's face, that one's body, another's mind and still another's performance in bed!

The profusion of different lifestyles in the modern world has produced a confusion about different lovestyles. Enjoying a satisfactory love relationship has never been more difficult. There are thousands of different occupations, compared to a few hundred familiar jobs a century ago. There are more than two hundred denominations of Christianity alone, to say nothing of other religions. Instead of everyone learning the same 'three r's' we are likely to find few adults with the same educational background. All these factors, together with the mass media, jet travel and the high mobility of urban populations, make men and women today more

19

different from one another than ever before. As a result, we are aware of a great many more choices than our grandparents knew.

Even if we do find someone whose style and personality are close to our own, so that we agree on the basics, neither of us is likely to be the same kind of person twenty years from now. More than a century ago, the French novelist Honoré de Balzac argued that anyone who grew tired of marriage in later years, had married too soon. In Balzac's time the average couple who married at twenty, could expect 10,000 days together before death parted them. The average life expectancy of an adult of twenty has nearly doubled since then. Can we now expect marriage to last two lifetimes?

One consequence of these modern conditions is the idea of 'creative divorce'. What used to be a stigma now seems on its way to becoming an expected stage in the adult life cycle. If a second and even a third or fourth marriage in a single lifetime becomes an accustomed pattern of love relationship, we need more than ever a clear distinction between the various styles of loving. In addition, as creative divorce emphasises, we need the ability to evaluate and learn from the previous marriage without blame and recrimination. Equal respect for different lovestyles can contribute to growth rather than shame and despair when a marriage ends.

An alternative outcome of the greater individuality of modern people and our extended life expectancy is the idea of 'open marriage'. Instead of the serial polygamy of marriage followed by divorce followed by remarriage, the advocates of open marriage want to remodel the traditional marriage to a accommodate a variety of love relationships. The spouses in an open marriage would have their cake and eat it too. They would enjoy the security and sense of continuity arising from a lasting one-to-one relationship, while at the same time granting each other the freedom to enjoy subsidiary love relationships without the deception necessary in the age-old practice of secret adultery. Success in such a marriage will also require an awareness of different styles of loving, as is explained in detail in Chapter Twelve.

Probably most readers will opt neither for open marriage nor for creative divorce. If you are among those who want a single partner with whom to share your kind of loving, in the hope that your choice will last a lifetime, then you certainly need to study the kinds of love. 'There is hardly any activity, any enterprise, which is started with such tremendous hopes and expectations and yet which fails so regularly as love', warns Erich Fromm. If we experienced the same dismal failure rate in our jobs, or in the investment of our money, we would certainly want to study the problems involved, and not delude ourselves that success comes naturally or is just a matter of luck.

Many people are colour-blind to the variety of different kinds of loving. This book invites you to abandon the black-and-white, love-me-love-me-not approach, and become familiar with the splendid colours of love. We begin with the primary lovestyles: eros, ludus, and storge.

Two

Eros – Love of Ideal Beauty

> I have sought love, first, because it brings ecstasy –
> ecstasy so great that I would often have sacrificed all
> the rest of life for a few hours of this joy. I have
> sought it, next, because it relieves loneliness ... I have
> sought it, finally, because in the union of love I have
> seen, in mystic miniature, the prefiguring vision of
> heaven that saints and poets have imagined ...
>
> *Bertrand Russell*

An immediate, powerful attraction to the physical appearance of the beloved is the most typical symptom of eros. Kierkegaard surely had such love in mind when he wrote 'to see her is to love her'. Thomas Gould spoke of the 'sudden inexplicable vision of what we pursue'. Stendhal called it a 'sudden sensation of recognition and hope'. Eros always depends on an initial attraction, even though an actual love relationship may not start until months later, if at all.

I began with the suspicion that eros was little more than a projection of the lover's imagination on to a suitable object: 'There is a period of thrill, anticipation, and tension, then a period of acquaintance, enjoyment, and ecstasy, then a decline into disenchantment,' I noted at the time. I expected eros to be superficial, motivated mainly by sexual drive, and quickly exhausted. It might produce an occasional permanent effect, as in Dante's 'new life' after meeting Beatrice – but that was only because the relationship was never consummated! I was sure that if Dante had married Beatrice he would soon have grown tired of her. With Anders Nygren and other Christian theologians, I expected to find eros 'egocentric and self-aggrandising'. Like Molière, I assumed that much of the lover's excitement over the beauty of the beloved was mere blindness: 'Lovers manage in their passion's cause to love their ladies even for their flaws'.

Interviews with actual lovers changed my mind. I uncovered stories of 'love at first sight' whose initial rapture survived years of life together. Their first recollections of their partners always included a sensation of recognition of beauty which to the lover seemed near-perfect. 'The first time I saw him was several weeks before we met', a typical erotic lover recounted, 'but I can still remember exactly the way he looked, which was just the way I dreamed my ideal lover would look.'

Lovers who reported experiences which I later classified as erotic usually recalled some physical symptoms of excitement, even shock, on first beholding the beloved. There was a chemical or gut reaction. Sweating, churning and tightening of the stomach, increased rate of breathing or heartbeat were among the effects reported. These reactions have long been familiar in fiction, but many readers have considered them nothing more than fiction. In successful erotic experiences – those which developed and endured – the first symptoms of attraction were followed by more profound physical rapport. These lovers spoke of delight in the smell, skin surface, hair texture, muscles, body proportions and other physical aspects of the partner.

Eros is a kind of loving motivated by great appreciation of beauty. But tastes vary, and a lover may be more or less 'purely' erotic in his kind of loving. Very few lovers are entirely typical of eros in their ways of thinking and acting. They tend to vary in the degree to which they are committed to exact specifications for a potential object of their love. This is just as well; the more specific the erotic lover's 'vision of perfection' the poorer the chances of finding a satisfactory partner.

Suppose, for example, there are five important qualities you seek in an ideal partner. Suppose that none of these qualities is naturally connected to any other. For instance, there is no natural reason for tall men to have smoother skin than short men, nor blonde women slimmer figures than brunettes. The chances of finding two unconnected qualities in one person is the multiple of the chances of finding each quality separately. If one in every five people you meet has the right figure, and one in every three has the right hair colour, then only one person in every fifteen will have both (3×5). It follows that if you seek just five qualities (not a very demanding ideal), each of which has a chance of one in

23

ten (fairly good odds), then the chances of finding one person who has all five, are one in one hundred thousand (10 × 10 × 10 × 10 × 10)!

Eros is not merely the pursuit of physical beauty, but the erotic lover does seem to make the risky assumption that the personal and social qualities he or she seeks will somehow go along with the perfect physical ideal. Obviously, erotic lovers are frequently disappointed! There may be a general relationship between basic human somatypes and personality characteristics – for example lean people tend to be more nervously energetic than stout people. But appearances are so often misleading that the erotic lover is often attracted to potential partners whose personality is far from that hoped for.

Erotic lovers with demanding ideals are often aware of the odds against them. Some have developed an uncanny ability to spot a person half-way close to their ideal, even in a large crowd. (When they are fortunate enough to encounter a person who is really close to perfect, erotic lovers may literally tremble with excitement, or go into what Dante called a 'stupor'.) But a chronic erotic lover will go on looking first for 'his type' even when his head knows that his eyes are betraying him and wasting his time. His hyper-sensitivity to touch does not help: most erotic lovers profoundly enjoy caressing and touching, but they are also particularly critical of the 'feel' of the partner. Such lovers may only be able to meet other kinds of partners by forcing themselves deliberately to ignore the people who first catch their eye, and deliberately to seek out those who do not.

Some kinds of love may be blind but eros is not one of them. The more typical the lover's approach is of the eros lovestyle, the more difficult it is for him or her to ignore even minor flaws. 'Her chin is too weak.' 'His legs are too thin.' The erotic lover may choose to overlook a flaw in favour of a generally acceptable appearance, but he will always remain aware that 'the nose is a little too large'. Eventually a serious flaw will force an idealistic erotic lover to break off. Among homosexuals especially I found erotic love to be fragile. After six weeks or so of warm and congenial intimacy, one male finally told his partner 'I just can't get used to the hair on your back. I've really tried, but it turns me off. I can't explain it, but I can't help it either.'

24

The erotic lover's pursuit of the ideal makes this type of loving a puzzling, impossible dream to those who do not share this lovestyle. There is no use saying to such a lover: 'I know I'm not your ideal, but if you only get to know me you'll learn to love me.' The erotic lover sees and feels the body first, and *then* decides whether it is worthwhile becoming acquainted. Most people have some idea of what constitutes an 'attractive' person, but the erotic lover's definition is unusually specific and demanding.

A predominantly erotic lover may have more than one ideal image. Some respondents had two complementary types. For example, a lover might be attracted to slim, fair-haired, smooth-skinned persons as the maximum ideal type. But failing this, darker hair would be acceptable provided the body shape was more attractive; or, blonde hair with a particularly striking face might compensate for a shorter, stouter build. Articulate erotic lovers can quickly arrange a series of photographs in ranked order of preference. They do the same thing mentally when running their eye over a line of potential dance partners to decide which to approach first and which second, or whether to ignore everyone. The more readily a lover can replace one near-ideal type with another, the more his 'eros' form of love is alloyed with ludus, which we will discuss under ludic-erotic lover.

Problems of Eros

Physical attraction serves as the driving power towards psychological rapport in erotic love. To 'know' the beloved is first to know in the flesh, as in the Biblical sense ('I have two daughters who have not known men' – Genesis 19: 8). Thus the typical erotic lover is eager to go to bed within the first few encounters, to discover whether the partner's disrobed body fulfils its apparent promise. This urgency is easily misinterpreted by a non-erotic partner as mere sexual lust. A mutually erotic partner will readily understand such urgency, because he or she will likewise want to *know* the beloved.

Even if a hopeful erotic lover encounters the 'one in a hundred thousand', luck may run out. Alas, the other person is 'already taken'. Or more heartbreaking still, the other is free, but you don't meet his or her expectations. Mutual erotic love may be the ideal for an erotic lover – finding someone who is as turned on about you as you are about him or her – but the odds against it are astronomical. Consequently most erotic lovers end by 'settling for less'. The all-or-nothing attitude gives way to compromise.

Eros may be compromised with ludus ('most people are basically alike') or with storge ('you can grow accustomed to almost anyone over a period of time') or even with pragma ('this is a sensible choice and it's time to settle down'). A compromise may last for years, even a lifetime, providing the erotic ideal image eventually fades and is not revived by some exciting encounter later in life.

In one case known to me, a businessman failed to find his erotic ideal by the age of thirty, and settled for a woman who was a sensible match. He was not physically attracted (though not repelled) and found it difficult to be enthusiastic with her, or even directly to say 'I love you'. This couple had a contented if unromantic marriage for twenty years. The wife was a good mother, homemaker and hostess. She contributed substantially to the businessman's successful career. When they talked, it was about the children, domestic problems, his work, her social clubs.

Then the husband met a young woman who incredibly fulfilled the precise ideal image he had sought years before. He was instantly and 'insanely' turned on, and stunned to discover that she was strongly attracted to him. To his wife's amazement (as well as that of his grown-up children and business colleagues), this man has abandoned the marriage of many years to return to the pursuit of his long-dormant dream. Others may feel that he has taken leave of his senses, but it is equally true that, in his new love, this man has really discovered his senses for the first time.

Typical Eros

The pattern of events and feelings which I have labelled the eros type of love is so distinctive that once you have encountered a single example, you can scarcely fail to recognise it. These short excerpts from a twenty-five-year-old woman's interview illustrate typical eros:

I was quite content with life in my early twenties – liked

my job, had good friends, got on well with my parents ... I'd seen Bobby around a few times ... I remember the first time I saw him. He was gorgeous. 'Just my type,' I thought, but there was no way to meet him – I couldn't just walk across the street and say hello to a stranger! I was sure he hadn't even noticed me. Then one day we were in a lift together. He smiled, then said 'Hello'. Just that ... imagine how different my life would be if he had not said that hello.

We got talking, and it turned out he'd noticed me before but was never bold enough to speak. We arranged a date for that very night, had a wonderful time and ... well, yes, we did end up spending the the night together at his place. I was a bit worried at the time, but now I'm absolutely sure it was the right thing to do. I can't tell you how much he turned me on. No drug could be as pleasant as the way I 'tripped' on his body. I wanted to cry and laugh and shout for joy at the same time ... and what made me really dizzy was, he seemed to be enjoying me just as much. ...

Oh, of course I worried that it was just a one-night stand, or at best a short affair ... but if we hadn't done it right away, maybe we would never have started. We were both busy people so we couldn't see each other every day, but we always phoned, and when we did get together it was terrific ...

No, I wouldn't say I worried about whether he loved me. I did think about him a lot, but I wasn't 'sick with love' the way I was with Jimmy a few years before. This time I was more confident, and more independent too. I mean, if it hadn't worked out I would still have treasured every moment with Bobby. ...

'Jealousy?' Well, I was sort of jealous, not in a possessive way; in fact, I think he had another girl friend at the time and I'm not quite sure when they broke off – that was his business and I didn't pry. But when we were together, there was always a kind of mutual possessiveness, a looking after each other which tended to exclude anyone around us.

No, we hardly ever had an angry argument. We disagreed, sometimes rather strongly, but one of us would always make a joke and the other would start laughing so it was impossible to stay mad.

Sex got better and better. He's so gentle and affectionate, and very sensuous, and of course I really like that kind of man. I enjoy touching him all over – there's no embarrassment ... Oh no, it's not sex that keeps us together. Sure it's important, but there's something deeper – a feeling of being really close, mentally speaking – how do they say, on

27

the same wave-length? We can often communicate feelings without a word spoken.

This woman's experience has been happy so far, though there was no guarantee that she and her beloved would marry, or if they did, live happily ever after.

Sometimes eros achieves joy for a short time, then disintegrates, especially when the partner is not mutually erotic. A builder in his late twenties, for example, recounted two years of loving cohabitation with a woman whose image he worshipped. Yet she occasionally supplemented her office-work earnings with opportunities as a call girl. My respondent was never jealous of this, he said, and their life together was ecstatic and rapturous for him. Unfortunately, his beloved eventually met a 'customer' whose qualities were closer to her tastes than those of my respondent. They separated, but remained 'on friendly terms' and occasionally went to bed together. This became rarer, however, as my respondent found that each such occasion left him feeling a greater sense of loss and loneliness. Now he is trying to forget her by finding someone new.

One of the most interesting cases of erotic love to come to light recently is that of Gay and Nan Talese, as reported in *Esquire Magazine* (December 1973):

> It was love at first sight. A mutual friend who went to Manhattanville with Nan and knew Gay in Louisville ... fixed them up. Nan was just recovering from ... London ... and Gay was starting out as a sportswriter for the Times. They got acquainted at lunch and closed P. J. Clarke's at four in the morning on their second date ... Nan and Gay saw each other constantly for the next two and one half years, yet never kept house together....

The eventual outcome of the Talese marriage (at least to the time of the article) is a particularly interesting example of ludic erotic love matched with storgic erotic, and will be discussed in Chapter Twelve, after these various styles of loving have been explained in detail.

Erotic Intimacy

Mere sexual intimacy with even the most desirable partner

will soon exhaust interest. The sensual delight which first caused yearning becomes blunted and satisfied, and leads to the conclusion that love at first was nothing but a temporary impulse to enjoy physical union with a beautiful body. The lover moves on to some other attractive person, again becomes disenchanted, and eventually concludes that eros is a romantic fiction. If eros is to endure, the impetus of the initial attraction must be harnessed, not exhausted. Successful erotic lovers among my respondents achieved this by first expanding the basis of sensual intimacy.

More than any other kind of lover they actively and imaginatively cultivated a variety of sexual techniques to preserve delight in the partner's body. This is possible only if the partner co-operates. If eros overcomes its first hurdle by uncovering no serious flaws in the beauty of the beloved (compared to its ideal image), it must then face a second hurdle of sexual exploration with the partner. Nothing is more deadly to eros at this point than a prudish or puritan lack of enthusiasm in the partner's approach to sex. The skill and patience of the lover may succeed in overcoming this hurdle; but if the partner's hang-up proves too stubborn, the would-be erotic lover must either transform his approach (to storge perhaps) or seek a new partner.

Sexual knowledge is profoundly related to personal knowledge on a wider basis. Much that the erotic lover comes to know about his or her beloved during the first stage of the relationship occurs simultaneously with, or as a product of, sensual enjoyment and genital contact. A successful erotic approach to love must include a willingness to reveal yourself to your partner openly and unashamedly, to express your feelings with great honesty, and to elicit a similar response from your partner. In time, this personal rapport cements the relationship after the original physical intensity has levelled off.

A profound knowledge of the partner takes time to acquire, even with the great speed of an erotic impulse. How then can we speak of eros as 'love at first sight'? This is merely a short-hand way of saying 'a kind of love which must begin with a powerful physical attraction'. It will become a relationship only if the attraction is converted into greater physical knowledge of the partner, and thereby into psychic and personal rapport. The erotic process of knowing the partner contrasts distinctly with that typical of either ludus or storge. As we shall see, the ludic lover needs to know much less about the beloved, and can acquire most of the information indirectly, rather than in intimate physical encounter. Even the preliminary sexual information can be garnered second-hand. 'What is she like in bed?' the ludic lover may ask a friend. No primarily erotic lover would dream of relying on vicarious evidence. He must directly and intensely experience the embodied personality of the beloved.

What happens if you consider that your attraction to another person is typical of the love I call eros, but the partner's approach to love is not eros but some other kind such as ludus or storge? One of the first problems of the erotic lover is to assess the partner's response. There is danger here, both the danger of being too analytical about something as delicate and uncertain as a formative eros relationship and the danger of over-committing yourself to a relationship which later may fall too far short of your ideal.

An early and useful symptom will be the partner's response to your urgent desire for intimate physical rapport. A compatible partner will understand and agree with early sexual intercourse in the relationship. Of course a willingness for sexual pleasure is also a symptom of ludic love, as we shall see. How can you know your partner isn't just playing games?

There's no way to be certain – about love or anything else in human relationships – but an erotic partner will express open, intense feelings for you, will want to see you every day (or at least talk on the phone), and will be prepared to discuss a possible future together. A typical ludic lover will be non-committal, unless he or she is a cheat at the game and is pretending eros to deceive you. That's a risk you'll just have to take.

There are some reasonably reliable indicators of the partner's ability to sustain the intense intimacy of eros. How does he or she view life now? A successful erotic lover tends to be content with life (though not apathetic), enjoys his or her work, and has some close friends. A likely partner will be ready for love but not desperate, and will have already experienced fulfilling love relationships (including those with siblings and parents). Your partner's self-esteem should be high, but short of vanity.

The typical erotic partner will be ready to shower you with joyful attention, but will not make demands on you, or constantly require reassurance of your love. If a partner becomes possessive, asking for a detailed accounting of your time when not together, or jealous, seeing rivals everywhere, then it is likely that he or she will develop manic eros or mania.

Hoping for the best, you will naturally reveal your own deepest hopes and feelings about love. At some point, it may become obvious that your partner is not feeling the same way. Perhaps you have hinted that the time for a definite commitment has come, but your partner answers: 'Of course I love you, but I'm not ready to make a lifetime decision yet. I haven't gone with enough girls to make up my mind. All right, if you want to put it that way, I'm still looking. You might be the right person, you might not. Do we have to rush things?'

This partner is revealing a ludic component in his approach, which diverges from a purely erotic type of love. Eros knows what ideal it is looking for, and whether it has found the ideal yet, while ludus has a range of satisfactory images. The partner is not purely ludic, because he is looking for a mate; but he is not purely erotic either. I call this approach ludic eros.

Your partner may make a different kind of response: 'Sure I find you attractive – in fact you're the most attractive person I've ever gone with. We have a lot of fun together but we don't really have much in common, do we?' At this point the partner begins to cite differences in education or social class, or other practical considerations. In short, he argues for a pragmatic approach to love.

Deciding what to do in situations where the partner is not mutually erotic is not easy. How often can you reveal the deepest feelings and ideas within yourself before the very act of revelation becomes tiresome? Some secret recesses of our personalities seem like film which cannot be exposed to too much light and still remain sensitive. On the other hand, not to risk opening oneself to a beloved who may prove mutually erotic is to take the risk of losing a rare opportunity for a happy erotic love.

There is something imperious and momentous in the initial ecstatic shock of eros which, fiction has assured us, often causes the lover to assume that the partner is indeed his ideal image. Stendhal called this process crystallisation. He believed that we begin very early in a relationship to project on to the partner all sorts of desirable qualities we want in an ideal lover, whether or not the situation warrants it. I did not find this process typical of the eros type of love, but rather, typical of mania.

Of course, an erotic lover is always in danger of slipping into mania (see Chapter Ten, manic eros), but the respondents who succeeded in eros did not blindly glamorise the partner; nor did they ignore early warning signs of shortcomings in the partner. Manic lovers tend to ignore the beloved's flaws (that is, they 'crystallise' the beloved), but my most typical erotic respondents were always conscious of both the assets and the liabilities of their partners, and ignored neither. Fiction has confused two apparently similar but in fact quite different styles of loving. The manic lover allows his obsessive preoccupation with the partner to blind him, though he is not happy in his blindness. He knows he is making a fool of himself, but, as manic respondent after manic respondent told me, 'I just couldn't help myself'.

It is not difficult to imagine how the fictional confusion between eros and mania may arise. If the erotic lover's partner has already conformed to the lover's ideal physical image, has initially responded with warmth and rapport, accepting the rapid intensification of the relationship impelled by the erotic lover's enthusiasm, and has engaged in sexual intimacy which seemed mutually delightful, then (and only then) the erotic lover runs the risk of making a mistake because he has already launched himself into an intense commitment. He may assume more reciprocity than is warranted and project his own hope for the future on to the partner; corrections in his course of action become more difficult, the more certain he becomes that the partner is his ideal. Thus, paradoxically, the greater your certainty that a relationship has the potential for the erotic fulfilment, the greater the risk that you may plunge into the anxiety of manic eros, and thence into the desperation of mania.

The process is rather like the intricate but powerful launching of a moon rocket. There is a moment, so Norman Mailer tells us in *Of a Fire on the Moon,* as the rocket is already lifting from its pad, when the slightest imbalance of thrust on one side, compared to the other, would collapse the rocket to the ground. The type of love I have defined as eros has a similar feature. At this critical stage a difference in approach by the partner has a shattering effect. Later, when a successful erotic relationship is in orbit, the same action would have much less impact. As an example of this critical phase, it may be that just as you reach the firm decision that this is the deep, ideal mutual love you have been waiting for, your partner may suggest a brief pause 'to think things over' or to 'straighten things out with the person I was going with until I met you'. You suddenly realise that only the first stage of a multi-stage rocket has fired successfully; you are barely off the ground yet.

When you realise that your beloved does not share your lovestyle, your relationship is in danger from that very realisation, as well as from the objective facts of a non-mutual relationship. Two responses are possible. You may retreat from your position, or retrench, for fear of becoming too dependent on the beloved, or you may attempt to compel the beloved to re-define the relationship in accordance with your conception. In either event, your confidence in yourself as an erotic lover is likely to be shaken.

A definite quality of self-assurance seems essential to successful erotic love. A lover who begins to doubt himself because the beloved does not requite his erotic form of loving, or who begins to distrust and even despise the beloved, will promptly undermine the basis of intimate rapport which is essential to lasting eros. The relationship will be forced back on to reliance on physical contact and sexual satisfaction to keep it going, and from that point on, it is almost certainly doomed.

Lasting eros requires that you have the self-assurance to risk revealing yourself openly and intensely to another person without excessive fear of the possible consequences. To show yourself, to surrender, to another human being is always a great risk. When you allow the powerful attraction of what appears to be a beautiful and exciting person to become an important focus of daily life, you are gambling with your independent existence.

All the successful erotic respondents in my research reported a solid foundation of contentment with life, a reasonably happy family background, close friends, and satisfaction with daily work before launching into the eros experience. Several even reported a waiting period of months between first sight of the beloved – at a party, for example – and actually finding the right opportunity to begin a relationship. During this interval these respondents did not lose their balance, become sick with obsessive desire, or try to force the issue. Their everyday life was sufficiently satisfying, and they felt no urgent need to be in love.

You cannot launch a space rocket from swampy ground, nor eros from a naïve, self-doubting and over-dependent personality. An erotic lover must be able to avoid wallowing in extremes of emotion, especially the self-doubt and self-pity typical of mania. The expression of such weakness in erotic love, for example in possessive jealousy, is likely to spoil the relationship. The frequent suggestion, in literature, that eros is a search for one's other half is misleading because it suggests that the lover is an incomplete person without the beloved. A half-developed personality has little hope of achieving a mutual erotic love. More apt analogies for eros are such poetic images as the sea touching shore, in contact at every point yet each separate in its own distinctive existence; or the image of two ships sailing side by side but not grappled together, lest they sink in the first storm.

Jealousy

The word jealousy, like love, covers several different kinds of behaviour. It is pointless to debate whether jealousy is learned behaviour or instinctive behaviour, without first clarifying what behaviour we are talking about. Some forms of jealousy exist in almost every society. Sexual jealousy is found in both highly sexist and relatively non-sexist societies, and in both puritanical and permissive cultures. But there are kinds of jealousy which relate to the different kinds of love.

Some jealousy is essentially fear of loss. Consider the individual's investment in a relationship and the difficulty of

34

replacing the partner, this may be quite rational. But when there is no real reason for such fears, or when the partner can be easily replaced, jealousy is irrational and unproductive for the particular lovestyle concerned. Thus, for different reasons, ludus and agape tend to exclude such jealousy.

In mania, fear of loss is usually reasonable from the point of view of the lover, since the partner is regarded as irreplaceable. Yet the very intensity of the manic lover is likely to alienate the partner's affections even when there is no rival in sight. As we shall see when we turn to mania in detail, jealousy is regarded as a proof of love. Nothing makes the manic lover more secure than a jealous partner.

Some jealousy is little more than envy, and may be resented by most kinds of lovers. But envy need not be begrudging in its attitude. Sometimes envy is simply admiration combined with a wish to have the thing envied, without denying it to the partner. A pragmatic or storgic lover, for example, may be 'jealous of' the partner's personal qualities or accomplishments, without resenting these. 'I'm sometimes jealous of his rapport with our children' is not an inappropriate comment within storgic or pragmatic lovestyle.

However, when envy becomes begrudging, it often becomes problematic for certain kinds of loving. For example, when we turn to ludic eros we shall find that it is unacceptable for a lover to begrudge his or her partner the opportunity to have other 'affairs'. In storgic ludus, we shall find it inappropriate to begrudge the partner's attachment to a spouse. Accusations of 'cheating' are out of place in these lovestyles.

Some jealousy takes the form of possessiveness. It argues that love has a right to be demanding of fidelity, since love creates needs and makes the lover vulnerable. In loving you, it is argued, I allow myself to become dependent on your love. Over a period of time I come to need you, and thus become vulnerable to any threat that you may withdraw your love. Therefore I have a right to protect myself against any possible alienation of your affections. Indeed, my possessiveness shows how much I love you. Only if I did not love you, could I become indifferent to your affairs with other people.

The other side of this coin is the fear that if my partner is not concerned to guard my love of him and prevent me from giving it to others, then perhaps my love is not really important to him. He is not afraid of losing me. Only in agape, as we shall see, might I admire such unselfishness, as a noble expression of the 'highest' style of loving.

The function of jealousy in the experiences of my erotic respondents was particularly interesting. Originally I did not expect eros to be a jealous form of love, I assumed eros to be essentially a sexual attraction, rather quickly exhausted and easily replaced by another attraction. My respondents divided into two groups. Some showed a form of eros with little or no jealousy. Others eschewed scenes, or attempts to compel fidelity from the partner, yet showed the most demanding exclusiveness. These lovers assured me that if the partner was unfaithful he or she would be dropped immediately. There would be no remonstrations or threats but a prompt and irreversible break-off.

How could the same type of love include two different conditions of jealousy? The witty French courtier La Rochefoucauld provided a clue when he said that there is a kind of love whose excess excludes jealousy. I re-examined the cases of eros and found differences in the previous love careers of the respondents. The non-jealous erotic lovers were those who had never experienced a failure or disappointment in previous love affairs, and whose current erotic experience was strongly requited by the partner. These lovers received so much reassurance from their partners that there was an 'excess'. If the partner was unfaithful, this did not seem to cheat the lover, who was already receiving more love than he needed. These non-jealous lovers believed that their love was appreciated by the partner and would not be discarded in favour of some supplementary diversion.

The jealous exclusive erotic lovers, by contrast, were in their second or third erotic experience, after at least one failure, and often lacked sufficient erotic requital of their love to make them feel secure. The relationship had not cemented enough to prevent it from coming apart under the strain of rival attractions. Since they were erotic rather than manic lovers, they still believed confidently in the worth of their love and held an all-or-nothing attitude towards love. Consequently, they would not reduce themselves to angry scenes or threats. They were not 'possessive' but were 'exclusive'. Their love was an ultimatum. Infidelity was sufficient reason to put an end to the relationship. In a sense, fidelity was the price these erotic lovers exacted for taking the risk of open intimacy and surrender to a partner.

Growth in Eros

In many ways, the pattern of growth in erotic love reported by my respondents was similar to that of a child's developing relationship with its mother. As Freud first demonstrated, a baby knows its mother intimately in a tactile and sexual context; this physical rapport then becomes the basis for the training of the child and the emergence of an independent personality. Eros is similarly dependent on close physical presence and the use of the five senses. A very young child is easily distressed by absence of the mother for any extended period; as long as mother is in sight, all is well. Eros, too, is severely strained by lengthy absence of the partner. I found no erotic relationship that had survived a total separation of even a few days if the relationship was begun, and in particular after the first acts of sexual intimacy. During the 'launching' stage, eros seems to depend on an especially rich mixture of fuel. It requires frequent physical presence, intense emotional expression, and a good deal of sensual, tactile contact.

After an erotic love is more fully developed it can tolerate longer periods of separation, but the lover will never lose his reliance on physical expression. Indeed, I found some evidence that lovers of a predominantly erotic type are individuals whose sense of reality in other spheres of life is basically physical or visceral. Their appreciation of sculpture and architecture, for example, seems to involve a distinctive tactile sense, and their reaction to artistic beauty is intense and passionate.

A person newly in love is often tempted to test his experience to prove that it really is love. Such tests are generally based on a dangerously simple conception of love. In the case of eros, testing the love by arranging a total separation of a week is likely to shift the type of love expressed by the lover into mania, while at the same time reducing the chances of a mutual erotic response from the partner.

37

Artificially postponing sexual intimacy is equally foolish. Such tests are about as useful to eros as depriving a baby of food or physical contact for its first week to see if it's strong enough to live. On the other hand, these would be appropriate tests for a ludic or storgic love, and could be an actual incentive to the development of manic love.

Almost by definition, the ecstasy of eros is not an experience which can be maintained at the intense level of its first few weeks or months. Eventually, you must emerge from ecstasy and return to the world. Thus, a more or less pure eros is likely to become weakened over time unless strengthened by combination with a few ideas and actions more typical of ludus or storge. The erotic lover's continuing problem is that of achieving an alloy in which the other components do not take over.

In the simplest case, that of mutually erotic lovers, if the alloy is ludus, a quality of conscious management becomes apparent in the lovers' behaviour. They arrange for spaces in their togetherness, to paraphrase Kahlil Gibran. One may occasionally encourage a rival to the other, in order to enliven the flagging erotic intensity. In this way lovers can avoid a drift towards taking each other for granted. Each must be careful not to become too ludic, of course.

The risks of a brief ludic adventure can rekindle attentiveness and mutual preoccupation in an erotic relationship which has become too placid for either or both partners. As Thérèse Benedek points out, a little 'jealousy' may relieve a period of boredom in love:

> If the suspense which initiated passion cannot be continued, the mutual sexual excitability decreases. Lovers know this instinctively and therefore often consciously seek to arouse a limited degree of hostile tension [to] render new stimulus [to love]. . . .[1]

Conversely, storgic qualities can be added to a relationship which is too intense. You bank down a fire that is burning so fiercely that it will soon exhaust its fuel. For example, you can spend less time talking about your love and relating directly with your beloved, and instead dilute the relation-

1. Thérèse Benedek, 'The Psychodynamics of Love', in A. M. Krich (ed.), *Anatomy of Love*, p. 136.

ship by the company of others. The birth of children can have the same effect by shifting some of the one-to-one intensity of eros towards a third love-object. But the lover must not go too far towards storge, for habit is the enemy of erotic ecstasy.

An erotic love may have to be 'put into storage' temporarily due to circumstances beyond the lover's control. For example, the beloved might be in prison for a while – as in the English film *Poor Cow*, or the song 'A hundred yellow ribbons'. In cases like this the love relationship need not cease, but it must be transformed to a type which does not depend on frequent physical contact. It could become manic or storgic erotic, and later, given favourable conditions on reunion, return to eros.

Consciously developing and directing a love relationship in these ways requires a high degree of self-assurance combined with intimate familiarity and mutual rapport with the partner. A contrast with mania (see Chapter Six) will make the important role of self-confidence in eros more apparent. No doubt the need for self-assurance has misled many observers to conclude that eros is egocentric. This is a mistake. There is a great difference between ego strength and egotism. The selfish, egotistical person is not really proud of himself at all, but self-doubting and anxious. His external self-assertion is a compensation for internal feelings of inferiority. Truly confident persons can afford to surrender themselves, because they do not fear what others might do.

The ego strength of the successful erotic lover is not boastful or vain, but serenely strong. He is aware that he can survive getting hurt, and can therefore take risks. He can afford to let down his defences because his strength lies in a deep inner core. At the same time, he can enjoy intimacy without overwhelming or compelling his beloved. None of the lasting erotic experiences among my respondents included any report of attempts to force the partner to show more love. Eros, like Aesop's sun, prefers to persuade the beloved through gentle warmth rather than through force.

Unsuccessful Eros

Those of my respondents who had had unsuccessful erotic relationships differed from the successful erotic lovers in

39

several respects. I would not argue that these differences necessarily 'caused' their failure, but the two were certainly connected. Unsuccessful erotic lovers differed from those achieving satisfying erotic relationships in their attitudes to childhood experience and the quality of life at the time of falling in love. They were basically discontented with themselves, and were often anxiously looking for love. They were not very optimistic about their chances so began to worry quite early in their relationship and borrow trouble in advance. Because they were uncertain of their own worth and abilities, they tried to postpone intimacy both in expression of feelings and in sexual encounter, but often the power of their initial attraction overcame their attempted restraint. In short, they were tortured by ambivalence and lack of self-assurance. Usually the erotic impulse triumphed over the attempts at self-restraint and caution, and these lovers experience what I have called 'loss of control'. They acted in spite of themselves, fell in love, and lost their balance.

These reports do not necessarily imply that it is impossible for a person discontented with life, or a product of an unhappy childhood, or searching for love, to achieve an erotic relationship. But lasting success will be much more difficult. Such persons will probably have to survive several disappointing eros-type loves before they have learned enough about themselves and developed the necessary self-assurance to win. Of course many will give up trying, and settle for some other kind of love; but unlike the lover who never believed in eros in the first place, the disappointed erotic lover will probably remain aware that he or she has settled for less than the ideal.

Like any living thing, a love relationship changes and grows, or dies. An experience which began as eros may become transformed into another kind of loving without losing all its primary erotic qualities. In this case the lover will not be plagued by lingering doubts about settling for less than his ideal, but will transform the ideal itself. For example, an erotic relationship may gradually become less physical and sexual in its expression, and grow more mentally or spiritually sensitive. In terms of my typology, it moves towards storge, forming a storgic-erotic type of love. In such cases, found particularly in married couples who began as mutually erotic lovers and aged happily together through life's many trials, the more tactile and genital intimacy typical of pure eros is replaced by gentle and unobtrusive expressions of feeling. I have seen older couples of this kind for whom a glancing smile, or the slight contact of hand, seem to convey more profound joy than most acts of sexual intercourse.

While eros may become transformed into storgic eros or, alternatively, into ludic eros, while still retaining its primary erotic impulse, I found no instances in which a type of love lacking the initial qualities of eros was later transformed into eros. Apparently one must begin with certain indispensable qualities. The most important seem to be the powerful physical attraction to the partner who embodies the lover's ideal image of beauty (which in turn implies that the lover does have such an image), and an ability and willingness openly to encounter another person, unhindered by fears or worries abut the possible consequences.

Eros and Sex

Modern usage tends to equate erotic with sexual. When the term erotic art is used, we are likely to think of pornography. Although my use of the term eros for the kind of loving described in this chapter is bound to create misunderstandings, I have not chosen the term out of a stubborn desire to revise the English language, but rather to revive and strengthen those uses of eros which stem from the original Greek meaning.

The interpretation of eros as an experience involving mental or ideal qualities, and not merely physical or sexual impulses, is faithful to the Platonic conception. Somewhere in history a misinterpretation arose by which 'Platonic love' came to mean sexless love, or at least love in which sexuality was thoroughly sublimated. Most dictionaries define Platonic love as 'devoid of sensual feeling', which is certainly not what Plato had in mind. On the contrary, it was sensual feeling for the beautiful body of another person which first evoked an awareness of eros as the ancient Greeks understood it. Their culture was permeated with an appreciation of the beautiful in its human bodily form.

Disembodied love is a conception which respondents in an erotic experience found it impossible to comprehend, let

41

alone accept. The fundamental experience of love for them, while erotic, was sensual and sexual. But to reduce erotic love to sexuality is to call a Picasso nothing but oil on canvas. The erotic lover is typified by an acute awareness of physical beauty which is much less specific and demanding in the ludic lover, and almost entirely absent or unexpressed in the storgic lover. Erotic love has no advantage over other kinds of love – indeed, the world has always been short on beauty, and many erotic lovers will never find their ideal – but it is certainly more than a refined lust. The erotic lover is a seeker of his particular mental image of 'the beautiful'.

Since the erotic lover knows what he wants, wants it very much, and realises how slim are his chances of finding it, we should not be surprised by the powerful feeling of excitement, anticipation and hope which the erotic lover experiences 'at first sight' of someone who seems to fulfil his ideal. He will want to discover as quickly as possible whether the promise is an illusion. At this point a confident easiness about sexuality is critical, but the erotic lover is not interested only in sex; it is his way of rapidly achieving knowledge of the partner. As one respondent put it to me: 'Our sex is good, sometimes it's really great, but it was never the most important thing and it's certainly not the thing that holds us together. We make love; sex doesn't make us love.'

My respondent's experiences indicate that success in eros is more likely if you are not a virgin at the time of encounter with the 'ideal' erotic partner, but have already had a variety of sexual experiences. The occasional person may be lucky enough to have 'natural' ability to communicate intense feelings through sexual intimacy without anxiety, and in a way which brings maximum gratification to him and his partner. Most of us are not so lucky; we discover that 'good sex' is an art that takes much practice and experience. Being at ease with your body, sensitive to the needs of another body, and free of any puritanical guilt during sexual intercourse are qualities which can be learned. You can learn them after meeting your ideal erotic partner, especially if he or she is more experienced and can teach you. Sadly, two sexually innocent would-be erotic lovers might miss a rare opportunity for happiness if neither of them could sexually communicate with the other. Their efforts to develop this intimacy might frustrate any hope of their relationship reaching the critical ignition point at which sensual attraction is converted into deeper psychological rapport. (There is also the danger of a virgin's over-idealising a pleasant first experience of sex; this may lead to later disappointment.)

Risks of Eros

Eros is not an easy kind of loving, even when you beat the odds and find a suitable partner to match your ideal image. The rapid disclosure of self, early sexual experience, honesty of emotion, and intensity of feelings all make this a difficult lovestyle. Of course, these qualities almost make it the most ecstatic, exhilarating and challenging kind of love for some people; but your chances of successfully enjoying eros are substantially reduced when you lack self-confidence, self-esteem and social stability. A would-be erotic lover should if possible first put his own psychological house in order, enjoy his work, surround himself with good and close friends, and have a good relationship with his parents, before attempting an erotic approach to love.

You might well say: 'If a person has all these advantages he doesn't need a lover anyway.' Precisely. The successful erotic lover must not *need* to be in love. Rather, he finds someone to love, and then allows himself to need that person. Eros is not a way of being happy, but of being happier.

People who have experienced an unhappy childhood, or are trapped in frustrating work, or lack close friends, may still attempt eros if they have a clear ideal image and the right person comes along. But they will be more likely to succeed if they delay starting such a relationship until they have first got themselves together psychologically. Several of my respondents saw or even met the eventual partner months before a relationship began, but instead of rushing into intense involvement, they attended to other urgent matters first – such as finding work they enjoyed, or moving to a more suitable environment – so that their self-esteem was sufficiently reinforced. They could then begin to love without feeling desperate.

Erotic lovers who have not yet found a suitable partner can scarcely avoid poignant emotions when they meet someone who fulfils their ideal but is for one reason or another not available or responsive. There is great risk on such occasions that the erotic lover will lose his or her balance.

Perhaps your partner will find you attractive and be willing to 'have an affair' as long as you don't 'get too serious'. The closer such a partner comes to your vision of perfection, the more tempted you will be. Yet, the more ideal the partner, the more difficult it will be to avoid over-involvement. It may seem like cynical advice, but the experience of erotic respondents who 'played with fire' indicates that you should avoid playful, short-term affairs with partners who come too close to your ideal. As the Spanish say, it doesn't matter whether the pitcher hits the stone, or the stone the pitcher – it's the pitcher that gets broken. Life may seem worthless after a brief ecstasy with a person who seems absolutely ideal yet remains beyond your reach.

The myth of Narcissus has often been misunderstood. He was not an egotist who unreasonably found his reflection beautiful. The myth tells us that he was actually the most handsome of men, and that he had an acute awareness of beauty. What could be more natural, then, than to want to achieve union with the ideal beauty he saw reflected in the pool? Narcissus was the classic case of an erotic lover whose ideal could never become his partner. The dream of perfect love will draw an erotic lover further and further into emotional surrender and commitment when an apparently ideal partner is met. If the partner is not responsive, then the erotic lover is leaning dangerously far over Narcissus' pool.

Breaking Off Without Smashing Up

The failure rate of eros has littered our fiction with bitter and cynical stories of love, and caused our conventional wisdom to be deeply suspicious of ideal beauty. Christian theologians have accused eros of representing irrational egotism and provoking inevitable disenchantment. Yet the experience of some of my respondents testifies to a continued hope that an ideal beauty can be found. The success of a few keeps the hope alive for many more. Several respondents had survived a dozen intensely intimate relationships in which the highest hopes were aroused, then dashed. They were still not prepared to compromise.

44

These respondents had learned the art of breaking off a relationship without smashing everyone up in the process. They did not 'blame' – for they realised that resentment does more damage to the hater than the hated. On the contrary, the most resilient erotic lovers numbered several of their past loves among their present close friends.

Repeaters in erotic love must learn how to face and survive the painful limbo between relationships. In freely letting go, one avoids being torn asunder; and the erotic lover who has not yet found his love, must be as capable of recognising a failure in a relationship as of recognising the ideal image when it is encountered. Refusal to acknowledge that a relationship has gone as far as it can, is a refusal to go on hoping. At this point it would be better for such a lover to abandon eros and pursue some other kind of loving.

For many readers, there will be no great problems or risks from eros, because you wouldn't even begin to think of choosing this lovestyle. You will not be interested in love as a grand lottery, where so many seem to have to lose in order that a few may win. Those of us who prefer to take fewer risks with the capital we have, will logically turn to some other lovestyle, such as ludus or storge.

Three

Ludus – Love as a Game

When I'm not facing the face I fancy, I fancy the face I face.

(*from 'Finian's Rainbow'*)

Ludus is the idea that love is a game, to be played by part-ners who can avoid taking their emotions too seriously. As a lovestyle, ludus can be summed up in the expression, 'love, like alcohol, should be enjoyed but never allowed to become necessary'. The ludic lover refuses to become dependent on any beloved, or to allow any partner to make demands and become too involved.

Other types of lovers will dismiss ludus as not a kind of loving at all, but a charade. Moralists will condemn it as a subtle form of seduction. Erotic lovers will reject its promis-cuity and lack of commitment. The believer in agape will attack ludus for its hedonism. Only the pragmatic lover will be tolerant of ludus – for pragma is a secondary of ludus – but even pragmatic love will hope to outgrow what it con-siders the emotional immaturity of ludic love.

With so many kinds of lovers aligned against ludus, the chances are you will not accept its inclusion in a typology of love. I can only observe that a significant group of respond-ents who reported this experience of love sincerely assured me that they considered themselves lovers. Moreover, there is ample evidence that numerous lovers in past ages have prac-tised ludus and called it love. Indeed, ludus has been a most socially acceptable form of love in some periods of western-European history. But the golden age of ludus may still be ahead, a time when individuals will be free to relate sexually to each other without fear of pregnancy or disease, and with-out moral and emotional hang-ups.

Ludus is one of the oldest concepts of love in our litera-ture, dating at least from the Roman poet known as Ovid. I have adopted (and adapted) his name for it, *amor ludens* – playful love. Ovid advised lovers not to get too serious or involved, but to enjoy love as a pleasant pastime. Like any game or contest, ludus is fun to play, even for the lover who doesn't win, because it challenges his skill in dealing with a variety of intimate problems.

Making a game of love does not necessarily diminish its value, the ludic lover argues. No skilled player of bridge or tennis would excuse inept playing because 'it's only a game'. Ludus has rules, strategies, and points for ability – as well as penalties for those who play it badly. Mutually agreed ground rules are important because there is rarely a neutral referee to arbitrate conflicts. When a partner ceases to be interesting or amusing, the game is called off and a more challenging partner is sought elsewhere. Once the game ends, neither partner has any claim on the other. During the game itself, the ludic lover makes no intense or exclusive claims on the beloved's affections. As Montesquieu wrote during a period of French history when ludus was in high fashion: 'A husband who wishes to be the only one to possess his wife would be regarded as a public kill-joy.'

Tactics of Ludus

Many games require a degree of insincerity: bluffing in poker, for example, or a finesse in bridge. The test of fairness is whether the tactic is permitted by the rules. In ludus, it is quite fair under the usual rules of play to pretend that certain situations or emotions exist when in fact they do not. 'Promise her anything', Ovid advised. Flattery, coyness, coquetry, gallantry – all are part of the ludic strategy. Like the permissible deceits of a card game, the deceits of love can add suspense and excitement to the game.

A typical example of ludic tactics is the lie about one's age. Its finest form is the impression created without telling an actual lie. You simply recount your life's major events in such a way that your partner makes a wrong assumption about your age. A physical appearance which belies your true age does the rest. Eventually you will be found out, but by that time you will have scored your points in the game.

Ludus is most easily played with several partners simultaneously. 'Play the field', an older generation put it. 'Don't let anyone get their hooks into you,' one of my younger respondents said; avoid becoming too involved with any one partner. Not telling each partner about the others is as fair in ludus as not showing your hand in cards. But if one of the partners becomes too involved, a favourite device for avoiding the consequences is to tell him or her about the other partners. Indeed, a ludic lover may even invent another partner – or a jealous spouse – to prevent a partner from coming on too strongly. But there are more pleasant ways. Most of my ludic respondents were careful not to date any partner too often; nor did they ever hint at including the partner in any long-range plans. On the contrary, if future events were discussed, the intention was to make it plain that they would not necessarily include the partner.

The arrangement of ludic encounters is generally casual: 'See you again some time next week'; I'll give you a call'; or, even more detached, 'Why don't you call me sometime?' This indefiniteness discourages the partner from building up intense anticipation of the next encounter, and hopefully reduces any tendency to become preoccupied with the relationship, a habit which is always annoying to a noncommittal ludic lover.

Gallantry was one of the most courteous forms of ludus ever to become fashionable. It traditionally required the lover to take measures to prevent his or her partner from feeling or expressing more emotion than the lover was prepared to requite. Contemporary readers of Flaubert's *Madame Bovary* joined the author in condemning Emma for ignoring the injuries done to her husband when she allowed him to love her too much. Stendhal's Julien, in *The Red and the Black*, was guilty of the same dishonour. A gallant lover must weigh even the most innocuous situation in terms of its ultimate implications. The partner's request for a token (in modern times, often a personal photograph) may have to be refused because giving it would imply a longer-term relationship than the lover has in mind.

As in many games, you must often be on guard against cheats in ludic love. There are cynical players who don't care how deeply involved the partner becomes, and who even exploit such unbalanced intensity. In the long run, such callousness will not only discredit the ungallant lover among his peers, it will make it difficult for him to perform a seductive role convincingly. In the short run, however, he will

48

probably get away with cheating, and you will want to avoid being numbered among his score of broken hearts! It *is* possible to play with a cheat – and particularly gratifying to outwit one. The best safeguard is to keep several relationships going, so as not to become too preoccupied with thoughts of any one partner, nor too vulnerable to any partner who proves ungallant.

Dating

Contemporary forms of ludic love are first learned in the patterns of behaviour we call 'dating'. Not all dating is love, even of a ludic kind, but the overall rituals of dating are much influenced by typical ludic concepts and actions. For example, in dating, no one has a claim on his or her partner beyond the enjoyment of the date itself, unless there is an agreement to 'go steady'. One's peers are expected to discuss openly the flaws and virtues of available partners in a process which sociologists have called 'rating the date'. Dating originally grew out of a relaxation of conventional courtship patterns, but as time passed, dating came to resemble courtship less and less. A decade or two ago a date was still a definite commitment to at least an evening's company with the partner. Recently, dating seems to have gone out of fashion. A casual 'See you at the party on Saturday' is not even a commitment to be at the party, should something more interesting come up in the meantime. If both partners to this casual arrangement do arrive, they can expect only the decent minimum of courteous interaction with each other. Beyond that, either partner is free to relate more intensely if he feels like it, or to develop an interest in someone else and leave the party with a new partner. These trends are thoroughly ludic in the attitudes they reveal towards intimate relationship.

Though ludus may sometimes appear close to seduction, it is rarely confused with rape or mere sexual assignation. Even in the most casual adolescent dating patterns a 'lay' or a 'trick' is not confused with a 'date'. A ludic lover doesn't steal the prize and run; he must first play the game. While I would not exclude from any definition of ludus a 'one night stand', the experience would have to involve at least an abbreviated ritual of encounter, including the typical devices

49

of ludus: flattery, wit, coyness, courtesy and non-committal admiration. If the lover is over-hasty, and anxious to get rid of the partner once intercourse has been achieved, or so disinterested that he fails to recognise the partner a few days later – or too embarrassed to acknowledge recognition – then I would not include such experience as even minimally ludic.

The rituals of ludus have sometimes become a style or fashion of social behaviour independent of sexual intimacy. The polished manner of the seventeenth- and eighteenth-century European gentleman included flattery and admiration of a lady, but this was not intended to conclude in sexual embraces. Indeed, such a gentleman would have been amazed if the lady had taken him seriously. I would not include this behaviour in the ludic lovestyle, since there is no intention to establish even a temporary intimate liaison.

Love as Fun

Ludus, quite simply is the idea that love should be fun. Not for the ludic lover the pangs and travails, the exquisite anguish and the broken heart. A medieval wit summed it up nicely when he said that love is like a well: a good thing to drink from but a bad thing to fall into. Some people play their roles in life with too much anxiety. They try too hard. The host who is too attentive makes the guests feel uncomfortable. Ludus sits lightly on lovers, as charm and wit sit lightly on a sophisticated host. Both know you can spoil an experience by taking it too seriously.

You may be scandalised by such an apparently frivolous approach to love, but the ludic lover argues that there is as much virtue in good manners and courtesy as there is in outright honesty. 'Sincerity' means no more than being taken in by your own propaganda. Honesty in love is too often an excuse for hurting, or starting an argument.

Perhaps ludus seems too manipulative to be considered a style of loving. Yet psychologists point out that we are manipulating ourselves and others all the time. Man is by nature a manipulator; the question is simply which kind of manipulation will be used, and to what effect. The most altruistic love, agape, requires the lover to manipulate his emotions as much as ludus. In the agapic lovestyle, people are expected to be kind and unselfish even when they don't feel like it.

The ludic lover argues that we use other people, and invite them to use us, every day of our lives. If the use is mutually beneficial there is no exploitation. Thus life may be viewed as a game or series of games, in which players take calculated risks to win desired payoffs. Ludus prefers rules for the game rather than allowing the players to interact with each other in emotionally unpredictable ways. To use an analogy, the ludic lovestyle is like the regulated, set-piece wars of medieval days, rather than the all-out struggle for unconditional surrender.

It has become less necessary recently for ludic lovers to pretend to be practitioners of some other, more socially acceptable lovestyle. Don Juan felt that he had to promise marriage to conquer his thousands. Today there is no need to mortgage intimacy by promising wedlock. Moreover, the pill has made the game of love more accessible to women, and penicillin has reduced the penalties of the game for players of both sexes.

Playing the Game

What sort of person makes a successful playful lover? The majority of my ludic respondents had had an average childhood (by their own definition) and were coping successfuly with life, though perhaps experiencing some frustration in accomplishing their goals. They did not consider 'being in love' as one of their priorities, and were certainly not ready to settle down.

Like the erotic lover, the ludic lover is quite aware of different body shapes and features; but, in contrast to eros, ludus has no ideal preference. The ludic lover thinks it rather foolish, with so many different kinds of people about, to specialise in one kind. However, ludus may enjoy the challenging pursuit of a particular species, and even ignore an easy catch in order to chase a more elusive quarry.

One of the first prerequisites for a ludic lover is the ability to get out and meet people. You won't win a prize in the lottery if you don't buy tickets. The accomplished ludic lover knows that it is remarkably easy to meet attractive strangers in any large city. In our more permissive, liberated

51

world of social encounters, women can use the same initiatives as men. In her advice on *How to Pick Up Men*,
Nicole Ariana claims that 'really the only thing it takes to
pick up men, is to talk to them'.

Good opening lines have long been a stock-in-trade for
the artful practitioner of the ludic lovestyle. 'Nothing ven-
tured, nothing gained' is as true now as it was in our grandparents' time. An amusing opener is all the more likely to
avoid an ego-bruising 'No, thank-you'. One of Ms Ariana's
best, for use at a crowded party or in a singles bar, is
'Weren't you my fourth husband?' One of my own favourites is 'Would you like to know what time it is?' (answer:
'It's time we met!').

If you're on the receiving end of a playful opener, but it's
coming from someone you don't care to know, then don't be
rude, if you want to be successful at ludus. Talk for a
minute, or accept one dance, then politely detach yourself.
This signals to the person you're really after that a show of
initiative won't be instantly repulsed. When you meet someone interesting, on the other hand, remember the name. It's
embarrassing to ask for it later. A manic or erotic lover
doesn't usually have this problem when the one-and-only is
met; and a storgic lover has usually known the partner as a
friend already.

An easy practice for forgetful ludic lovers is to employ the
partner's name, with emphasis, several times in the first conversation after you meet. 'I like your suit, Bill.' 'Would you
like to dance, Ann?' You may be grateful later for this little
tactic. What could be more embarrassing than to use the
wrong name in a moment of passion?

What to say after you say hello? Anything agreeable, and
keep it that way. Playful love is not for ever, so there's no
need to settle the world's problems. Leave it to husbands
and wives to score off each other and win points in an argument. Your objective is to keep talking until you make up
your mind whether to pursue this partner further, or, with
a friendly disjoinder, move towards someone else who has
caught your fancy.

Most people like to talk about themselves, so a good ludic
lover is a creative listener who leads the partner on with
stimulating, non-controversial questions. 'How do you like
your work?' 'Have you found people in this town friendly?'

Avoid stupid questions like 'do you come here often?' How should I answer that? If I say Yes, it means I'm always out on the prowl, and if No, that you're not likely to meet me here again – and maybe you'd like to.

Compliments are double-edged swords which the ludic lover handles with care. They should always be slighty conditional and tentative. She is *one of* the prettiest, he is *one of* the most interesting people you've met. If the affair develops, the experienced ludic lover knows that three little words are always to be excluded from an enjoyable game. You can ruin a perfectly pleasant affair by saying something stupid like 'I love you'. The ludic lover expresses approval of qualities, but never total love of the person. 'I love the way you laugh' (cook, smile, kiss, whatever). Even 'I love the way you make love.' Never an outright 'I love you', unless the partner is that rare person who will understand you to mean 'among a number of people I love'.

Ludic lovers will try to avoid writing letters at all (the less evidence of commitment the better); but if a note must be sent, 'yours truly' will hardly do. How to sign off without saying 'love?' Some cute expression will suffice – 'your teddy-bear'. The expression 'luv' serves nicely without misleading.

If your partner tries to spoil the game by using the forbidden words, there's no need to feel trapped. 'That's awfully sweet of you, but isn't it a bit soon?' Or, 'I take that word too seriously to let it spoil a great friendship.'

The successful ludic lovers among my respondents always avoided discussions about a joint future. A non-committal 'I haven't the faintest idea what I'll be doing then' can remind your partner not to start planning for two.

Likewise, ludic lovers carefully limit the frequency of encounter with the partner. On occasion it may be necessary to use gracious but deceitful tactics to prevent the partner from getting too involved: 'I'll be busy this weekend but we may see each other next week.' If necessary, the ludic lover refers to other involvements (including other partners in love) as important priorities. He or she is not about to let an emotional attachment become the centre of life.

A significant problem reported by my ludic respondents was the extent to which they suffered from a Victorian moral hangover. Many of those I interviewed did not really believe, deep in their hearts, that ludic love could be fully justified or is 'fair' to the partner. Intellectually, they accepted the value of ludic experience, but emotionally they were torn by doubts, of romantic origin. They played the ludic role without identifying with it. This ambivalence, evident in vestigial feelings of guilt after a relationship had been broken off, robbed most of my ludic respondents of the cheerful simplicity of the game. It was as if they somehow thought of themselves as cheaters.

Lisa is a sweet-faced woman in her late twenties. The disarming simplicity of her face, framed by long, black hair, would lead most men to conclude that she was an unsophisticated woman, looking for eternal romantic love. Nothing could be further from the truth. Lisa is a self-confident, successful career woman, who has little inclination to get married, and no desire to be dependent on a man. Some would classify her as a 'liberated' woman. Certainly she is happy-go-lucky in matters of love.

'I keep telling my boyfriends that I am definitely not looking for a husband, but they don't seem to listen,' Lisa told me. Perhaps they were paying more attention to her warmth, which Lisa expresses not from commitment, but because she likes men. That warmth, combined with her disarming features, could easily lead a hopeful lover to the wrong conclusions. She is apparently too gentle and euphemistic with her warnings. Instead of bluntly telling a male friend that he is getting too involved, she will suggest that 'there are other women around, you know'. She will avoid saying 'I love you', but she is unable to reply to a lover's declaration with something like 'Have you ever noticed that I don't say that to you?'

The result of Lisa's carelessness about playing the game of ludus by the rules is that she is often accused of 'leading a man on'. In the case of Michael, things really got out of hand.

Michael was a merchant seaman. He met Lisa early in a six-week shore leave. They saw each other often, as Michael had little else to do, and Lisa happened to have no other affairs at the time. As a result, Michael soon concluded that Lisa was really in love with him, but afraid to say so.

When Michael went back to sea, he entered a living condition favourable to mania (loneliness, discontent with surroundings, even sexual frustration) and began to write love letters every day. He could only mail these in port, so suddenly Lisa found herself receiving a bundle of passionate declarations of love. We'll take up the story as Lisa told it to me in her interview:

I was absolutely dumbfounded when that batch of letters arrived. I was already going with another guy, and had more or less forgotten about Michael. Sure, I expected a postcard from him once in a while, and perhaps we'd go with each other on his next leave. But these letters – I just didn't know what to do.

My parents were staying with me at the time, and they asked about the letters. When I explained, you know what? They took Michael's side! They said I had probably led him on, and he sounded like a fine young man. 'You're not getting any younger, you know,' my mother warned me; and my father chimed in with 'By the time you decide to get married all the good men will be taken.'

I was furious – at my parents, at Michael, and I guess most of all, at myself. Then I began to feel guilty, so I wrote Michael a short, nice note, saying I would enjoy meeting him again next time he was on leave. Then another bundle of letters arrived. He'd gone on writing without even waiting for my reply. Finally he returned, and we went out together again.

Then I did something really stupid. There were only a few days left in his leave, and Michael kept asking me to be engaged to him. Just to have some peace, I said something like 'We could talk seriously about that next time you're home.' So he went away thinking I'd tentatively agreed, but I'd already decided not to answer any more of his letters once he was gone.

His letters started coming again, and I didn't answer. So he telephoned – all the way from Cape Town! – and my parents happened to be with me when the call came. They heard every word I said. Michael broke down, and I tried to quiet him, and finally hung up on him. I was so annoyed and frustrated, and my parents started at me, so I told them to get out too.

Lisa was so unnerved by her experience with Michael that she spent a month on tranquillisers. She discontinued her other affairs, and went into seclusion. It was six months before she was able to get over her feelings of shame and guilt, and begin again to enjoy happy-go-lucky relationships with men. She still prefers the ludic lovestyle, but her manner during the interview suggested that she had not really learned how to manage this style without breaking yet another heart, some time in the future.

One of the main failings of many modern ludic lovers is a tendency to get too involved. Whether from laziness or lack of skill – or conviction – my respondents neglected the precautions and observance of simple rules which would have made ludus more fun. Quite often they allowed their partners to become too preoccupied and attentive. When a showdown became inevitable, the ludic lover had to detach himself with more cruelty and injury to the partner than would have been necessary if earlier warnings had been issued and insisted on. Many of my ludic respondents showed a poor sense of timing, and resorted to techniques of control which were clumsy. As a result they got out of their affairs only at the expense of angry scenes, pleading and accusations, which, no matter how much the ludic lovers tried to rationalise, left a residue of guilt.

Another common failing is a reluctance to declare, early in the relationship, the nature of the game you are playing. Such duplicity is unwarranted in today's free market of lovestyles. Not only is it unfair to trick a partner into intimate encounters by pretending to be interested for life – it is also unwise. How can you expect your partner to avoid becoming too involved, if you don't make it clear that you're not playing for keeps?

The burden of controlling your partner's emotions, as well as that of the eventual guilt for misleading the partner, are hardly worth any temporary advantage. You may win an early trick in bridge by reneging, but before the hand is out your offence will be uncovered. In ludus, the only permissible deceptions are those which are intended to be discovered in due course. Clever deception without malice will give both parties pleasure, or at the very least will be accepted as fair play by both.

Ludus, like tennis, is best enjoyed by closely matched partners. Two predominantly ludic lovers, each fully understanding the rules of the game and competent to limit his or her own personal involvement (rather than relying on the partner to do so), can play a mutually enjoyable game of love. But when one partner must do all of the 'cooling out', assert all the controls, and issue all the reminders about not getting serious, the game loses much of its pleasure. The worst possible combination is a ludic lover with a manic partner. As we shall see, a manic lover absolutely thrives on difficult love and non-requital of affection. He clings to an unwilling beloved with the most unbearably possessive tenacity. Nothing wearies gallant love like passion love from the other side, Stendhal observed.

Breaking Off

Even when the partners are fairly evenly matched in their preference for a ludic approach to a love relationship, the timing and operation of 'breaking off' is not an easy matter. The fact is, most ludic lovers enjoy being loved. It's flattering to the ego. Ovid noticed it twenty centuries ago. The same vanity which makes a ludic lover self-sufficient enough to be casual and detached about his beloved is boosted by being loved.

Self-sufficiency, or what some would call vanity, is psychologically essential to competent playing of gallant or courteous ludus. Theodor Reik points out that the individual who is fairly satisfied with himself is less likely to fall dependently in love with someone else. The self-satisfied ludic lover has a wide range of tastes, and any one partner who falls within that range is about as good as another. This substitutability of partners reflects the fact that a ludic lover has a much less specific ideal image of the beloved than is true of eros.

Brinkmanship can be fun, but remember that many a playful lover has lost his grip and fallen into the well. You're in danger whenever a particular partner has become someone special, someone you no longer feel could easily be replaced. You're already leaning too far when you begin to put up with anxieties, abuse and arguments in the relationship rather than break it off. Because you are afraid to start back at 'Square One' looking for a new partner, you may be holding on to a love you no longer enjoy.

A ludic lover who becomes serious about a partner soon finds that love isn't fun any more, but hard work and sometimes real pain. Of course, adherents of other lovestyles would argue that this is the way true love should be. But the ludic lover, even at this point, will look for a way out. One escape route suggested long ago by Ovid, is to discover what it is about your partner that is fascinating you so much. Then concentrate on that quality until it becomes tiresome to you. Instead of maintaining the usual intermittent pattern of ludic encounters, begin seeing your beloved every day, as much as possible. Go to bed often. You'll soon find that boredom makes the prospect of a lifetime relationship with this person so uninviting that you'll happily face the problem of finding a new partner.

If this remedy fails, then only one cure remains – that suggested by Robert Burton more than three centuries ago. Live together. A few months of domestic tedium will probably restore your playful vigour. If not, then ludus is no longer your appropriate lovestyle.

Love in the Plural

Typical ludic respondents were surprisingly undemanding in their preferences of partners. They considered the pursuit of an ideal image naïve and unrealistic. Aware of a variety of needs and tastes – and perhaps aware also of human imperfection – the ludic lover prefers to satisfy some needs and tastes with one person, some with another, and so forth, whether simultaneously or in succession. This mobility in intimacy, combined with 'vain' self-sufficiency, makes breaking off with any one partner fairly easy, so long as the supply of alternatives is obvious and plentiful.

In past centuries the elaborate practice of ludic love tended to be limited to the aristocracy, who had leisure and money for such diversions. Not all aristocrats were ludic lovers, of course, but it was a style of life more acceptable at court than among the bourgeois or lower classes. In the present democratic age, ludus is more freely available to every class, but the aristocratic grace and polished manners are not easily duplicated by today's middle-class swinger or neurotic jet-setter. The worthy courtier of the past earned his reputation by executing a time-consuming and complex ritual of love. Progress from salon to bed-chamber called for a precise and charming display of the best manners, innumerable witticisms, flattery and noble gestures, to say nothing of costly little gifts and extravagant promises. Finally, after near-misses, and hints at open physical contact, the lover accomplished his goal. His beloved was naturally expected to be equally diligent and polished in the game of love.

Once gained, the gallant lover's prize was not hastily ravished, or left unattended while he returned to work at the office! He could withdraw as graciously and ceremoniously as he had advanced, with more flattering admiration appreciation and tokens of affection. Whatever his intentions, there would always be allusions to possible future encounters. If his object, once undressed and bedded, had proved disappointing, not the slightest hint of this disenchantment was revealed. Not only would such behaviour be insulting – and damaging to one's gallant reputation with other ladies – it would also have mocked the lover's long campaign by suggesting that he didn't know how to pick a prize worth winning. Incidentally, though I have spoken of male ludic lovers, any reader of Flaubert, Laclos or Tolstoy will know that gallantry has had its lady players too.

Today's clumsy ludic rituals are a peasant's boorishness in contrast to the gallantry of European court life: 'Want to come up for a cup of coffee?' 'Like to stop by for a drink?' 'My place or yours?' The transparency, haste and superficiality of modern ludus would appal a courtier. Perhaps the recent rash of how-to-bed-your-man (or woman) paperbacks is evidence of the desire for more skill in the rituals of ludic love. Even the use of a little wit adds some mutual pleasure to the game: 'Like to try my new waterbed?'

The most polished ludic style is sometimes to be found in older homosexual men. The younger gay male is often so eager for a sexual 'trick' that he is unwilling to perform the ritual dance of ludus; or else he is so seriously seeking 'true love' of the manic style that he shuns playful love entirely. Gay women still tend to share the female distrust of ludus inherited from Victorian times.

Tom is the most accomplished ludic lover I know. He is

67 now, a man whose once-handsome face has mellowed to a kindly smile. His charming and engaging manner is difficult to resist, and this gallant lover knows how to combine great patience with an instinct for the opportune moment. He forces himself on no one, yet is rarely alone at a social gathering. His urbane manner and aristocratic bearing attract the company of good-looking younger men. I asked Tom the secret of his style.

'Well, I never try too hard,' Tom smiled at me. 'And I let the other person do most of the talking. There aren't many people who really *listen* to a lot of younger men, so they appreciate a good listener. Usually older men are too busy doing the talking.

'When I first meet someone I ask him something about himself. You know, most people really like to talk about themselves. Especially vain young men – and most good-looking men have reason to be vain! Everyone's always trying to get them into bed, but no one is paying any attention to their personality. Vanity is often a result of frustration, you know. A person who feels he is really accepted can be self-confident without being vain.'

'Do you mean that you exploit their vanity, their frustration?' I asked.

'Well, I think *exploit* is too strong a word. These are adults, after all, responsible for their own behaviour. I'd rather think of myself as providing something they need – and hoping for something in exchange.'

'You mean sex?'

'Oh, sometimes, yes. But not every time. What I really want is company, the attractive, alive company of younger people.'

Tom's approach would earn most older men the label of 'dirty old man' but I have never heard it even hinted in Tom's case. Talking to some of the young men who are his companions, I find that Tom rarely takes sexual initiatives, and is quite content to talk, perhaps touch lightly, or cuddle for a few moments. And despite the most diligent probing, I have not discovered beneath Tom's charm, what many would expect – a sad and lonely old man. Tom seems to really enjoy his ludic lovestyle.

Sexual gratification was only a minor part of the total time
and effort involved in the gallant practice of ludic love. It
was the reward for a suitable performance of the ceremonial
dance. As much, perhaps even more, pleasure was gained
from playing the game well, surmounting the obstacles while
never once becoming entangled in unseemly emotions. I
found a much greater emphasis on the sexual aspects of the
ludic relationship among my modern respondents than
seems to have been typical of gallant love in the past. Today
there is an impatience to go to bed which not only telescopes
the preliminary pleasantries, but also diminishes the lover's
enjoyment of any future encounters with the partner. Ludus
is not merely 'having sex', any more than good sex is just
reaching an orgasm as fast as possible. Even if the partner
proves to be exceptionally good in bed, the accomplished
ludic lover knows that the pleasure of sex is multiplied when
contained within a larger social relationship.

Ludic respondents showed the lowest level of interest in
the mutual study and improvement of sexual techniques and
pleasure with their partners. Their attitude seemed to be
that it is easier to find and bed a new partner who might
prove more enjoyable than to spend time trying to work out
sexual difficulties with a present partner. This attitude contrasts sharply with that of erotic and storgic lovers. Even
pragmatic lovers were more willing to try to work things
out.

Whenever a typically ludic lover encounters a partner
who has ideas about sex, commitment, honesty, or other
features of the love relationship which are typical of some
other kind of loving such as eros or storge, the ludic lover is
likely to depreciate the importance of these differences. His
argument will run: 'But I don't expect to settle down with
you anyway. We can just have some good times together and
then go our own ways. I won't interrupt your search for the
perfect mate.' Needless to say, the typically erotic or storgic
lover is likely to regard this approach as superficial and
shortsighted, or even promiscuous and immoral.

This judgment, may be somewhat unfair to the ludic
lover, for his calculated control of involvement should not
be confused with a lack of involvement. On the contrary,

well-performed ludus requires the most subtle management of self, and this cannot be accomplished instinctively. It calls for involvement of a different kind from the emotional attachment and rapport the erotic lover expects, but there is an interpersonal relationship none the less.

Self-assured Ludus

Just as the erotic lover requires considerable self-confidence to be successful, so does the ludic lover, but his self-assurance differs in its psychological composition. The erotic lover is sure of his ability to encounter others openly with some risk, yet not endanger the ultimate survival of his ego. He swims in a fast current because he is a strong swimmer. The ludic lover prefers shallower water. He knows his limitations and is not prepared to allow himself to become too dependent on others. Perhaps experience has taught him that risks are not worth the taking. At the same time, he believes in his own assets and self-sufficiency and convinces himself that he does not 'need' other people the way other kinds of lovers seem to do.

I have found it quite futile to suggest to a convinced ludic lover that his self-assurance has a hollow ring to it, or that he is really missing a great experience by not taking a few risks. Indeed, I soon came to regard it as unethical in my research even to hint at an alternative approach to love. The most successful ludic respondents seemed quite happy with their detachment from intense love relationships, except for the occasional bout of guilt feelings after a partner had become too involved. Perhaps as these respondents grew older they would, like *Alfie*, come to regret their type of love, as Burt Bacharach's song of that name suggests. Even lovers with as long and varied a career as that of George Sand may eventually wish they had more deeply requited some past partner's intensity.

A confident ludic lover enjoys a challenge, but he will never pursue a losing game, least of all to the point where he loses his dignity. The able ludic lover knows when to take his losses and quit graciously. For example, the swinging secretary may make a play for her happily married boss, just for the fun of it; but to the extent that she is typical of ludic love, she will never push her luck by over-ardent efforts. She will not cut off her own retreat should that become necessary. On the contrary, she will probably have several other affairs going at the same time so that she does not allow victory in any one of them to become too important or defeat too injurious to her vanity.

Many readers who would not define themselves as lifelong ludic lovers will nevertheless take this approach in at least one love relationship at some time. If you happen to choose ludus, perhaps while waiting for a partner to come along who will fulfil the requirements of another, preferred definition of true love, it will probably be most enjoyable if you select a partner who is about equally inclined to a ludic adventure. This is especially true if you are less self-sufficient (less vain?) than is necessary for uncomplicated, guilt-free ludus. When some of my respondents had the misfortune or carelessness to select manic or erotic partners for a ludic adventure, their attempts to keep the relationship pleasantly casual were often exhausting, and the final break-up quite painful. These respondents vacillated between efforts to cool the partner down and attempts to soothe the partner's hurt feelings. Such love becomes 'one long tacit apology for itself'.[1]

Manic Ludus

When a lover alternates between a detached, devil-may-care attitude with the partner, and a worried, lovesick desire for more attention (an attitude most unbecoming in a gallant lover!) I refer to this condition as *manic ludus*.

Often this is a case of a lover wanting to be more purely ludic, but for some reason lacking the vanity or self-sufficiency necessary to remain independent of any intimate involvement. Perhaps work has not been going well. Perhaps the lover is showing disturbing signs of age, or finds fewer partners available or responsive to his ploys. When it becomes less certain that there are always more fish in the sea, it's more difficult to throw back the fish you've already caught.

A would-be ludic lover whose self-sufficiency is being undermined by everyday experience, personal problems, or

1. Aldous Huxley, *Point Counterpoint*.

mere ageing, will often become more cavalier about his partner's feelings even while he becomes more dependent on the partner for attention and affection. He both needs and resents love. The patience and polish of gallantry come easily when one is young and beautiful and well-to-do, with few cares and much leisure time. It's easier to be kind and gentle while dropping one partner in favour of another who is already waiting. When promising new encounters become rare, the ludic lover may grow more cynical and ruthless, and at the same time more anxious.

Joanne, a professional woman in her late thirties, had enjoyed a series of pleasant, uncommitted relationships over the previous decade. Recently she had experienced more difficulty replacing cast-off partners with new ones. Thus she was less self-assured than usual when Bill, a night-school classmate, began making advances. She allowed herself to become more emotionally involved than usual. Joanne began to want to see Bill every day, and became preoccupied with thoughts of him when they were apart. Unthinkably for a ludic lover, she indulged in fantasies of life together with Bill sometimes in the future.

One night while making love, Bill let it slip – by calling Joanne by another name – that he was married. Joanne was amazed to find herself deeply hurt. In previous relationships the fact that a partner was married had never been a handicap. On the contrary, it was something of an assurance against the partner's becoming too serious over her.

> This time it really stung [Joanne told me]. I accused him of being dishonest with me, which was pretty silly, considering the number of times I've been dishonest in various ways with men. Besides, no one expects a lover to mean everything he says anyway. It's all meant to be taken with a pinch of salt. But this time it was like having salt rubbed in a wound – and was I surprised how much I got wounded!

After several attempts to persuade Bill to love her – attempts, so unlike ludus (and so much like mania) that Joanne hardly knew herself – she finally dropped Bill:

> Not politely like I did with past lovers, but with a thud. I *hated* him. It was so stupid of me. I had a good reputation as a

cool person, an easy-going companion the guys could enjoy without either them or me getting hung up. In fact several of my affairs were men who knew each other and when I let one go, another started in. Not just for sex – in fact there was one guy I went with for six months and we never had sex. But with Bill I really blew it. No one who knows how I treated him will want to go with me now. They don't understand what could have come over me – to tell the truth, I'm not sure I understand either. I was so mad at Bill I cut him dead at a party, hung up the phone on him. . . .

The funny part is, he finally divorced his wife. Going with me made him realise he wasn't very happy at home. He's married another woman now. If I'd handled things properly I could have been in her place.

Joanne, like many older ludic lovers, was tired of the game and wanted to stop playing. She feared *Alfie's* fate. But perhaps she wanted to change lovestyles a little too late. Playing ludus is rather like blowing a balloon to its fullest capacity without bursting it. To stop short of the full capacity is to have missed something – 'One more fling, then I'll settle down.' But go one puff too far and it's impossible to back off. The balloon has burst.

Ground Rules

Competent ludic lovers often lay out explicit ground rules early in the relationship to forestall unwanted involvement. The partner is told not to expect to see the lover every day, and contact by phone or letter is made difficult or 'inconvenient'. The understanding is established that the lover is not accountable for his time when not with the beloved, and vice versa. Nor should the partner expect the lover to make any basic changes in his life style – and he won't demand any of her.

'Love several persons', a seventeenth-century manual advises; for three lovers are safer than two, and much safer than one, when playing ludus. After three, the marginal benefit declines, while complications multiply. Three is better than two, because many lovers expect to contend with one serious rival; but if there are several rivals it's easy to conclude that the beloved isn't ready to be serious about anyone.

Jealousy is not a permissible emotion in ludus except as a ploy in the game. It must be of the teasing type, not serious. Any jealous scenes are likely to bring 'game over' from a ludic lover. After all, he considers one partner in love about as good as another once certain minimum requirements are met, so why put up with the hassles of jealousy? The typical ludic lover is a lodger or tenant of love, not an owner or freeholder. He is no more concerned with whom his partner becomes involved with after his interest is exhausted than with who occupies his hotel room after he moves on. Equally, the ludic lover is not impressed by promises of future improvement. If you don't perform very well in bed or amuse him with your conversation, your best intentions to improve will meet with little patience. He is more likely to move on to someone else.

Those who expect to play an enjoyable game of ludic love must adopt the appropriate attitudes. To suggest that such an approach to love is cynical or immoral is simply to argue one's preference for another kind of love. No use trying ludus in that case. 'You can't cart a wagon-load of ideals and romanticisms about with you,' one of Aldous Huxley's ludic characters warns. If you want ludic fun and variety, if you want to cover the ground, you can't have old-fashioned baggage holding you back.

Some of my respondents who reported ludic loves were better able to accept the ground rules of ludus than to put them into effect. Intellectually, they agreed with the possibility of loving several persons at once. They were even willing to pretend more intense emotion than they actually felt, just for the pleasure of the game. Yet most of them baulked at admitting that one must always reserve the right to end the relationship when it ceases to be interesting, and to do so without any feelings of obligation beyond courtesy. They shied away from conceding that it is better to be first and drop the partner, rather than let the partner have the initiative. Their experiences obviously told them otherwise – that one's vanity is better maintained by being the first to break off – but they could not accept this as morally right. As a result, a significant number of my ludic respondents failed the acid test of ludus – the ability to break off with a partner they were 'through with'. Instead, when the partner held on, several of my respondents let the relationship go on until the inevitable break was much more painful for the partner, thus producing greater guilt for the ludic lover.

Ludic love is never surrender or ingenuousness. It is always more enjoyable when conducted with self-control. The lover who passionately reveals his need for the beloved thereby surrenders control of his destiny to the beloved, and could never be ludic. The approach to loving taken in the style I call ludus is similar to our modern scientific approach to nature. Man does not surrender to nature today, nor intimately commune with it. Instead, he marshals his powers of control and exerts mastery over nature. Method, never impulse, is the ludic lover's guide.

The Future of Ludus

In past centuries ludus has probably been easier for men to practise than for women, but this is changing. Removal of the fear of unwanted pregnancy has certainly been a factor in the change. Ludic love does not depend on an inequality of the sexes. It has been practised by women in the past. It is widely practised among homosexuals. Medical control of venereal diseases, combined with a generally more permissive attitude to sexual relationship, will probably increase the possibilities of ludic love in the future. But the most important factor in enjoyable ludic love in the coming decades will be our general conception of the nature of intimate human relationships. Are we prepared to replace single, fairly intense, long-lasting intimate relationships with multiple, rather superficial, but also more pleasure-centred, short-lived relationships? This trend is already evident in our relationships at work, in the places where we live, even in our physical intimacy.

If the popularity of ludus threatens to undermine the traditional monogamous lifetime marriage, and the family built around it, the practitioners of ludus would simply reply that the viability of such marriage and family forms in modern society is debatable anyway. At the same time, the cultured and civilised practice of ludus is considerably more attractive than unbridled hedonism and promiscuity. Whatever our prospects, Ovid, if he were alive today, would certainly feel vindicated. He was banished for life to the remote edges of the Roman Empire for publishing his scandalous poems on *amor ludens*; but his ideas are far from banished from the Western practice of love.

Four

Storge – Love as Friendship

> Love without fever, tumult or folly, a peaceful and
> enchanting affection. . . .
> (*Proudhon*)

Storge is love without turbulent emotion, a feeling of natural affection such as you might have for a favourite brother or sister. An unexciting and often uneventful lovestyle, it is rarely the stuff of dramatic works or romantic novels. When depicted in fiction, storge usually takes the form of a background love or one of sober second thought, as in Somerset Maugham's *Of Human Bondage*. The hero, Philip, finally concludes six anguished years of manic love with Mildred, during which time he has also been a sort of 'older brother' to Sally Athelny. Philip and Sally never 'fall in love'. The forced marriage they expected from their single lapse into sexual intimacy proves to be a false alarm. Yet, almost without realising it, they subside into matrimony.

'I wonder if you'll marry me, Sally. . . .'
'If you like.'
'Don't you want to?'
'Oh, of course I'd like to have a house of my own and it's about time I was settling down. . . .'
'There's no one else I would marry.'
'Then that settles it. Mother and Dad will be surprised, won't they?'
'I'm so happy.'
'I want my lunch,' she said.

In many instances of storgic love, Mother and Dad probably will not be surprised at all. Indeed, they will probably have been wondering for years why two people who seemed so well suited and comfortable with each other haven't got married. The reason of course, in the Maugham novel, is that at least one of the lovers believed for a long time that love, true love, should be more ecstatic, dramatic, and occasionally anguishing. Or perhaps more challenging, playful and promiscuous. To the lover whose dominant lovestyle is eros, mania or ludus, a storgic relationship is not really love at all, but 'just affection'. To a typically storgic lover, by contrast, the ecstasy of eros is an allusion, the suffering of mania a self-imposed torture, and the playfulness of ludus a mockery of serious love.

Reading the existing literature of love originally caused me to think of storge as friendship gradually growing into a committed love. As C. S. Lewis describes storge: 'We can sometimes point to the very day and hour when we fell in love or began a new friendship, but I doubt if we ever catch Affection (storge) beginning.'[1] Classic examples would be children of neighbouring families who grew up together, or met as schoolmates, and eventually married without ever falling 'romantically' in love. In my interviewing I encountered a few such cases, especially among respondents whose love began in semi-rural areas. But in modern cities few people live near each other, or go to the same schools, long enough to develop, over a period of time, the un-self-conscious affection which is typical of storge. So I originally discarded from storge those instances in which a respondent began a love relationship with a stranger in adult life. When further data-processing made it apparent that except for the shorter time span some of these relationships resembled the growth pattern of the classic examples of storge, I revised my definition of the ideal type.

As I now use the term, storge is a kind of love which can begin even with a stranger. It is not the existence of prior friendship which distinguishes storge, but the quality of the experience as it develops. Among my urban respondents, who usually had few surviving contacts with their childhood or adolescent peer groups, storge began after an encounter with a person of the sort one *might* have grown up with, that is, someone with similar background and interests. If the lover and beloved had known each other in childhood they would very probably have been close friends. This characteristic clearly distinguishes storge from lovestyles in which the partners may not treat each other at all like friends.

The storgic lover never *consciously* selects a love partner.

1. In *The Four Loves*.

He is not 'looking for love'. Instead, he selects activities he enjoys, and thus meets others with the same interests. The activities are selected for their own sake, not as a means to meet a partner. Storge thus differs from the lovestyle I call pragma (see Chapter 8): for the pragmatic lover, the activities are a means to an end and will be dropped in favour of other activities if they do not pay off with a suitable partner.

Sustained by common interests, storge is not as direct a form of interpersonal encounter as eros. Mutually erotic lovers gaze into each other's eyes, talk endlessly about themselves, and are intensely aware of *being in love*. Such behaviour would seem ridiculous to mutually storgic lovers, who treat each other basically like 'old friends'. Perhaps neither will be able to recall when 'I love you' was first said, if indeed any special declaration of love was ever made. Not that they deliberately avoid such statements; more likely they simply reserve them for very special situations, such as the eve of a long separation. After all, how often does one say to a close friend, 'I am your friend'?

This attitude also distinguishes storge from that more managed, artificial lovestyle, ludus. Rituals of coyness and witty conversation would be out of place between those who relate to each other like old friends. Storge may superficially resemble ludus in its lack of great intensity or passion, but the origins are quite different. The typical ludic lover avoids or controls intensity of feeling, because he is consciously aware of its risks. The typical storgic lover is largely unaware of intense feeling in the first place. It simply doesn't occur to him that a lover should be sentimental and dewy-eyed. Storgic love 'just comes naturally' with the passage of time and the mutual enjoyment of shared activities. You grow accustomed to her face.

One of the storgic lovers I talked to, Nancy, lives in a comfortable Brighton flat with two girlfriends. She comes from a happy family where she was one of six children, growing up in a small town in the North. At 19, Nancy left home to join relatives in Brighton and find work in an antique shop in the Lanes. She eventually met two other shop workers, and they took a flat.

'I really like our life together,' Nancy told me. 'Each of us has a boyfriend, and we often go out together, or have dinner here in the flat. We have a lot of fun, without getting too intimate, if you know what I mean.'

It transpired during the interview that Nancy had never had intimate sexual relations with her boyfriend, and, to her knowledge, neither had her flatmates, both of whom came from happy, but fairly religious families in the North. 'We don't go in for that sort of thing,' Nancy explained. 'It's not right until after marriage. Sure, I could see myself trying it out with someone after we were engaged and definitely going to get married. But not just for fun.'

Nancy's boyfriend apparently 'respects' her approach. 'I think he's had sex with a girl or two, but that doesn't matter. He wouldn't want to marry any of them. He's very serious about being in love and really promised to each other, before we do anything like that.'

Nancy and her friend spend their time visiting each other, going to the Front for long walks, shopping together, listening to records, and in many similar forms of companionship. Neither has said anything so definite as 'I love you', yet Nancy already feels that they will probably marry.

> We're in no rush. We want to grow together, and get used to each other. I think loving begins with liking. My parents really *like* each other, after all these years. That's not so common nowadays. I want to have that kind of marriage too.

Not only the pace but the purpose of storge differ from those of the eros and ludus lovestyles. Storge is a companionate kind of loving. Its goals are marriage, home and children. How nice to avoid all the silly conflicts and exhausting sentiments of other lovers, the storgic lover sighs. Theodor Reik clearly has a storgic type of love in mind when he contrasts passion 'like a house on fire' with the love which is a friendly, warming fireplace.[1] But to the would-be erotic or ludic partner, the storgic lover is a stick-in-the-mud, a stay-at-home, a bore, a drag – or whatever the current slang provides.

Sex in Storge

Sex is one of the most revealing aspects of intimacy. It is not

1. In *Of Love and Lust*.

surprising that sexual contact comes late in the slow development of a storgic love. Intimate petting or nudity on the first night of encounter with the partner would be unthinkable. Not that the storgic lover takes a puritanical attitude to sexual pleasures. He simply considers the rapid exposure of one's body to be quite out of keeping with a gradual process of emotional and intellectual contact. Sex does not become important in storge until the releationship has reached a level of intimate knowledge of the partner in other respects. The storgic lover does not expect great sexual ecstasy with his partner any more than he expects emotional intensity. Sexual disappointment is far less likely to break up a mutually storgic love than it is an erotic or ludic relationship. One of the frequent difficulties of storge in contemporary society is the constant emphasis in our mass media on ultimate orgasms. It's not easy for the storgic lover to go on believing that sex is not really important when everyone keeps telling him that it is.

Psychologists might attribute the lack of intense feelings and sexual expectation in storge to the absence of any powerful sex drive. While this may be part of the explanation, my impression is that the typically storgic lover has a slower 'internal clock' or calendar. My storgic respondents seemed to view the passage of time with less anxiety and urgency than did those respondents who were more erotic or ludic. There was less lust for life, in terms of the number of experiences they expected to encompass in any given period of time.

Absence of impulsive emotions makes storge a hardy love, capable of surviving long dry-spells. The physical absence of the beloved, or the absence of strong emotional rapport with a physically present partner, seem much less distressing than in other lovestyles. Just as you may have a 'very close friend' whom you have not seen for a year or more, so a storgic lover can continue to define as a partner someone he has not seen or even heard from for a long time.

A classic example is the love of Ulysses and Penelope, but there are numerous modern instances among partners separated by work, prison or war.

Storge is a slow-burning love, rarely hectic or urgent, but it is not without its disagreements and conflicts. Even the best of friends sometimes argue or fight. But over a period of time, storgic lovers build up a reserve of stability which, like a deep water table tapped by an artesian well, may be drawn on during times of difficulty that would quickly kill a ludic relationship and greatly strain an erotic love. Yet mutual storgic relationships do not always survive. Among my respondents were cases in which a new experience of another, more intense kind of love had shattered the calm of storge. Even if a break up occurs, storgic lovers are very likely to remain good friends. It would be inconceivable to a typical storgic lover that two people who had truly loved each other at one time could hate each other simply because they had ceased to be lovers.

Whole weeks or months may pass in a storgic love with nothing interesting happening, so far as an outside observer can detect. No wonder this kind of love is neglected by novelists! In a ludic or erotic relationship, and most of all in a manic love, something is happening all the time. In eros, there is some little misunderstanding to correct, some secret to share, or a separation to survive by urgent and repeated assurances of love. In ludus, the absence of activity soon leads to boredom, and the lover begins looking elsewhere for amusement.

Storge is a love in which sympathy rather than desire makes the match; so there are fewer campaigns to fight and fewer wounds to heal. An absence of tumult nicely compensates for the lack of ecstasy. While love is a more important or central activity in the life of the storgic lover than it is for the ludic, it is less vital to storge than to the erotic lover. Love becomes more of a basic habit than a conscious effort for the storgic lover. No one typical of this lovestyle could have written 'How do I love thee? Let me count the ways.'

Unreciprocated Storge

A lover whose ways of thinking and acting in love are typical of storge may find himself puzzled and confused by a partner who expects a more dramatic experience. The story of one of my respondents illustrates what may happen. He and his beloved had grown up in the same small town, started dating in high school, and eventually became identified by the community as a couple. Shortly before they planned to announce their engagement, the girl met a boy who was new in town. At first the girl's preference was obviously for my respondent:

I'm sure she was in love with me, but this new guy came on very strong – flowers, poetry, the whole bit. He had a knack of saying just the right things – sort of flattering without being obvious. Then one day he hinted that he was falling in love with her. Ann told me about it, and I could tell she wanted me to compete with this guy – to do some of the same things, tell her how much I loved her and so on.

Well, of course I told her I loved her, but in a matter-of-fact way ... I couldn't think of any fancy ways to say it. Friends started telling me how different Ann was when she went out with this other guy ... all sentimental and moony. Ann and I went on dating, but she started treating me more like a confidant – sort of brother – instead of a future husband. She kept telling me about this other guy and the things they did together. Then Ann and he started having lovers' quarrels, and she asked my advice about him. One time when they weren't speaking, I actually took a message from her to ask him to call. Stupid of me – but I'd have done anything to make her happy. Unfortunately, he wasn't too proud to call – I was hoping he would be – and they started again.

Eventually this respondent lost his beloved to his rival, who offered Ann a more exciting kind of loving. Centuries ago, social custom, family opinion, the church, and even the traditional love stories were allied in opposition to 'romantic' forms of love and in support of the storgic types. In such an age, the community would have rallied to my respondent's support. His girlfriend would have been warned of the dangers of dramatic love: 'Look at the fate of Romeo and Juliet, Tristan and Iseult, and the misfortunes of our local examples of love-struck youth!' But today there are at least as many social forces *supporting* the girl's adventurism, urging youth on to more ecstatic emotions and orgasms. Nor are older married couples immune from the effects of these social forces. I have interviewed numerous respondents who broke up a comfortable, contented marriage because it seemed dull and predictable. A new love with a younger or prettier person was risky, but the risk was part of the attraction. For many ordinary people, falling into an exciting kind of loving is the only adventure open to them.

There are fewer distinctive symptoms, either by presence or absence, for storge than for other lovestyles. Storge has a lower profile than eros, ludus or mania. It is sometimes difficult to distinguish from ordinary friendship. A gradient of friendly relationships exists, from instrumental acquaint-anceship (getting along with someone for some purely ul-terior purpose such as sharing adjoining airplane seats), through friendship of varying degrees of intensity, to the form of affiliative love called storge. Obviously there is no sharp dividing line between a very close friendship and stor-gic love, except insofar as a society provides *rites de passage* from one to the other, such as engagement and marriage. In my interviews, I established an arbitrary line: if the respond-ent believed the experience was love, not simply friendship, I included his experience among my data.

Storge is often identifiable by contrasting it with other lovestyles. For example, storgic lovers depend on their part-ners in a manner which contrasts with ludus, eros and mania. The ludic lover depends on the partner to stick to the rules of the game. Once the relationship is over, this love-style prescribes total independence: 'I got along without you before I met you, and I'll get along without you now.' At the other extreme, the manic lovestyle involves excess-ive dependence on the beloved: 'I'm nobody without you.' When the beloved is lost, the lover is devastated.

In eros and storge, the relationship with the partner is one of *interdependence*, rather than independence or de-pendence. However, the interdependence in eros is direct and intimate, while that of storge is mediated by shared ac-tivity. When the erotic lover's partner is absent, no amount of activity will fill up the void left by the missing voice, motion and touch of the beloved. Photographs and long dis-tance calls may help, but only temporarily. In storge, if the absence of the partner makes the shared activities difficult or impossible, the lover will pine for the partner's return; but if the activities can be continued, they tend to compensate for the partner's absence.

It is as if the daily round of habit preserves something of the beloved's physical presence. Sometimes, when a long storgic marriage has been ended by the death of one partner, the other will go on for the remaining years doing almost exactly what the couple did together. The house will be kept exactly as it was before the partner died. The same daily routine will be repeated, in a manner which may seem 'weird' to outsiders, but perfectly meaningful to the storgic lover.

Lovers who prefer storge as a lovestyle are often those with happy memories of childhood. Many storgic respondents came from large families and enjoyed close relationships with brothers or sisters. Children in such families learn to spread their emotional needs among a greater number of intimates, avoiding the magnified focusing of emotions which leads to eros and mania. Thus storge was a typical lovestyle of the traditional rural or small-town society. Living in settled communities where economic interdependence underlined emotional relationships, lovers grew up expecting love to be a matter of companionship and shared activity rather than sudden discovery and ecstasy.

Today's mobile urban family with one or two children is a less favourable environment for the development of storgic attitudes to love. The child may have to acquire a new set of friends several times in a decade, and is often cut off from relatives. The child often learns to depend on a single significant other for all major emotional needs. This early conditioning is reinforced by popular songs which persuade young people to find 'someone who loves only you'.

Modern urban social conditions tend to produce lovers who expect bells to ring when true love is encountered, while at the same time making us more suspicious and even cynical about the possibility of distinguishing the true from the counterfeit. People who have grown up in settled surroundings are more confident of their ability to decide whom to trust, and more willing to take a reasonable length of time to decide. The typical storgic lover already enjoys the companionship of good friends and neighbours, and does not expect to abandon these relationships when love comes along. Rather, the partner will be included in the friendship group. The storgic lover does not become preoccupied with the partner, nor attempt to monopolise the partner's time.

Since love is seen as a part of kinship and social life, the storgic lover naturally pays attention to the opinion of family and friends about the new partner. This contrasts sharply with the erotic or manic lover, both of whom believe that the 'rightness' of a love choice can be decided independently of 'what other people think'. The manic lover may even conclude from social and parental opposition, that this *must* be true love, which Fate is putting to the test.

The true test of storge is not the ability to 'find a way' by sheer emotional force, but the ability to wait patiently. This lovestyle does not ignore social convention and defy tradition. The 'truth' of love is proved by outlasting trouble through quiet fortitude. 'All things come to him who waits'. 'Time will tell'. 'Rome was not built in a day'. These are the watchwords of storge. Novelists sometimes try to make storge more dramatic, as in the case of Tonya's love for Doctor Zhivago. But these literary efforts rarely succeed in making drama out of a lovestyle whose pace usually moves too slowly to seem romantic.

No Impossible Dreams

Storge contrasts sharply with eros on the question of ideal images of the beloved. Most of my storgic respondents were incapable of sorting through a set of photographs to choose which physical appearances were their 'type'. The storgic respondents reported no strong physical attractions to their partners, nor any sense of recognition in the partner of the embodiment of an ideal. Typically storgic lovers do not seem to construct an ideal physical image of a beloved. Also unlike eros, they are quite unlikely to become deeply preoccupied with thoughts of the beloved. In these respects the storgic lover seems like the ludic; but he can be distinguished by further comparisons. The storgic lover does not consciously load the dice in his own favour by 'allowing himself to be loved' while holding back on his own involvement to protect himself, as a ludic lover would. Though both ludic and storgic lovers show reserve in display of feelings, the reserve is a *calculated* restraint in the ludic lover, who has no intention of letting the relationship go beyond a certain point. Sexual gratification is no test of the worth of the relationship for a storgic lover, but it certainly becomes such a test for the ludic lover.

Sometimes a person whose basic approach to love is typical of storge will be drawn into a more frantic form of love by a serious threat to his relationship. Instead of responding to a rival with the confused apathy of the respondent reported on p. 75 ff., the lover may temporarily manifest many of the symptoms of mania. This form of loving I have called manic storge, a 'tertiary' lovestyle discussed in Chapter Ten. However, once the threat is removed, or the relationship actually broken off, the storgic lover is likely to return to his previous definition of true love. Thus, storge and mania are usually in sharp contrast to each other.

Homosexual Storge

The pattern of companionate love found among heterosexuals has its parallel among gay lovers. Andy and Alan, for example, have been together for fifteen years. They first met and became friends in the same college residence. But it was more than two years before each discovered the other's sexual orientation, before they 'became lovers'.

It was in relation to the other that each of these men realised his own gayness. Andy and Alan are not so much homosexual, as homosexual in relationship to each other. Neither has had a gay relationship with any other man. Sexual activity simply emerged out of a long-term mutual affection and trust; it seemed but the final and logical step in disclosing themselves to each other.

Among lesbians the storgic pattern is a familiar one, much more typical than the ludic and erotic patterns found frequently among gay men. This may be a product of acculturation. Young gay women tell me that there is now more 'cruising' for partners. However, new love relationships are still more likely to develop with friends or acquaintances than with complete strangers. In this respect, gay women share the same heritage as heterosexual women. It is difficult for them to 'pick up' partners by taking the initiatives which, until recently, have been a male prerogative.

Loving is Caring

A storgic lover believes that true love is a deep feeling of respect, concern, compassion and solicitude. This lovestyle knows nothing of the thoughtless precipitateness of mania or the self-conscious intensity of eros. Life goes on as usual, but now includes the partner. Loving is caring and sharing. Where the erotic lover would want a romantic dinner for two with candlelight, or the ludic lover a witty conversation in an impressive restaurant, the storgic lover prefers home cooking.

This does not mean that the storgic relationship is devoid of emotion. 'Still waters run deep.' But the typical storgic lover is embarrassed by an obvious display of emotion. Thus, if the partner is not mutually storgic in lovestyle, mis-understandings may arise. A manic or erotic partner, for instance, expects frequent and conspicuous expressions of feeling, and may easily charge a storgic lover with 'not really caring' or 'taking me for granted'.

Storgic lovers expect the behaviour of a lover to be much like that of a close friend or relative. This lovestyle recog-nises that love is sometimes hard work, rather than a spon-taneous rush of attraction – an attitude which emphasises, the element of compassion in storge. Com-passion, 'suffering with' another person, is part of a lovestyle in which difficulties are made lighter by being shared. The stor-gic lover is not one who seeks difficulties in order to test love, as the manic lover would.

A typical storgic lover is reserved about expression of his feelings for the beloved, but this does not require a restraint on physical encounter. Indeed, they have probably seen each other daily for years, as neighbours or workmates. They do not manipulate the relationship by *not* seeing each other too often, as ludic lovers would; nor do they feel impelled to see each other daily because of the intensity of their attraction, as erotic lovers would. When absent from each other, storgic lovers are not constantly assessing the relationship or re-dramatising episodes to themselves, as manic (or, in a different manner, pragmatic) lovers would.

Storgic love is relatively undemanding and readily for-giving. The lover may sometimes attempt to elicit a greater show of affection from the partner, but there is none of the unremitting pressure typical of the manic lover. Nor will the storgic lover readily blame his partner for difficulties in the relationship. The typical storgic lover is not a compulsively possessive lover. Taking the partner's commitment almost for granted, he will ignore potential rivals and refuse to believe that his partner could be unfaithful. While the manic or erotic lover tends to consider three a crowd, the storgic lover thinks 'the more the merrier', so he is glad to have company around, not thinking that he may be opening the door to a rival. Even after repeated infidelities by his partner, the storgic lover will still be ready to forgive and forget, assuming that the bonds of lasting friendship are more powerful than temporary indiscretions.

The storgic lover's basic attitude to his partner is one of familiarity: 'I've known you a long time, seen you in many moods.' This familiarity breeds realistic candour and insight, not of a probing, analytical kind, but quiet and stable. When Tonya says of Yury Zhivago '. . . for you have no will', she is not making a penetrating psychological diagnosis. She is simply stating something she had known about Zhivago for a long time and has accepted as a fact.

Like most lovestyles (mania is the significant exception), storge requires a certain kind of self-assurance on the part of the lover. In eros, ego strength is expressed as the capacity to risk rapid and deep involvement, and depends on a realistic knowledge of one's self. In ludus, ego strength is expressed in observance of the rules of the game. It rests on the less secure base of vanity and self-defence in interpersonal relationships. In storge, ego strength is expressed as a patient and generous trust in the basic decency of people. It rests on the lover's past experiences of secure relationship in family and community. When life seems reliable and predictable, why make it more complicated by engaging in emotionally exhausting lovestyles? The typical storgic lover is quite content to ignore the 'bright but branding fire', or prefers to read about it in romantic novels and enjoy it from afar.

Five

The Love-Spectrum

Nothing is more disastrous between lovers than a misunderstanding which involves a widely divergent conception of love.

(*Dallas Kenmare 'Love the Unknown'*)

Eros, ludus and storge -- these are the basic lovestyles. But few love affairs, and few colours, are pure examples of one type. Most reds have a little yellow or blue in them, and most cases of eros have a little storge or ludus. As we shall see, there are many more than three possible 'shades' of love.

Mania is probably the most familiar of the 'secondary' lovestyles. As the next chapter explains in detail, mania is a combination of eros and ludus. A primary love has qualities which are not reducible to any other kind of love, just as red is in no way reducible to blue. The ideas and actions typical of the eros lovestyle are clearly distinct from those of a ludic lover, and it would be difficult to confuse the two. But mania can be accounted for in terms of ideas and actions stemming partly from eros and partly from ludus. Agape is another secondary love, in this case the combination of eros and storge. Pragma is the outcome of combining ludus and storge. Each of these loves will be explained in turn.

The colour analogy only goes so far, however. The combination of two primary colours can produce only one secondary: no matter how you mix yellow and blue, you get some shade of green. But in love, each pair of primaries can produce *two* secondaries. At first I found this difficult to explain, especially when the two secondaries were somewhat unlike each other, and in one instance very unlike. No two lovestyles could be more contrary than mania and ludic eros. Yet both can be understood most easily as combinations of eros and ludus. Likewise, eros and storge can combine to form storgic eros, a lovestyle somewhat different from agape, the other combination of the same two primaries. Both pragma and storgic ludus are combinations of ludus and storge.

A solution to the puzzle of double secondaries came from chemistry, where we learn that it is possible to combine the same two substances in different ways to get two different products. Chemists speak of a *mixture* when two substances are mingled in varying proportions in such a manner that each ingredient retains its individual character. However, when two substances are combined so that they 'fuse' with each other chemically to produce a new substance which is rather different from either component, chemists speak of a *compound*. Substances which can be mechanically mingled at ordinary temperature and pressure to form a mixture, can be made into a compound when, for example, heat is applied.

Cooks (who are really chemists in the kitchen!) may prefer another explanation. You can combine several ingredients into a mixture; but each ingredient retains its own character, and, over time, will separate out again, as in salad dressings. On the other hand, you can blend and cook some ingredients together so that many of their original qualities disappear, and the new combination can never be separated again to its original ingredients.

Chemistry, then, is the means by which we may analyse a compound or mixture into its basic components. Who would have guessed that everyday table salt is actually a compound of two deadly poisons, chlorine and sodium? Likewise, few have guessed that mania is a compound of eros and ludus. My analogy does not suggest that a lover consciously combines two lovestyles called eros and ludus to get mania, any more than you mix sodium and chlorine to get your table salt. But mania becomes more understandable when it is explained in terms of eros and ludus.

What is especially interesting about compounds is that certain qualities may appear in the compound which were never apparent in the ingredients. Or, to turn it the other way round, a knowledge of the compound may give no clue to the nature of its ingredients. Some famous recipes have never been successfully analysed, despite the easy availability of the finished product.

Schematic Summary

To sum up, there are three primary lovestyles, each of which can be paired with another in two days – to produce a compound or to produce a mixture. In the chart below, a compound is represented by a secondary colour, and a mixture by an unblended combination of the two primaries, in varying amounts. As we shall see later, secondary lovestyles can be more typical of one primary than the other – a ludic eros, for example, which is more playful (ludic) than preoccupied with ideal images (erotic).

Classification	Names of Types	Colour Analogy
Primary	eros	red
	ludus	blue
	storge	yellow
Secondary compound	mania	violet
	agape	orange
	pragma	green
Secondary mixture	ludic eros	blue and red
	storgic eros	yellow and red
	storgic ludus	yellow and blue

In colour, of course, there are also *tertiaries*, formed by combining all three primaries to make browns. So too in my theory of love there are tertiaries – but, to avoid confusion, I will leave discussion of these until Chapter Ten.

Lovestyles in Motion

Most readers have probably detected a certain amount of each of the three primary lovestyles in their own experience. Yet, in every case I have analysed, a preference for one lovestyle has stood out above the others at any given time in the lover's history of relationships. A lover may want affection and friendship from a partner, but finds his or her eyes constantly drawn to 'ideal images' which do not offer such friendship. Eventually such a lover must decide which considerations are more important. At that point, one lovestyle becomes a more obvious choice than any of the others.

Alternatively, in a love relationship which began with actions and ideas most typical of one lovestyle, such as storge, the lover may, in response to a partner whose ways of acting and thinking are, say, mainly ludic, be drawn into a compromise whereby he becomes storgic-ludic. In time, the originally storgic lover may even come to prefer a fully ludic style. Some lovers jump about the love-spectrum, trying first one lovestyle and then another, just the way some people experiment with lifestyles.

It is also possible to have two love relationships going at the same time, with different lovestyles. In one relationship the lover may wish to be 'affectionate', while in the other, intense and urgent. Needless to say, it takes a certain emotional agility to combine those kinds of loving which are farthest apart on the love-spectrum. It may also require some fast explanations to the partners, if they should happen to meet and compare notes!

Now that the basic structure of the love-spectrum has been outlined, we can turn to a detailed analysis of one of the most common, yet most complex, of the compound loves: mania.

Six

Mania – Obsessive Love

> He did not know what it was that passed from a man
> to a woman, from a woman to a man, and made one
> of them a slave. . . . It was irresistible; the mind could
> not battle with it; friendship, gratitude, interest had no
> power beside it.

(*Somerset Maugham*)

'I hate and I love. And if you ask me how, I do not know. I
only feel it, and I'm torn in two.' So wailed the ancient
Roman poet Catullus. His affliction was familiar to Greek
and Roman civilisation. The Greeks called it *theia mania*,
the madness from the gods. Both Sappho the poetess and
Plato the philosopher recorded its symptoms: agitation,
sleeplessness, fever, loss of appetite, heartache. The manic
lover is 'siezed by the power of exclusiveness', so that his life
centres on the beloved, day and night. He staggers helplessly
under the spell of excruciating, tormented love. The slightest
lack of response or enthusiasm from the beloved becomes
an occasion for anxiety and resentment. Each tiny sign of
warmth or approval brings instant relief, but no lasting
satisfaction. The manic lover's appetite for attention and
affection is virtually insatiable.

Mania is demonic love, a concept as primitive as sorcery
and spells, potions and star-crossed destinies. Yet mania is
as modern as neurosis. Freud compared it to a state of hyp-
nosis, and traced its origins to a lack of sexual gratification
which produced an excessive idealisation of the love partner. Psychologists have labelled it narcissistic, neurotic and
pathological. Yet it still holds great popular appeal, whether
in the form of an ancient myth like Romeo and Juliet or a
modern *Elvira Madigan*.

Manic love is the theme of innumerable romantic novels.
Its familiar characteristics – extreme jealousy, helpless obsession and a tragic ending – are used in literature to build
up a picture of human conflict and noble self-sacrifice. The

manic lover is a writer's delight because he is full of paradoxes. Having found the one true love in life, he is unable to relax and enjoy it, but instead becomes gripped by fear of losing the beloved. His love relationship, far from supporting and fulfilling his other roles in life, begins to subvert and consume every portion of his activity. He is wracked by yearning and moodiness. He alternates between momentary highs of irrational joy and depressing bouts of loneliness whenever the beloved is absent or angry. He knows his insufferable possessiveness defeats his own cause, but he can't help feeling it – and worse – showing it.

Rational observers throughout the ages, from Lucretius to Robert Burton to Denis de Rougemont, have described mania as nothing but a state of melancholy to be avoided like the plague; but romantics have celebrated the self-sacrifice and self-revelation often associated with mania. Overwhelmed by his own emotions, the manic lover cannot comprehend how his beloved could be indifferent to the sheer power of his devotion. Before blowing his brains out in despair, Goethe's *Young Werther* complains 'I simply cannot understand how she can love another, how she dare – since I love her alone, so deeply, so fully, and recognise nothing, know nothing, have nothing but her!'

Mania's obsessive devotion becomes sufficient excuse for any action. Possession of the beloved becomes the measure of all worth, the arbiter of all morality, the only meaningful life activity. Little wonder that this kind of loving has long been opposed by the organised Christian church. It challenges God, priest, gospel and sacrament, replacing them all with exclusive human love. It excuses adultery and even encourages it. Manic love overrides all social restraints and religious duties, makes nonsense of family feuds or traditions, and denies the sanctity of the marriage contract.

The manic attitude towards unmarried, and often adulterous, love dates at least from the legendary Court of Love under Marie, Countess of Champagne, in 1174:

> We declare and we hold as firmly established that love cannot exert its powers between two people who are married to each other. For lovers give each other everything freely, under no compulsion of necessity, but married people are in duty bound . . .[1]

1. Andreas Capellanus, *The Art of Courtly Love*.

Unconditional surrender is the demand of mania. 'I want all of you, physically and spiritually, and if there is more of you left over after I am completely sufficed, I want that too.'[1] In exchange, the manic lover offers himself totally to the beloved. This kind of loving seems so often destined to produce unhappiness that some psychologists have argued that the manic lover's desire is to be unhappy, that he is masochistic in love. They note the propensity of manic lovers to create hazards and difficulties in the way of possible success and happiness with the beloved. The manic lover, these analysts say, is not in love with the beloved but with Death.

Analysts of human behaviour have diagnosed mania as 'melancholic depression', or 'transitory imbecility' or 'a paralysis of consciousness'. The manic lover seems possessed by some strange demon, or hypnotised by the beloved. 'He can't get her out of his mind.' Mania rarely ends happily. Few lovers go to extremes of disappointment such as suicide or violence, but most remain troubled by the experience for months, and even years, after. One never fully gets over a manic experience. Like malaria, it may return to seize the lover with moods of nostalgia and unrest. Recollections or souvenirs of old times together with the beloved can throw the manic lover into a mood of depression. Memories of the beloved are etched deeply in his mind. In later years, if the two meet again, the manic partner will discover that he can clearly recall many specific details of events the lovers shared, while his erstwhile beloved will have forgotten all but a few highlights.

A Compound Love

When first developing hypothetical kinds of loving, I found it difficult to distinguish clearly between mania and eros. The literature of love was certainly no help, for these two types have often been lumped together under the general rubric, 'romantic love'. Mania was considered an unhappy romantic outcome, while eros was at least sexually satisfying. In ancient Greek thought, however, the two loves were quite distinct. Eros was the pursuit of the beautiful; first, in personal embodiment, and ultimately, in spiritual essence.

1. Doris Lessing, *The Golden Notebook*.

Mania was a madness from an apparently external source, seizing the lover and producing a torment of unsatisfied desire and humiliation.

I have already noted in Chapter Four how eros emerged from my empirical research with rather different characteristics from those commonly associated with it in our literature of love. In the case of the obsessive, jealous love which I eventually labelled mania, the lover's experiences were often similar to those associated with eros as I had redefined it, but there were some important differences. Both types of lovers were emotionally upset by early encounters with the beloved; but in eros the emotions were hopeful anticipation and delight, while in mania, they were emotions of hesitation and self-doubt. Eros and mania also shared intense preoccupation with the beloved, but in eros the thoughts were optimistic, while manic lovers went halfway to meet trouble.

Respondents who had reported experiences which included the characteristics I had hypothetically clustered under the mania label had also stubbornly included some quite *un*-manic behaviour. Two qualities in particular stood out. First, these 'manic' lovers (if they were that) had indicated that in many ways they didn't really 'like' the beloved at all. Yet they were intensely preoccupied and obsessed with desire for the partner's love! I had taken Catullus' 'I love and I hate' poetically; now it seemed to hold some literal truth. There was a partial detachment in these lovers that was more typical of my hypothetical ludus than of mania as I had constructed it. Second, these lovers reported a wide range of behaviour aimed at self-control of expression and display of emotions. Again, such behaviour had been hypothesised under ludus, not mania.

The literature of love portrays the typical manic lover as a person whose feelings are beyond rational control. He is swept about by winds of fortune, by his own self-doubt, or even by some love potion or demonic impulse. Whatever the cause, mania has traditionally been viewed as a love-madness, characterised by self-defeating extremes of behaviour. How then, in these respondents' experiences, could it also show qualities typical of ludus, a love so rational and self-controlled?

A startling fact appeared when I laid out these problematic cases of mania on a chart. The feelings of intensity reported by the lovers, when looked at in isolation from the self-controlled behaviour, would have made me predict these cases to be eros. Yet when I ignored the intensity data and looked at the self-control factors alone, I would surely have called them ludus. Up to this point in the research I had regarded mania as a primary love, one of the six originally hypothesised. The idea of 'secondary' loves made up of primaries had not yet occurred to me; nor had the use of colour as a structural analogy. Mania was the most common and best-described love in fictional literature. It had not entered my mind that it might not be primary at all, but instead a paradoxical mixture of eros and ludus. Yet this is what the interview data suggested. It was like realising for the first time that the most common colour around us in nature, green, is not really a basic colour at all, but a mixture of yellow and blue.

How could mania be a combination of eros and ludus? It showed none of the confident rapport of eros and none of the confident self-control of ludus. True, there were the intense emotions typical of eros. There were signs of attempted self-control, but these were often last-minute acts of desperation, full of futility, with none of the relaxed sophistication of ludus. Even more puzzling, mania contained qualities not found in either eros or ludus: self-defeating extremities of emotion, desperate attempts to force reciprocal feeling from the beloved, and inability to enjoy whatever mutuality the beloved did show. Mania almost always has an unhappy ending followed by deep bitterness and a long recovery period. By contrast, ludic lovers easily recover from their involvements, with perhaps a residue of guilt if they have mismanaged the partner's intensity. Erotic lovers tend to be reasonably self-confident and emotionally independent of their partners when break-ups occur.

It was at this point that I was first inspired by the analogy with colour. I began to examine colour theory and apply it to my data. If eros was thought of as red, and ludus as blue, then the combination of them produced a new colour, violet, which was neither red nor blue but did 'contain' both. A pure violet would look quite unlike either primary, just as pure mania looked unlike pure eros or pure ludus. In cases of a very reddish violet, or bluish violet, there would be difficulty in distinguishing the secondary from a primary, but in such cases the colour was much less distinctly violet and more closely associated with the predominant primary. Returning to my data, I sought an analogous pattern among the manic lovers, and found it. The distribution ranged from manic love quite close to eros to manic love quite close to ludus. A few cases in the middle of the spectrum still contained both erotic and ludic elements, but were clearly different from either eros or ludus. These were the 'pure' mania cases, which would never be confused with either primary.

The idea that certain qualities typical of two distinctive patterns of human behaviour – which I call eros and ludus – can also combine in such a way as to produce a third, equally distinctive, but very different, pattern, at first seems rather outlandish. Yet recognition of such a process – the 'theory of emergents' – has long been a part of philosophy and chemistry, and has been accepted by some psychologists. Of course the theory is not a direct description of what happens in reality, but a way by which 'what happens' may be rationally understood. As I noted in first explaining this theory on page 84, we don't mix sodium and chlorine to get our table salt, yet it is helpful to know that these are the components of salt.

One difficulty remained even after the theory of emergents and the analogy with colour had provided a useful means of explaining the structure of mania as a secondary of eros and ludus; for I already knew that patterns of behaviour typical of eros could be partially mixed with those typical of ludus to form another lovestyle, ludic eros. This was where my puzzle of double secondaries came in: how could two primaries form two different secondaries, especially secondaries as different (as we shall see) as mania and ludic eros? Two primary colours can produce only one secondary. Chemistry again came to my rescue with its distinction between compounds and mixtures. Mania was like a compound; ludic eros like a mixture.

Most readers will have found my descriptions of eros, ludus and storge not unusual, or difficult to accept. These types of loving have been a familiar part of life and literature for many centuries. If I went on to describe mania as a fourth primary lovestyle, you would probably find this equally acceptable. Indeed, mania is the most familiar type of love in fiction. But to argue that mania is best understood as a compound of eros and ludus is – to my knowledge – a novel idea. Yet literary treatment of mania as a compound of antagonistic elements dates at least from the time of Catullus. Aldous Huxley's *Point Counter Point* provides one of the most vivid descriptions I know: 'And he wanted her against all reason, against all his ideals and principles, madly, against his wishes, even against his own feelings, for he didn't like Lucy, he really hated her. . . .'

Symptoms of Mania

The distinctive symptoms of mania are so familiar that little explanation is needed. An individual who is lonely and insecure falls – or more accurately, jumps – into love with a partner who, from an observer's point of view, probably appears to be a most illogical choice. At the outset of the relationship the typical manic lover feels a great need *to be in love.*

This predisposition to 'fall in love with love' generally arises from the lover's discontent with life. The typical manic lover feels that he has had an unhappy childhood. He is often on poor terms, or out of contact, with his parents. He frequently has no close friends and dislikes his work. In short, he is looking for someone to give him a reason for living.

One manic respondent summed up the lovelessness of her condition by noting a safety-campaign billboard which read: *Drive safely. Somebody needs you.* 'Not me,' she said. 'No one would even notice I was gone.' Within a few weeks she found someone to love. She set out to make sure he noticed when she wasn't around. Unfortunately, the partner of a manic lover all too often gives a sigh of relief when the lover is not around. The pressure of an anxious manic lover is more than many mortals can bear.

In sharp contrast to the self-esteem, vanity, or quiet self-confidence which are typical of eros, ludus and storge, respectively, it is a deep sense of insufficiency and dependence on others which generates mania. The manic lover feels he is nobody until someone loves him; so he must find someone to love, and then urgently implore that someone to love him in return. This dependence on others for one's self-worth may be viewed as a negative and even neurotic quality by self-reliant individuals. But the manic lover makes dependence a positive virtue: 'People who need people are the luckiest people in the world.'

Frequently the manic lover's choice of partner is a stranger. Often lover and beloved have hardly anything in common. But it is precisely this gap which helps to generate manic intensity, for under the circumstances a gradual storgic friendship is less likely to develop. Far from discouraging the manic lover, the gap between his social background and that of the partner convinces him that this must be true love, intended by Fate. How else could they have met? Ordinary life could not have been expected to throw them together.

The manic lover is usually aware of the improbabilities of the relationship but chooses to ignore all warnings. With determination and almost inexhaustible emotional energy, the manic lover proceeds to bridge the gap. 'Nothing else matters, because I love you.' In fact, if there are no mountains to climb and chasms to bridge, the manic lover is likely to be disappointed. After all, true love should be difficult. Where no problems exist, they can be invented. The lover can begin to see rivals everywhere, question the sincerity of the partner, and worry endlessly. Reassurances of being loved may be demanded from the partner, then rejected as unconvincing. The smallest misunderstanding can be inflated into an all-night argument, hopefully leading to a tearful reconciliation. The manic lover loves drama!

This lovestyle, in contrast to eros, rarely includes a clear notion of the ideal physical appearance of a suitable beloved. Almost anyone is acceptable, and the most unlikely beloved may be chosen. The lover's first reaction may be one of repulsion rather than attraction. For example, both Philip in Somerset Maugham's *Of Human Bondage* and Cathy in Edna O'Brien's *Girl with Green Eyes* begin by disliking the partners with whom they eventually become obsessed.

The manic lover is often looking for contradictory qualities in the same beloved. Whenever one desired quality is displayed, the lover can then complain about the absence of the other. The partner's calm is labelled apathy, but when the partner shows excitement it is called nervousness. Strength becomes stubbornness but submission is weakness. Nothing a partner can do will ever fully please a manic lover. Since mania is a lovestyle in which one test of true love is emotional agitation, what better way to produce this agitation than to be constantly torn between opposing expectations?

Mania is not a lovestyle than can easily tolerate long dryspells. Once the obsession with the beloved has begun, the lover will be anxious to see or at least telephone the partner daily or even more often. Postponements become unbearable. Delays of even a few minutes are upsetting. Manic lovers can walk off in a huff when the beloved is just ten minutes late for a rendezvous. Yet a few minutes later they come running back to see if she has shown up.

Periodically the manic lover will realise that he or she has become too dependent on the beloved. Suddenly the lover will back off, throwing the initiative to the partner. 'I'm leaving it up to you – you decide what to do.' Of course this only increases dependence on the beloved. You can be sure that if the partner takes more than a few minutes – or at the very most, a few hours – to decide in favour of the lover, then the manic lover will rush to take the initiative again. One thing a manic lover cannot do is really leave it up to the partner to love him. He can't leave the fires of love alone, and must constantly be stirring the embers.

If, as is often the case, the hapless beloved does not respond enthusiastically to such overwhelming and possessive attention, the manic lover will attempt to please her at whatever price to his pride or identity. He will take her hints as commands, change his style of clothing or manner of speech, leave his family and friends, submit to her ridicule, perform any favour.

At the same time the lover will be conscious of making a fool of himself, and will attempt to restrain his emotions. He may even try to become involved with some other love partner. These attempts are almost always futile. Even when he is with another partner, his mind will be seized with anxiety about his beloved. He will be worried that she might be doing the same to him. Instead of slackening, his jealousy will be more aroused than ever.

As the manic lover escalates the intensity of his attention,

94

protesting love more loudly and more often, he will naturally want more commitment from the partner. If such a response is not forthcoming, then bitter accusations and disputes become the daily menu of manic love. Even if the partner tries to sympathize and reassure, the manic lover may remain unpacified. Calm may seem too much like indifference. If the partner would become angry, involved, combative, then that would be evidence of real caring!

Sometimes mania will progress from verbal to physical combat. The manic lover may lash out with words *and* hands, striking the beloved while exclaiming 'Don't you realise how much I love you?' These fits of rage may alternate with remorse, and attempts at reconciliation in which the manic lover pleads willingness to 'do anything' to be on good terms again. It is not unknown for excesses of mania to lead to homicide followed by suicide.

Mania can become almost an addiction, nearly impossible for the addict to end on his own initiative. The partner must usually make the final break. If you are the object of a manic obsession, you will hope in vain for the lover to lose interest finally and go away. If you are a manic lover, you will probably have to persuade your partner to make the final separation. I have known manic lovers who emigrated to another country because it was the only way they could prevent themselves from asking for 'one more chance'.

Among my manic respondents there were many who reported a typically unhappy outcome; but occasionally a more enduring relationship develops. Let us consider two examples, one ending unhappily, another leading to marriage.

Dianne arrived at the door of my London office for her interview quite out of breath and visibly upset. She had forgotten her purse, and had to ask a stranger in the Underground for money for her fare. Arriving for her appointment quite late, she was afraid I would not have waited. It soon developed that Dianne had ample reason for her disorganised state. She had undergone an abortion just the previous week; the lover involved was no longer with her, but still painfully present in her mind. Dianne had met Alex several years before, at 18, just after coming to London. Behind her was a history of unhappy home life. When she first arrived in London she knew no one.

I got a job in a theatre, where I met Alex, who was acting in the play. He was 25. I took an instant dislike to him. He was always teasing and mocking everyone around him. After a while I began to notice that he mocked himself more than anyone else, and in all of his mockery there was a lot that was very true, and at the same time very funny. In spite of myself, I found Alex amusing, then fascinating, then attractive. Before I knew it, I was in love with the guy.

Neither of us was earning much, so we got a flat together to save money. That was a mistake. He drank a lot, and borrowed money from me. We began to quarrel almost every night. I got very jealous if he stayed out late.

Soon Dianne was walking out on Alex after arguments, but inevitably returning to the flat. She had nowhere else to go, no other friends or relatives to turn to. 'Besides, Alex would always make up with some cute, funny remark, and I would decide that he really liked me after all.' But eventually an argument occurred for which no reconciliation followed, and Dianne went her own way, finding a new job and moving in with two women in a larger flat. She had other boyfriends, but could not seem to get Alex out of her mind. One day she noticed Alex's name in the paper, and a chill of sorrow and nostalgia swept through her.

Alex had apparently 'reformed' and was now becoming a successful actor. The more Dianne heard or read about him, the more she blamed herself, and wished that they were together. Then they met again, at a party, and she took the initiative in rekindling the relationship. But now Alex was living with his mother, a dominating woman who was the driving force behind his increasing success. She was possessive of Alex and his success, and unwilling to share it with anyone – or so it seemed to Dianne. It was impossible for Dianne and Alex to spend a night together comfortably. She was not welcome at Alex's home and there was no room for him in her flat. All the same, though they had few nights together, Dianne became pregnant. With his mother's insistence and support, Alex broke off, abandoning Dianne to her fate. It was at this point that I had encountered her on the street, and asked her for an interview.

Her story complete, Dianne broke into tears. 'What should I do now?' It was not the sort of question my research anticipated. I provided what comfort I could, and urged her to consult a therapist. 'So long as you desperately need love, it seems to me that you are not going to be able to enjoy it,' I advised.

The story of Ronald ends more happily, perhaps because he came from a happier childhood background and a close circle of friends. For him, mania was a response to crisis, rather than to a deeper, long-term condition.

At the age of 18, Ronald's previously contented existence as a university student was shattered by failure in a major examination. His way seemed blocked to the career of his choice, school teaching. He came to London to work in a shop in Notting Hill, where I encountered him and suggested an interview. He was lonely now, distant from his friends and home, working in a job he really hated. At the shop he had met Velma, also 18, and also very unhappy, though for quite different reasons. Velma suffered from acute acne, and all its attendant adolescent anxieties.

Though he did not find Velma physically appealing, Ronald felt an immediate sympathy for her. They began to spend time together. Ronald found in Velma a salve for his own disappointment in life. He began to become dependent on her, then possessive of her. It was not an easy relationship. They argued often, bôth at work and when going out together, but Ronald always took the initiative to make up. In spite of himself he found that he needed Velma's company almost constantly.

> I can't explain it. I don't really *like* Velma – well, maybe I do – yes, I like her, but I don't find myself attracted to her. We haven't slept together, you know. But whenever she's not around I feel lonely; incomplete. Yet when I'm with her, I feel slightly annoyed – at myself perhaps. more than her – annoyed for needing her, and for not being what I want to be.

It seemed likely that this typical manic muddle would have either eventually worn off, or reached a crisis of confrontation and break-up. But I learned later, through an accidental re-encounter with Ronald, that events had taken an unexpected turn. He had managed to win an appeal for a new examination, and had passed with honours. Velma's acne had cleared up. She became an attractive, charming woman in Ronald's eyes, and he a successful teacher in hers. In one of those resolutions of human destiny which are so ordinary as to seem trite, and certainly not the stuff of great fiction, Ronald and Velma had passed through a mildly manic lovestyle, and become quite devoted to each other. They are now happily married.

The War Within

A manic lover seems to be at war with himself. Because a part of his consciousness of the beloved is the awareness that she is not really a suitable partner, and not mutually in love, he tried to remain detached. He makes attempts to restrain his own feelings: 'I knew I shouldn't have done that but I couldn't help it'; 'I knew she was making a fool of me but I couldn't break off'; 'I tried not to think of her but I couldn't get her out of my mind'. (Of course my use of the male and female pronouns is for simplicity – there are just as many manic female lovers.)

Another part of the manic consciousness involves the yearning to be loved by, and a need for the approval of, the beloved. The manic lovers interviewed wanted to be with their partners every day, to share every secret, to enjoy sex with the beloved, to make their love the centre of existence. In short, they showed a pattern of love typical in many ways of eros.

Why don't manic lovers combine the advantage of both eros and ludus in that other secondary love, ludic eros, which is pleasant, intimate and satisfying? Their background seems to provide the answer. They lack both the self-confident ego strength of the successful erotic lover and the self-sufficient vanity and detachment of the successful ludic lover. Ludic eros requires a degree of both these assets; the manic lovers I interviewed could draw on neither.

Consider the telephone caper, a typical manic experience. You realise you have been taking the initiative too often by telephoning your beloved. You calculate that a more balanced relationship requires the beloved to take some of the initiatives; so, you ask him or her to phone you next time. This process shows a ludic consciousness. Neither erotic nor storgic lovers keep count of whose turn it is to show commitment, but ludic lovers invariably do. It's part of the game not to let your partner realise that you are more dependent on her love than she is on yours. However, a ludic lover plays the game all the way. A manic lover cannot.

The hour of the expected phone call arrives but the phone doesn't ring. Barely a minute or two past the time, you begin worrying. You may try to occupy your mind with something else, but your behaviour becomes increasingly fretful. Within a few minutes you begin to weaken, and reach for the phone to make the call yourself. Then you think. 'No, I won't do it. She's got to show whether she loves me enough to remember. . . .' Perhaps you will stick it out until the call comes, but the longer you wait, the more frantic you become. When you answer, you will be completely incapable of the ludic detachment required at this point. Instead of acting as if you were hardly aware that the call was late, or as if you'd simply assumed she was prevented from making it, you will break down with emotion: 'I was so worried. Why didn't you call? I'd never do a thing like that to you. Don't you ever think how much you hurt my feelings? . . .'

A ludic lover would not only have successfully pretended that the delay hadn't bothered him; he would actually have *felt* that way to a considerable degree. The interval, especially if a long one, would have been occupied with thoughts of other girlfriends. What better way to punish a tardy caller than to present a busy signal because you are already making a date with someone new? If your partner failed to phone within a limited time, you would never break down and call her. Instead, you would simply go out for the evening. There are other fish in the sea!

If you were an erotic lover you would not become entangled in such games in the first place. Confident of the worth of your own love, and convinced of the good intentions of your partner through the medium of your close rapport with her, you would often leave it to chance to decide who called whom tomorrow. If a specific agreement was made and a delay occurred, you would assume it was unavoidable or would make the call yourself. The manic lover has a similar impulse: if the call doesn't come, why not make one myself? But he can't really believe in his partner's reliability – mainly, psychologist Theodor Reik argues, because he doesn't believe he is lovable.

Reik argues that the extreme and obsessive behaviour typical of mania arises from a profound self-despisal. The lover knows he lacks certain qualities he very much wants, and he attempts to compensate for this shortcoming by fanatically attaching himself to a beloved who *seems* to have the missing qualities – often these are more projected than real. Ironically, the single-minded devotion of the manic lover may appear to be utterly unselfish. He will go anywhere, do anything, for the sake of his beloved. All of my manic respondents described the great sacrifices they felt they had made for their partners, but always in vain.

The manic lover is like a swimmer already struggling to keep his head above water when the beloved comes into view. He is anxious for the security of someone who cares. He throws himself so forcibly on the beloved that she is in danger herself; she will attempt to withdraw, or at least prevent herself from becoming fully committed. At this point the manic lover becomes panic-stricken and clings desperately. To save herself, the partner must be cruel. The manic lover certainly will not willingly let go. Some psychologists have argued that mania is a self-defeating, masochistic love motivated by an unconscious desire to fail. I find this an inadequate and unprovable explanation. A drowning man does not choke the lifeguard because he wants to drown – but because he wants so terribly to live that he has lost his self-control. This was precisely the case with my manic respondents.

The obsessive power of mania originates in an erotic impulse. The lover yearns for intimate, absorbing union with a beloved. But the erotic lover knows who he is and what he is looking for. The manic lover knows neither. He feels himself an incomplete and unworthy person who desperately requires union with a more admirable beloved. His attachment is dependent and self-immolating. Unlike the erotic lover, he is enormously impatient, and careless in his choice of partner. Once my manic respondents had made their unlikely choices, they feverishly projected on to each partner an image of qualities which they felt the lack of in themselves. Almost invariably the beloved could not live up to these projected idealisations, and the manic lover met inevitable disillusionment, but blamed the beloved, not himself. Sociologist Willard Waller concludes that in such glamorising, obsessive love the lover is always in love with an imaginary person.

A frequently heard explanation of the manic lover's exaggerated attachment to his beloved is the argument that he (the lover) is suffering from sexual frustrations. 'If he would only take her to bed a few times he'd soon stop admiring her to such a ridiculous extreme' the argument runs. This cure for mania was a popular remedy long before Mercutio suggested it for Romeo, or Freud included it in his theory of romantic love. Unfortunately for my manic respondents – as well as for Romeo, and probably most other manic lovers – it doesn't work. Sexual intimacy within the context of the manic lover's anxious and impulsive obsession with the beloved merely intensifies the crisis-consciousness of the relationship. Uncertain of his own attractiveness or ability to perform in bed, dubious of the beloved's commitment, and lacking in honest psychological rapport with the beloved, the manic lover effectively frustrates any possible relaxation of tension which sexual gratification might bring. Instead, he creates one more problem to worry about. If the lover was typical of the lovestyle I call manic-ludic (see Chapter Ten), the sex cure might work, but in the case of full-blown mania it is most unlikely.

As the manic lover comes face to face with the incompatibilities of his relationship with the beloved, whether social, intellectual or sexual, we might logically expect him to decide that this was not a divinely destined love after all, but simply a mistake. His friends will certainly try to persuade him to recognise this, by means of rational argument. In the case of pure mania, they are only wasting their time. The typical manic lover does not concede to difficulties or crises. He takes them as proof of the existence of true love, and a challenge to his devotion. Instead of hedging his bets, he gambles everything on the beloved. Naturally, these risks evoke great anxiety. The lover becomes unbearably possessive of the beloved, and fearful of any possible rival. From his point of view, extreme jealousy is only reasonable; he has invested everything in his beloved.

'Everything' in this case, means more than just his time, emotional energy and mental preoccupation. The lover also remakes his personal identity in an effort to please. When the beloved rejects this new identity, the manic lover is in a desperate condition indeed. What is he? Who is he now? In *Wuthering Heights* Catherine described the predicament:

> If all else perished and he remained, I should continue to be; and if all else remained and he were annihilated, the universe would turn to a mighty stranger. I should not seem a part of it. Nell, I *am* Heathcliff – he's always in my mind – not as a pleasure, any more than I am always a pleasure to myself – but as my own being.

Jealousy in Mania

The line between 'reasonable' jealousy and so-called pathological jealousy blurs easily in mania. What sort of evidence is good grounds for jealousy? To the self-assured ludic lover, even the partner's sexual involvement with others is not sufficient grounds. The playful lover expects the partner to have other affairs. An erotic lover may find his guts churning with anxiety when the partner shows an interest in others, but his self-esteem assures him that open, honest discussion of his feelings is better than a jealous scene. The storgic lover counts on companionship and shared activities to keep the partner mindful of 'where home is'.

But the manic lover cannot draw on these reassuring conditions. Part of the reason he has adopted the manic lovestyle is his own uncertainty about his own desirability. If he delivers an ultimatum, as an erotic lover might, and the partner ignores it, the consequences become unthinkable. If he tries to smile away the partner's infidelity as a sophisticated ludic lover might, the partner may take this as permission for further indiscretion. Besides, the manic lover's smile is rarely convincing when he is feeling anxious. There is hurt written in every line of his face.

The only way out for the manic lover is to justify the jealousy – to insist that a true lover is a jealous lover. His possessiveness is evidence of his love. In short, he needs no evidence whatever to justify jealousy. Love itself is sufficient grounds.

In addition, the manic lover will probably plead that he 'can't help' feeling jealous because he is 'so much in love'.

This lovestyle involves the belief that some external power has somehow seized control of the lover. The modern notion of mania still owes much to the ancient Greek notion of 'madness from the gods'. Recent studies of the relationship between compulsive personality and four of our lovestyles (eros, ludus, storge and mania) have found that mania is the only lovestyle strongly associated with compulsive behaviour.

Homosexual Mania

Mania is a lovestyle as familiar in gay relationships as in heterosexual love. Among gay males who advertise for lovers there is often a note of lonely desperation. 'Isn't there anyone who is tired of the bar scene and ready to settle down in a sincere relationship?', pleads a typical ad. Two gay women I interviewed experienced so much tension and argument as a result of manic obsession and jealousy on the part of one of them, that they have broken up and reunited five times in a single year

In addition to the ordinary factors which predispose certain lovers towards mania, homosexual men and women suffer a tendency towards low self-esteem as a result of internalising the prejudice in our society. It is common, for example, to find gay men insisting that their partners appear 'straight' or 'masculine', because they want to pass as heterosexuals whose partners are simply room-mates.

Self-despising gay lovers are likely to despise their partners too, at least unconsciously, because the partner is an accomplice in the homosexual act. Thus it is not unusual to find gay people seeking absorbing, committed relationships while at the same time rejecting any association with the gay subculture. When such gay men and women are liberated from 'the closet' their self-esteem is increased, and they are much less likely to be drawn into mania. I have observed both an avoidance and a disapproval of manic behaviour among members of gay liberation groups. In his *Gay Manifesto*, Carl Wittman argues against possessiveness and 'promises about the future . . . which prevent us from growing'.[1]

1. In J. A. McCaffrey (ed.), *The Homosexual Dialectic*.

When the last attempt at reunion fails, the last plea goes unanswered, the last threat is ignored, the manic lover may destroy himself – perhaps along with the rejecting beloved – in an act of violence. More commonly (and this was obviously the case with all my respondents!), he begins the long road to recovery. For most of the manic lovers I interviewed, months and even years were required. A period of hatred of the former partner is almost essential if the lover is to recover a sense of self-worth. To reassert his own ego, he must deny and attack the rejector. Most eventually outgrow this period of hatred and achieve the condition of indifference which is the sure sign that mania is finally dead.

During the recovery period the manic lover is often in a condition popularly known as 'on the rebound'. This can be a dangerous period for any new partner whom the manic lover seizes on to assuage his injured self-respect. He is now likely to take a quite ludic role, 'allowing himself to be loved' by the new partner: as soon as he has fully recovered from his previous injury he will very probably drop her. That evens the score in his mind. He loved and was not requited, and now has been loved and refused to requite. If the new partner is primarily ludic, no one is likely to get hurt. The ludic partner will simply enjoy and exploit the situation to mutual advantage, then go his own way. But if the new partner is manic, the cycle of broken heart and heart-breaker will begin another round.

Another common feature of recovery from mania is the denial of the partner's love. 'You never did really love me,' the disenchanted lover accuses, ignoring all the affectionate or sympathetic acts of the partner because they were less than 'real love' as mania defines it. A manic lover may even mentally rewrite the history of a relationship so that actions of the partner which, at the time, were interpreted by the manic lover as evidence that the relationship was going well, now become 'warnings I was stupid to ignore'.

Manic lovers are rarely strong on consistency. In the same breath that the disappointed lover denies that the partner ever truly loved, he or she is likely to assert that the partner led the lover on. 'But you told me you loved me,' is a frequent accusation. Old letters may be resurrected to quote to the rejecting partner. Manic lovers do not give up easily.

The Positive Side of Mania

It is theoretically possible for a manic attachment to develop into a lasting love, but the instances are rare indeed. If the attachment is to last, the idealisations which the manic lover projects on to his beloved must not be so unreasonable that the partner cannot possibly fulfil them. The partner must find the manic lover sufficiently attractive as a person to be willing to ride out the manic storms of emotion and slowly enable him to transform his basic approach to love towards a more stable lovestyle as eros or storge. This process requires an unusual beloved indeed. Most manic lovers are not lucky enough to choose a partner who has the patience, ego strength and wisdom so fully to requite the lover's emotions that eventually the lover begins to believe *he is lovable*. For example, the partner must always telephone promptly, or, better still, call early. Only a beloved who is typical of eros is likely to support a manic lover until his self-despisal is replaced by a feeling of worth. A ludic beloved will never tolerate the manic lover's extremes. A storgic lover may try to be kind, but will be unable to reciprocate the manic lover's intensity. The lover will find fault with mere kindness, for it falls a great deal short of the total embrace he desires.

Christian theology has traditionally regarded mania as a dangerous condition, provoking irrational acts which ignore accepted social virtues in favour of a fanatical devotion. Mania is ultimately a heresy, for it places adoration of another human being above that of God. Only a few Christian writers, such as Charles Williams, have recognised that mania is also a potentially liberating experience, provided the lover does not remain possessed by the beloved but instead begins to develop the newly-discovered intensity of emotions in himself.

Most of my manic respondents, even those not yet fully recovered from a traumatic break-up, believed that the experience had been of some benefit to them. Only a very few, if given the choice over again, knowing what they know now, would rather not have fallen in love manically. The extremes of manic emotion had enabled most respondents to realise for the first time how much they could care about another person.

The transcendental power of manic love can lift you out of yourself. New talents may be discovered, new perspectives opened. You may even conclude that you could not have become a mature person without a manic experience. Instead of discarding your manic experience as a juvenile stage or a neurotic illness, it is possible to recognise this experience as a major contribution to your capacity to love. In this sense, mania is akin to religious conversion. Most converts do not remain in the exalted state of transfiguration which initiated the conversion – and you are probably glad now to be 'over' mania ! but the fact that this transitional stage may be left behind does not invalidate the conversion experience.

Of course it is possible to learn nothing from a manic experience, and to go on repeating the pattern of magnificent obsession in one love relationship after another. Some lovers make a lifetime vocation of this lovestyle. Continuing to suffer from loneliness and lack of self-esteem, they become lifelong addicts of the exquisite anguish of mania. Most of us, however, will learn from one or two bouts of mania, that we prefer affection without affliction.

Seven

Ludic Eros – Pluralistic Love

> It is absurd to say that passion is augmented by depression and langour. It is not so. Laughter and lightness of heart feed love best. . . . Yes, my dear, we will marry, all in good time, but don't let us be in a hurry, lest, indeed, marriage prove the grave of love.
>
> (*Casanova*)

The lover who wants to combine eros and ludus in a happy compromise without 'snapping' into mania must maintain a smooth balance between two quite different lovestyles whose potential conflict threatens to pull him in opposite directions. Just as a circle could not be formed of elastic held out at only a few points (that would merely form a polygon), so the ludic lover cannot avoid manic difficulties by an occasional correction of imbalance. There must be a consistent, overall approach.

What enables one lover to mix eros and ludus in a pleasant compromise, while another finds his troubles compounded into mania? Previous experience in interpersonal relationships is a major factor. Although the ludic-erotic respondents I interviewed did not consistently show a recollection of happy childhood, they certainly differed from the manic pattern of unhappy memories. Even sharper was the contrast between manic discontent with life at the time of the love encounter and the ludic-erotic lovers' basic contentment. All the ludic-erotic lovers had experienced at least one prior love relationship. They had formed a fairly clear ideal image of the kind of people who attracted them as possible lovers, while manic lovers had no such images, and instead projected qualities they lacked in themselves.

Ludic-erotic ideal images differ from those of eros, and resemble those of ludus in their plurality; but they are still clearly defined images. The ludic-erotic lover knows what he likes best and does not easily accept substitutes, as is the case with the ludic lover. On the other hand, he is not as demanding as the erotic lover.

The ludic-erotic lovers I encountered were in no desperate need to be in love. Thus, they neither forced the relationship nor became worried by it. The successful ludic-erotic lover is balanced between the self-esteem of eros and the vanity of ludus. He certainly will not submit to the self-effacement, ridicule and abuse borne, martyr-like, by the manic lover. Unlike the manic lover, the ludic-erotic lover retains the ludic capacity to play the game all the way, including the ability to break off the relationship when it ceases to satisfy. The manic lover could never be the first to break off.

Ludic-erotic love is no cakewalk, but an exacting tightrope balancing between intensity and detachment. When a lover allows his attraction to become exclusively focused on one beloved who is not willing to requite this attachment, he is in danger of losing his capacity for ludic control, and may be drawn into manic torment. On the other hand, the lover who over-emphasises ludic detachment will undermine the possibility of erotic rapport. Efforts to recover intensity may become frantic and preoccupied, again causing the lover to slip into mania. Alternatively, the lover may move towards a purely ludic role, rejecting the advantages of erotic intimacy. The classic example of long-successful ludic-erotic love is Casanova. His own account of his adventures typifies ludic eros. Only rarely, as in the case of Henriette, did Casanova nearly succumb to manic yearning. But towards the end of his life he began to grow weary of the effort of mixing erotic intensity and ludic detachment. He wrote of losing 'some of the delicacy and power of idealisation', and became more purely ludic and calculating.

A Collector of Loves

The ludic-erotic lover is prepared to take the risky erotic jump into rapid, open encounter because he believes he can land on his feet with ludic self-sufficiency whenever it proves necessary. Unlike the manic or erotic lover, the ludic-erotic lover enjoys love as one among a number of satisfying life activities (love becomes the manic lover's only important activity, the erotic lover's major activity). Though he resembles the ludic lover in this regard, he puts more emphasis on physical and sexual gratification than does the gallant ludic lover. The successful ludic-erotic lover builds up a repertoire of sexual techniques. His numerous experiences (some would call them affairs) enable him to captivate readily the attention of many of those who attract him. Failure in any particular campaign does not seriously upset him as long as there are alternative opportunities. But when Casanovas grow older, they may find it difficult to retain this equanimity.

In the best of all possible worlds a ludic-erotic lover may encounter someone close to his erotic ideal image (he *does* have one, since he is erotic as well as ludic), and his beloved may be *mutually* attracted. In that happy event, the ludic-erotic lover may lose his balance of eros with ludus and become primarily erotic. But as long as a lover cheerfully collects love relationships the way others collect antiques or souvenirs of foreign places, he can be confidently diagnosed as still partly ludic. The successful ludic-erotic lover avoids deflation of his ego, or manic disappointment, by selecting partners who, his experience tells him, are likely to appreciate his attention. His self-confidence and self-sufficiency, a combination of erotic and ludic assets, enable him to become intensely and profoundly involved, yet – much to everyone's surprise – free to disengage himself later with no apparent wrenching of emotions. Some will envy him, but most will suspect him of hypocrisy and heartlessness. They will argue that he (or she, for there are certainly female ludic-erotic lovers) should either become deeply committed in a permanent way or else make it perfectly clear that he is only having a little fun – in short, play either the erotic or the ludic role, but *properly*! Most people think having one's cake and eating it too is somehow immoral. To the ludic-erotic lover, it is just good sense.

Unless the ludic-erotic lover keeps moving from community to community, he is likely to build up a reputation reflecting his approach to love. If he becomes known for leaving a trail of broken hearts, his potential market will soon dry up. Even Casanova, who travelled widely in Europe, knew that word gets around. He therefore took considerable pains not to leave his partners sorry for having known him. In a gallant ludic manner he took care to disengage slowly and courteously. Often, he managed to replace himself with some other lover before leaving the beloved, thus easing the pain of his departure. But unlike the more ritualist ludic lover, the ludic-erotic lover retains a personal interest in former partners, and tends to enjoy repeated encounters with the beloved with intervals of detachment between.

One of my ludic-erotic respondents had continued a relationship over almost a decade without ever having lived with the beloved. When circumstances threw them together, they enjoyably passed a day like erotic lovers, went to bed, brought each other up to date on the intervening events of life, then parted again with no pain or sorrow. Their encounters in love were similar to those of two friends having dinner together from time to time with the utmost intimacy and rapport. They enjoy the experience tremendously, yet neither would dream of moving into the other's house for all meals.

The ludic-erotic lover allows himself flights of erotic intensity and ecstasy with the confidence that he can land when he wants, and take off again later in some other direction. He expresses intensity and delight *openly* – not in the coy, manipulative manner of the ludic lover – yet without implying that he feels any permanent commitment. This requires a very fine balance indeed between eros and ludus. In bed, he approves of the partner's body enthusiastically without suggesting an exclusive attraction: 'You've got one of the nicest bodies I've ever seen'; 'That was one of the best times I've ever had in bed'. In short, I like you very much but you're not the only one.

A ludic-erotic lover never becomes jealously possessive of his partner. Indeed, he may encourage the beloved to become involved with someone else in order to prevent her from becoming too much involved with him. By granting both freedom and intimate rapport to the beloved, he claims both from her.

A Tightrope Act

A tightrope walker develops many small, almost unobservable muscle reflexes to maintain his balance. He does not walk stiffly or precisely on a vertical axis, never leaning to either side. Such inflexibility would be fatal. Likewise, the ludic-erotic lover attempts no constant, exact balance between the two types of love he mixes. At one point he leans to the erotic side – short of the point of toppling over – then back he swings in a countervailing motion to the ludic side.

Brinkmanship can give ludic-erotic love a delightfully 'tangy' or 'bittersweet' taste. The lover may spend a whole evening in the most intense intimacy with his partner. They talk endlessly, cuddle and embrace; he feels a profound personal rapport with his partner and remains in close physical contact with her. Then he makes love, passionately and with enthusiasm, his non-verbal behaviour expressing a deep attraction to the beloved. But if you watch closely (or happen to be the object of such attention!), you will see that this apparently erotic lover is repeatedly making small 'corrections' to maintain an overall balance between erotic, rapportive sensuality and ludic, controlled detachment.

For example, just at the moment when you, the beloved, are about to interpret his enthusiasm with a comment, or a question such as 'Do you love me?', your admirer hops up from the couch to make a cup of coffee. Or he will put his finger to your lips when you are about to 'say something stupid' (as Frank Sinatra's song put it), and whisper 'Shhh . . . don't say anything!' The ludic-erotic lover not only helps his partner to avoid breaking the bittersweet spell; he must also restrain himself at critical moments and back off in a ludic direction. Just at that ecstatic moment of intimacy when he is most tempted to blurt out 'I love you', he bites his lips and says something less binding: 'You really turn me on.' (Needless to say, an erotic or manic partner will not be satisfied with such conditional affection.)

When the lovemaking is over, the lover may stay with you for the night, but he is sure to let it be known that there will be an interval of several days before your next encounter. On the other hand, if he wants to avoid going too far in the ludic direction, he will swing back towards eros, perhaps by making a definite date, together with warm embraces and kisses.

Maintaining a satisfying practice of ludic eros over a long period of time, and with a series of partners, is nothing short of fine art. It requires the utmost craftsmanship in mixing

111

intensity with control. How often to see each beloved? How many other partners to see in the intervals so as not to think too much about any one of them? Should one write letters, or avoid putting anything on paper? There are so many risky moves, so many 'somethings stupid' which could topple the relationship.

Several of the differences in background and attitudes to life which distinguished the successful ludic-erotic respondents from the manic are obviously critical to the balancing act in ludic eros. Ludic-erotic lovers tend to have more close friends, a happier relationship with parents and siblings, and a greater contentment with life and work. All these activities help the ludic-erotic lovers avoid the self-despisal and extremism of the manic type of love. Instead of mooning over a lovely partner who might easily drive him to jealous possessiveness and obsessive preoccupation, the ludic-erotic lover throws himself into his work, spends an evening with a friend (without boring the friend with talk about the beloved!), or dates someone new. He knows instinctively that to feel lonely or depressed will weaken his ability to walk the tightrope.

Not too many of us want to be acrobats in love, or to be urged to such balancing acts by ludic-erotic partners. Ludic eros has generally been the preferred type of love of only a small part of the population in past societies. Ludus, mania, and perhaps even eros are more familiar loves than ludic eros.

Marriage and Plural Love

The idea of combining a central, lifetime love relationship with occasional short-term affairs is far from new in human history. For example, the upper and upper-middle classes in nineteenth-century France enjoyed a 'mistress and lover' system. The husband was permitted to supplement his marriage by a discreet love affair with a mistress. The wife was allowed her lover.

These arrangements reached a high level of sophistication familiar in French novels and such plays as Jean Anouilh's *The Rehearsal.* The 'affair' of each spouse was no secret from the other and was not considered 'cheating'. However, these supplementary love relationships were expected to be kept polite and restrained. They would not excuse neglect of the obligations of marriage, either sexual or social.

It was considered the mark of a great lady or gentleman to meet the spouse's lover socially and give no offence – indeed, to give no clue at all of knowledge of the affair. Husband or wife might even invite mistress or lover to a 'salon' or party just as they would invite any other friend. The husband might make a sly joke among his closest friends about 'my wife's lover', but his behaviour to the lover at such social gatherings would be above reproach. It was considered the vilest of manners to show any resentment or jealousy.

Mistresses or lovers, for their part, were expected to behave according to the rules of polite society at such gatherings, and never embarrass by a show of excessive affection. The wife's lover in Anouilh's *Rehearsal* becomes the butt of jokes because he allows himself too much passion. Not that the affairs involved were secret – everyone knew what was going on – nor were they resented. quite the reverse, they were expected. A husband who could not find a suitable mistress, or wife a satisfactory lover, placed their own desirability in question. And it was especially boring to be tied to a jealous, possessive spouse.

What *was* expected was that such affairs should never threaten the continuity of the marriage, one's reputation or 'good name' in polite society, and the children's heritage. When a lover went beyond the bounds of discreet affection and tried to woo a woman away from her husband, he would certainly be warned, still with politeness, 'Sir, you go too far.' When a husband became involved with a mistress to the neglect of his family, not only his wife but all his best friends would caution him.

Although these arrangements involve plural relationships around the marriage, they do not usually qualify as examples of ludic eros. Instead, they fall within the lovestyle of storgic ludus, which is discussed in detail in Chapter Eight. Both lovestyles have one primary in common – ludus – but the other primary makes the difference. The combination of ludus with storge emphasises companionate playfulness, while with eros the result is playful intensity. In the mistress and lover system, intense emotions were usually avoided. Polite restraint was expected. Society was shocked by Flaubert's *Madame Bovary* partly because Emma allowed herself to become too serious about Rodolphe. Her delight in having a lover is acceptable, but her proposal to abandon her husband for her lover is outrageous. That was certainly not what Rodolphe had in mind and he abandons her.

There is a further difference. In storgic ludus, relationships are known about but not openly acknowledged. In ludic eros, the married couple are more open and candid about the existence of their 'affairs'. Indeed, as in the Lobell autobiography, *John and Mimi*, the married couple may even compare notes on each other's adventures outside the marriage.

There is little or no effort at pretence in a ludic-erotic relationship, and intense feelings are much more acceptable than in storgic ludus. In Somerset Maugham's *The Painted Veil*, Townsend becomes annoyed when Kitty begins to take his expressions of love too seriously and threatens to embarrass his wife Dorothy, who has shown the good taste to ignore the affair. Townsend warns Kitty she must not 'take literally the things a man says when he's in love'. When Kitty objects that it's not very pleasant to realize she was 'only an episode' he retorts:

> Of course it wasn't an episode . . . One can be very much in love with a woman without wishing to spend the rest of one's life with her.

It is clear that Kitty has not understood Townsend's love-style. He is expecting her to remain friendly and neighbourly, as storge would prescribe, not to become erotically intense.

Within the traditional definition of marriage as a monogamous lifetime relationship, storgic-ludic affairs may continue to find their place without undermining the marriage system. However, ludic eros would seem less compatible with marriage. It is less discreet, more open, more potentially disruptive in its intensity.

Those who favour a ludic erotic lovestyle are often unprepared to commit themselves to any single, lifetime relationship, and may therefore refuse to marry at all. Their personal needs for stimulation, whether social, intellectual, or sexual, are so varied that no one person is able to gratify more than a portion of these needs. The dedicated ludic-erotic lover will not be satisfied with a diet of supplementary affairs of the storgic-ludic style, because these affairs must not become emotionally expressive relationships.

Open Marriage

A new concept of marriage has been developing, first in fiction and more recently in real relationships, which attempts to combine the freedom of plural love affairs of intense and yet short-term quality with a marriage of longer-term, dependable attachment. The fiction of Robert Rimmer (*The Harrad Experiment, Proposition 31*) is probably the best-known example. In these works the traditional married pair is opened out to involve larger numbers, in 'corporate' marriages and families. Rimmer's *Adventures in Loving* reports letters from actual couples experimenting with new models of 'liberated marriage'.

George and Nena O'Neill's *Open Marriage* attempts to provide a manual for couples seeking to liberate their marriages. Their *Shifting Gears* deals with the transition from old model to new. In all of these recent developments there is an effort to combine a more open, honest and intense intimacy (eros) with a reduction in jealousy, a capacity for playful attachment, and an acceptance of the impermanence of relationships (ludus).

Our generation may be witnessing the emergence of a genuinely new social invention – the ludic-erotic marriage. This is almost a contradiction in terms, and certainly won't be easy to implement. If both the intensity and pluralism of ludic eros are to be combined with some kind of continuing relationship which still deserves the label of 'marriage', the couple involved must be committed to each other without being bound.

A central solidarity is essential if ludic-erotic or 'open' marriage is to remain *marriage*. Otherwise the relationship will fly apart any time either partner becomes involved with a lover who seems more interesting or attractive than the spouse. Yet this central solidarity cannot be marriage as tradionally understood – particularly the pragmatic marriage which was usually the counterpart of the mistress or lover system. That would prevent either spouse from really enjoying erotic intensity and intimacy with other people. It would also prevent the couple from sharing with each other the emotional growth and insight which each gains by having open and honest extra-marital relationships.

The problem is rather like that of keeping a satellite in orbit around its planet: its speed must be sufficient to keep it aloft, against the pull of the planet's gravity, yet not so great as to fling it into space. The fine and delicate balance of a ludic-erotic marriage would be in danger especially at those inevitable times when one partner has an affair and the other does not. When one stays home while the other plays, the 'loser' is likely to experience a decline from ludic-erotic balance into manic possessiveness.

Successful practitioners of ludic-erotic marriage would have to be like a pair of acrobats who take great risks on the high wire because they absolutely trust and depend on each other's movements, can predict each other's actions, and know that the partner will 'catch' them at critical moments. Nervous practitioners would almost certainly fail whenever one partner became more involved in extra-marital activity than the other. If one partner's overall life-conditions (family, friends, work) became unsettled, there would be a tendency towards mania. At such times, the other partner would have to recognise the need to abandon outside adventures temporarily, until both are able to walk the tightrope together again.

The ultimate measure of the psychological capacity of a couple to perform the tightrope act of ludic-erotic marriage together, is a test which will probably shock some traditional married couples. It is simply this: could you allow your spouse to bring back to your own home his or her lover for the purpose of sexual relations, while you are present in another room of the same house? And without any jealous anguish or recrimination? Could you sit down for coffee with your spouse and the lover, and behave as if an ordinary guest was being entertained in your home?

The storgic-ludic lovestyle might say 'Do as you wish, but I don't want to know about it'; but in ludic eros, the partner gives full permission, not a mere turning of a blind eye. Of course some couples may find it difficult to handle the actual physical presence of a lover in the sacred territory of the

116

home. Possible compromises which I have encountered in open marriages include one spouse going out for the evening, or away for the weekend, while the other uses the home to entertain the lover, and agreements on 'nights out' when the spouse sleeps at the lover's place.

Life is Outlasting Marriage

The traditional lifetime monogamous marriage is the social invention of ancient generations whose life expectancy was well under fifty years. Even a century ago, one partner in a marriage contracted at twenty would, on the average, be deceased before the marriage had lasted two decades. A fifty-year marriage rated a 'golden' anniversary because it was statistically rare – not because people were divorcing each other, but because few couples lived that long.

Society has not yet developed a new model of marriage to accommodate the reality of a 75-year life expectancy for the young person who reaches twenty. Perhaps it is no more reasonable to expect an average marriage to last fifty years, than to expect an average automobile or an average job to last that long. There will be exceptions, of course – but should we continue to raise our children as if a lifetime marriage were the rule?'

For married couples caught in the present period of transition from the outmoded marriage of the past to the new models of the future, life may be difficult indeed. Many married people of 45 or 50 are thoroughly tired of their marriages. But they have no pattern on which to base their behaviour, other than to stick with the partner. Psychologically, such married people are unprepared for the limbo of separation, the return to the search for a partner (a search they happily abandoned several decades before), the competition with younger people, and the long nights and weekends alone.

Nor are they likely to get social support for their attempts to abandon a moribund relationship and strike out again in pursuit of new experience and personal growth. Their separation is regarded as a threat by all other married couples in the same boat. Stan and Diane, after twenty-eight years of married life, decided to 'call it a day' and seek new relationships. Both were still young-looking and lively. But

117

their decision was greeted with dismay by married friends. No invitations came for dinner to either of them, from those who had formerly entertained Stan and Diane as a safely married couple.

Solicitous inquiries and veiled hints came from friends who kept reminding Stan or Diane that the other one was still unattached. 'Wouldn't it be best to try to get back together again?' Neither Stan nor Diane found 'the world of the formerly married'[1] an appealing existence. They felt old and out of place in dance clubs and bars. Within a year they resigned themselves to reunion.

New books and night classes on such things as 'creative divorce' and 'how to enjoy being single' are obviously a response to the social needs of couples like Stan and Diane. The women's liberation movement is also campaigning for career opportunities for older married women who want to abandon the housewife role – which can become particularly meaningless after the children leave home. However, the statistics indicate that most couples who break up promptly marry new partners. Divorced men and women seem to conclude that it was the choice of partner which was a mistake, not the fact of marriage itself.

If the later years of our extended existences are to be years of continued personal growth and new experience, but at the same time free of the shock and pain of divorce, we need a new model of marriage. The O'Neill proposals for 'open marriage' are intended to meet this need. Ludic eros is the lovestyle which would make open marriage possible.

An analogy may help to contrast the lovestyle of ludic eros in marriage, with the traditional lifetime marriage based, usually, on storge or pragma. These traditional lovestyles tend to define married love as if it were a barrel of water. When you draw a jugful from the barrel, there is that much less water remaining. If the spouse gives someone else a share of his or her time, money, social attention or sexuality, there is that much less for the spouse: 'You've already seen that movie? But I wanted to go with you to see it'; 'You're too tired to make love tonight? I bet you weren't too tired with your boyfriend this afternoon!'; 'What do you mean, we can't afford it? You always seem to have money

1. Morton Hunt, *The World of the Formerly Married.*

118

to take your secretary to lunch. I know what goes on in that office of yours'. This conception of the resources of marriage defines extra-marital activity as cheating, because limited resources which are properly the shared property of the couple have been unilaterally diverted to some outside person. The ludic-erotic affairs of an open marriage must function on a 'water well' analogy of love. A well is kept fresh and cool by frequent drawing of water – though not *too* frequent, obviously, or else the bucket will hit the bottom! The greater the resources of the couple, in leisure time, income and sexual drive, the more often the well can support withdrawals.

Certain ground rules are required in this open form of marriage in order to prevent exhaustion of the mutual resources, as well as to leave time for the partners collectively to assimilate the experiences each is enjoying outside the marriage. (Time for the well to refill itself.) A simple example of one such ground rule would be an agreement to inform your partner at least a few days in advance that you are going to be out for the night, so that your partner can also arrange something for that evening and thus avoid the potentially manic anxiety of feeling alone and abandoned.

In the old-fashioned monogamous union, Jack and Jill usually experience only those personal qualities in each other which each is able to elicit from the other. If Jack or Jill has an extra-marital affair and keeps it secret from the other, the addition to the total relationship is minimal (and possibly destructive). Jack may add to his own enrichment by fooling around with lovers A, B and C, but his personal development arising from these affairs must be hidden from Jill. By contrast, if Jack openly shares his extra-marital experiences with Jill, by discussing them, introducing A, B and C to Jill, even sharing some social (and possibly sexual) experience among them all, then not only Jack, but also Jill, has the opportunity to diversify her personality. Jill experiences Jack's character not only as evoked by herself, but also as evoked by A, B and C. Truffaut's film *Jules and Jim* presented an excellent example – at least until the implied moralism of the finale. The lives of Jules, Jim and their common amour were interwoven and passionately enlivened because they related as three (and three sets of two) rather than as only two sets of two. If the relationship had

119

grown to four or five, the possibilities of mutual interaction would have increased accordingly.

A ludic-erotic open marriage is not merely a contract to live with a partner while exploiting this relationship as a home base for one's extra-marital sexual games. The very quality of the ground rules required to make open marriage work contrasts sharply with the affairs typical of storgic ludus. There is no way a husband engaging in a storgic-ludic affair with his secretary (or his wife with the infamous postman) would actually tell the partner about such liaisons in advance so that the partner could go and do likewise.

Obviously, I am defining open marriage in somewhat different terms from those used by the inventors of the term. Indeed, it is possible to imagine a variety of forms of open marriage, depending on how secure each spouse feels about the other's mutual love, which in turn determines the safe limits of permissiveness, i.e., how far each spouse can go without destroying the marriage. It may take quite some time for a couple in open marriage to reach the stage where each is so assured of first place in the other's hierarchy of affection that he will actually permit the partner to bring an extra-marital lover home for dinner – or for love-making in the spare bedroom. The weaker the internal solidarity of the partners, the more elaborate the ground rules necessary. Some open marriages may require rules against staying out overnight, or against bringing the extra-marital lover home at all. The O'Neills provide an elaborate set of 'guidelines' for their model of open marriage.

Homosexual Open Marriage

Ludic eros is a kind of double-thought, since it requires that the lover psychologically and physically treat each beloved as if he or she were the only one – the erotic ideal – yet simultaneously remain capable of detaching at any time, without lasting anxiety. Among homosexuals there is often a great tension between the lovestyles of eros and ludus, because they are motivated by the ideal ('Strangers in the night, exchanging glances') but compromised by the reality ('All the sad young men'). The tightrope-walk between eros and ludus becomes particularly difficult, and the plunge into mania all too common.

120

The frequency of game-playing among gay males has even produced a gay vocabulary of intimacy. The 'trick' is a very short affair, or the person involved in such an affair. He may also be called a 'number'. Looking for a trick is called 'cruising'. This jargon often leads observers who are strangers to the gay world to conclude that all or most gay relationships are short-lived, calculating games. This is not so. Quite a number of gay males are earnestly searching for an ideal image. Some even advertise a detailed description of their dream:

> San Francisco white male seeks a lover. You must be 19 to a youthful 30, goodlooking, no beard or mustache, blond hair and brown eyes, slender, under six feet, well shaped very hairy legs, and masculine looking.[1]

Torn between the dream of eros and the games people play in the gay subculture, lovers will not find the open marriage an easy option to practise in gay relationships. Nevertheless, some try. Jim and Paul managed an open marriage for about five years. Their ground rules included sacred home territory, a return from the night out before breakfast at 8 a.m., and advance notice of dates with partners. But when Jim became involved with Fred, Paul sensed a real rival, not another 'trick'. He reacted by losing his emotional balance, and expressed manic jealousy and resentment. Jim assured Paul that Fred was only an affair. Fred himself insisted he had no intention of stealing Jim.

Paul was unable to believe these assurances and began to renege on the open marriage agreement. Jim moved out. This upset Fred so much (he was being honest about having no lasting interest in Jim) that he stopped seeing Jim. After a few months Jim and Paul got back together, but the injury done to their relationship by the crash from the tightrope of ludic eros has never been healed.

Ron and Rodney have been more successful. Their open marriage has survived for ten years and is still going strong. Perhaps this is due to their tighter rein on the affairs outside their 'marriage'. Ron and Rodney go out to a bar together, rather than in separate directions as Paul and Jim did. As soon as one of them has found someone interesting

1. Advertisement in *The Advocate*, Los Angeles.

and interested, he introduces that person to his mate. Only if the potential 'trick' is about equally interesting to both Ron and Rodney, do they continue the engagement. If the hunt is unsuccessful, Ron and Rodney return home together.

This does not necessarily mean a 'threesome' when this couple find an interesting third party. They may date him alternately; but no one is allowed to come between them emotionally. Obviously there are fewer potential partners available who will please and be pleased by *both* Ron and Rodney than there would be for either singly. But they prefer this limitation to the risks of separate cruising.

When Ron and Rodney find a mutually acceptable partner, they are open, honest, intimate and affectionate with the partner as with each other. I have interviewed former partners and found that they generally have a high respect for this couple. Several had actually moved into Ron and Rodney's home for a period of time and felt very much 'part of the family'. They sensed no competition between Ron and Rodney on the one hand, and no manipulative exploitation of themselves on the other. Instead of jealousy, Ron and Rodney feel mutual protectiveness for each other and extend this to the third party when there is one.

The Future of Ludic Eros

Open marriages of various kinds will probably merge with other contemporary phenomena of marriage such as key clubs, wife-swapping (surely a male-chauvinist label!), and group sex. In general, an era of moral permissiveness may increase sexual activity of ordinary kinds to the point where it becomes boring and stimulates greater interest in so-called 'perversities'. In the same way, permissiveness in marriage may bring greater flexibility in the definition of love, and an awareness of the great variety of lovestyles. This change could either wreck marriage and marriages, or lead to new forms of intimate relationship. For a time, at least, the trend will probably continue towards open marriage: life expectancy is increasing, as are the availability of extra-marital partners, the leisure time to meet them, and the medical safeguards against discouraging circumstances. Fewer and fewer married couples are likely to be satisfied with the prospect of fifty years of monogamous marriage, or with the emotionally disruptive alternative of 'sequential polygamy' through a divorce and remarriage cycle.

On the other hand, a ludic-erotic style of love combined with open marriage will certainly not be universally acceptable as a solution to contemporary marital problems. Indeed, it may work for some *only* if it is neglected by others. Maintaining one central relationship while at the same time engaging in – and more importantly, sharing with the spouse – a series of extra-marital affairs which are fully ludic-erotic (not merely ludic, in cynical, manipulative form, or even discreetly storgic-ludic) will demand a great deal of self-confident maturity from tomorrow's married couples. Aside from the safety which can be achieved by an adequate set of ground rules, such couples may accumulate additional assurance against dissolution of their own marriage if most other marriages remain relatively closed. A Jack who tells Jill about his involvement with Jane is less likely to drop Jill in favour of a new marriage with Jane if Jill is willing to let Jack go on having his fun, while Jane asks for fidelity. It is likely, since most lovers lack the ability to maintain the delicate balance of ludic-eros, that most of the Janes that Jack becomes involved with will want Jack all to themselves. Thus, the success of a few open marriages as *marriages*, not merely affairs, may ironically depend on most people continuing to prefer closed marriages. If too many lovers become ludic-erotic, the institutions of marriage and family as we know them may be destroyed.

The dangers posed to our conventional experience of marriage and family life are abetted by the weaknesses developing in the traditional closed marriage. There appears to be a tendency for duration and commitment to undermine the pleasure of the closed, single-partner marriage. The boredom and habitude so movingly described by Simone de Beauvoir in *The Second Sex* spell an increasing probability of dissolution, at least up to the point in a marriage where the partners are too old to throw themselves on the market for new mates. With fewer commitments to children in the future, greater residential and job mobility, and all the other features of the over-choice society drawn by Toffler in *Future Shock*, closed marriages are likely to pall with time rather than become enriched.

A ludic-erotic marriage built on the new 'open' model would be likely to increase in internal stability with the passage of time, providing the appropriate guidelines were applied. The partners would gain more by incorporating new experiences into the existing relationship than by starting all over again with someone new. For example, if, after your open marriage has already functioned well for five years, you meet someone who is considerably more attractive, pleasant and intelligent than your present open-marriage mate, it will probably *not* pay you to drop the present mate in favour of the newcomer, since you would also lose the five shared years of experience. Only with a potential mate who offered so much more than the present mate that in, say, two years, you would be as far ahead as in seven (five plus the two) years with the present mate, would it be worthwhile to switch.

It is far from clear yet what the next several decades will bring us in new modes of marriage. The present monogamous marriage may seem as obsolete by the year 2001 as the parentally arranged marriages of past centuries seem to us. Present signs are that the conception of love as defined by ludic eros will play a major role in our changing patterns of marriage.

Eight

Pragma and Storgic Ludus – Realistic Love

> All our data bearing on this question point to the con-
> clusion that on the average, marriages resulting from
> comradely affection turn out happier than those
> chiefly inspired by romantic attitudes. . . .
>
> E. W. Burgess
> The Family from Institution to Companionship

Some of my respondents had clearly decided that the time
had come to find a suitable marriage partner, or to settle
down to raise a family. Some of them were lonely and
wanted a compatible mate; others got hints from their
superiors at work that the bachelor state was not helping
their chances for promotion. A few were 'parents without
partners' looking for a new mate who would be a good
parent for their children.

When considerations like these are foremost in the lover's
mind, his or her basic approach to love can be called
pragmatic. Pragmatic love doesn't have to be exciting or
especially interesting or unusual. Nor is it casual and adventuresome; and it is certainly not uncommitted. Pragma is the
love that goes shopping for a suitable mate, and all it asks is
that the relationship work well, that the two partners be
compatible and satisfy each other's basic or practical needs.

The invention of electronic computers has greatly en-
hanced the possibility of successful pragmatic love. Old-
fashioned matchmakers had to rely on astrology, family
histories, local traditions or property arrangements to determine whether a proposed union was sensible and workable. Often one's parents looked after such things. They
knew the ways of the world better than youth. The result
was called an 'arranged marriage'. Today anyone can arrange his own marriage with a reasonable probability of
happiness, the dating agencies claim, by applying computer-
matching processes to the same kinds of basic family, personality and biographical data that the old-fashioned

matchmaker considered. Of course, a computer isn't essential. Some of my respondents arranged their own introductions. They joined organisations where they thought they were most likely to meet a compatible mate. They unobtrusively conducted their own 'interviews' to determine whether a potential partner would be suitable: 'How old are you?'; 'Are you from around here?' (that's important; no use getting involved with someone who lives a thousand miles away); 'What do you do for a living?' (also important; a suitable pragmatic partner must be socially compatible with your career and acceptable to your friends and colleagues).

The pragmatic approach is not as cold-blooded as it sounds. Once a sensible choice has been made, more intense feelings may be developed. Oriental matchmakers are fond of noting that in romantic love 'the kettle is boiling when the young couple first start out' and can only cool as time goes by. Romantic love makes post-marital disenchantment inevitable, they argue, while an arranged marriage is like a kettle that starts cold but gradually warms up. Love grows as the years go by.

The Typical Pragmatic Lover

Pragmatic lovers come from a variety of personal and social backgrounds. There is no common pattern of experience in prior love relationships such as is often found in eros or mania. And since the pragmatic lovestyle has been socially approved for generations, it is easily adopted by many individuals. After all, our society tends to say 'if it works, it must be good', whether the field is science, industry, education, or marriage.

The key word of this common-sense lovestyle is *compatibility*, which is measured not so much in sexual as in social and personal terms. The pragmatic lover, like the erotic, has a clear ideal image of the partner he or she seeks, but this is rarely defined by physical appearances. Instead, the pragmatic lover will have in mind qualities of character, vocation, social standing and social attitude. A thoroughly pragmatic lover may even write down a list of desired qualities, and compare possible partners on how well they score. One of my respondents had this list:

a. education – must be at least a college graduate
b. vocation – must be in a profession
c. social skills – must be able to entertain well
d. politics – must be middle-of-road to conservative
e. religion – must be same as or similar to my own
f. appearance – must be slim and healthy.

A pragmatic choice in lovestyles might seem rather calculating, and most of us are likely to make our approach a little less obvious by avoiding *written* lists. We keep our lists in our heads, because popular literature and social values suggest that we should be romantic rather than level-headed about love. We tend to ridicule those who are too practical in their choice of mate, as in this old joke:

WIFE WANTED: farmer, steady, hard-working, good provider, seeks level-headed wife who is sober, strong, and owns a late-model tractor . . . send picture of tractor.

Yet our common sense often tells us that we should be more practical about loving. We instinctively realise that the pragmatic lover is generally not faced by the odds confronting an erotic lover. The qualities sought by a pragmatic lover are somewhat more likely to be found together in the same person. For example, finding someone who has both a college education and a professional career is not that difficult. The pragmatic lover wants a love relationship which is workable within his or her social milieu, so will tend to select qualities which already appear in that milieu. Pragma is not a search for an impossible dream or a vision of perfection.

Nevertheless, a lengthy list of desired qualities can require the pragmatic lover to sift through a number of possible partners before coming up with the appropriate candidate. Parents and friends may be recruited to help locate and assess potential partners: 'Jim and Bill are both good looking and both have good jobs. Jim likes children more, but Bill seems more dependable. Which would you choose?'

Calculations include not only present assets but also future potential. 'You've got possibilities', the song has it. A sensible young woman from a lower class position may attach herself to an ambitious young man who is likely to become a top executive some day, taking her up the social ladder with him. The lower-class male can marry the boss's daughter if he wants to find 'room at the top'. The young activist in the peace movement marries a girl involved in women's lib, because each wants a help-mate and fellow traveller, not someone who will abandon youthful principles to make more money.

A pragmatic selection often begins with those with whom one is already acquainted, whether at work, in a church or club, or in some social or sports activity. That way, the partners are more likely to have 'things in common'. In past centuries, young people travelled little and had only a small pool of acquaintances. Parents and matchmakers broadened the choice by arranging introductions and even formal 'coming-out' parties.

An erotic, manic, or ludic lover is not ordinarily interested in a potential partner's family, friends, and associates. Love is concentrated on the partner. But the pragmatic lover is very much concerned with the family background, friends and colleagues of the partner. These are all useful sources of information about the probable compatibility of the partner. If in-laws are going to figure significantly in the pragmatic lover's future family life, then each potential partner's parents must be rated along with the partner. On the other hand, a pragmatic lover who is highly independent of his or her own parents will probably steer clear of an otherwise suitable candidate who is still too closely tied to Mum or Dad.

While other lovestyles might choose to ignore advice about the acceptability of a partner – or even consider the opposition of parents and friends as all the more proof of the reality of love – the pragmatic lover pays close attention to the opinion of others. After all, the selected partner must 'fit in' and be accepted by people who matter to the lover. This is just as true of the working class pragmatic lover who wants a mate acceptable to 'the boys' or 'the girls' as it is for a young executive whose partner must be acceptable in company circles.

The same considerations which launch a pragmatic relationship must continue to support it, or the pragmatic lover is likely to conclude that the relationship is no longer useful. For example, a young salesman married a clerk in his office. She was useful in providing him with leads and inside information. With her help, he excelled the other salesmen and was promoted to a managerial position. His wife, however, continued to work at a clerical level. Gradually, the office friends they had originally shared became only her friends. The husband adopted a new circle of friends at a higher social level. He deliberately improved his accent and manner of speaking to impress his new friends. He dressed more carefully, and bought a more expensive car.

Soon the wife who had been a pragmatic asset to this young man's career became an obvious liability. He was nervous about her possible mistakes in etiquette when entertaining his new business friends. He was troubled by the intangible, yet nagging realisation that his wife did not 'fit in' with his new lifestyle. Although, in the words of C. P. Snow in *Homecomings*, his wife had never given him a bad hour to hold against her, 'never done a thing to me or said a thing to me that isn't as considerate as it could be', he eventually found it possible to say to her, 'Thank you, you've been good to me, now for no reason that I can possibly give you, I intend to leave you cold.'

After the divorce, the young manager found a new wife, chosen with equal pragmatic care, who would contribute to his continued success. Of course, if she fulfilled her role in time she too might find herself 'out in the cold'. However, not all pragmatic matches are nearly so calculating, nor dependent on 'keeping up' with one's spouse. Besides, in these days of women's liberation, it might as easily be a social-climbing wife who matches and dispatches one husband after another as she reaches for the room at the top.

Jealousy and Sex

Jealousy in pragma is the protection of vested interests, without the possessiveness of 'scenes' found in some other lovestyles. 'I've invested money, time, property, attention, in this relationship. I have a right to expect a reasonable return on this investment.' As in a business relationship, the income should at least match the expenditure. The relationship can even stand a little cheating, if there are no other serious problems, just as most businesses can tolerate a certain amount of employee theft! Indeed, it might be worse that the partner become an alcoholic or gambler, than that he or she should occasionally stray into infidelity.

If the mental book-keeping of pragma indicates that the relationship is operating at a loss, then a review is in order. There may be a 'serious talk' in which the aggrieved partner indicates how the 'other half' is not contributing enough – whether it be money, time, sex, or whatever. The help of a third party such as a marriage counsellor, may be called upon. The basic question is simply 'Can the relationship be made to work, or should it be abandoned?' In this context, jealousy is much the same attitude an investor would take to a dubious stock investment: sell, or hang on? Much the same common-sense approach is taken to sexual difficulties in the relationship. In other lovestyles – especially eros – sexual incompatibility may create grave doubts about the validity of the love experience. But the pragmatic lovers among my respondents approached sex as a problem to be worked out.

A pragmatic lover does not live for the sake of others, or ask anyone to live for his sake. This lovestyle does not assess the reality of love according to sacrifices made for another. As long as the potential gains of continuing the relationship are greater than those offered by an alternative investment, then the pragmatic lover will continue jealously to protect the relationship.

A Science of Love

Modern psychology and sociology have made a science of the old matchmaker's impressionistic practice of pragmatic love. By analysing the statistical characteristics of 'happy', long-lasting marriages, social scientists have developed a shopper's guide for the pragmatic lover. The marriages considered most likely to succeed in modern urban society are those contracted between persons in their mid-twenties, after an engagement of not less than eighteen months and not more than three years. The couple should have a common religious and social background and about equal educational achievement. If one is somewhat dominating in personality, the other should be correspondingly submissive. I could continue, but any reliable guidebook to marital happiness will provide you with details. Successful dating agencies have simply applied these statistical facts for their clients. They know that an inter-ethnic or inter-religious match is not as likely to survive. They will discourage marriage at a younger age than twenty-one because statistics show that such matches have a higher divorce rate.

Survival of a marriage is not necessarily proof of happiness of course. The spouses may merely have settled for the best they could find and resigned themselves to the habituating effects of domestic life. You may not be willing to settle for less than great beauty, marvellous sex, exciting conversations and other aspects you consider essential to 'true love'. Yet it was clear from my pragmatic respondents that they considered their lovestyle the most valid and sensible choice.

Here is a portion of a typical interview, with a woman who, in this case, had met her husband at work.

We met a few times in the cafeteria, and at the company picnic. I knew he was about my age and had a good job with good chances ... He had such a nice smile, nothing passionate you know, but kindly, and so well-mannered. A gentleman with just the right touch of boldness. After we started going together, if I said stop, he stopped ... but he'd try again later, which made me feel good. That way I knew he wanted me and respected me too.

After a few months we got around to more serious topics like children and furniture and houses. We'd be shopping together and commenting on different styles. I could tell he liked much the same thing I did. He met my parents and they liked him; so did most of my friends.

Our first sex? Yes, I can remember ... it was after a company party; we were both a bit happy that night and when he dropped me off home I invited him in for a last drink ... My parents were away. Well, one thing led to another you know. ... Oh, it went fairly well ... I guess first times are always a bit rough, but he was very gentle and considerate. We both felt we could work it out, given time. ... Oh, of course I was on the pill already. Be prepared, I always say.

I was hoping he'd soon ask me to marry him and he did. We began to plan about a house, when to have kids, how long I'd go on working – though of course we'd really planned those things already, in a way, by talking about them. If his ideas had been really different from mine I wouldn't have held on to him. We're quite happy now. It was a sensible match. He has a good job; I've got three nice children. No,

I'm not passionate about him or anything...just content. Yes, I did have a big crush once, a few years before I met my husband. Very beautiful it was, and very sad. I'll never forget it, but that wasn't meant to last. My husband and I are really quite happy. Well matched, you might say.

Pragma Compared to Other Loves

A pragmatic approach to love is frustrating to those who rely on direct personal encounter and emotional impressions as sources of knowledge about other persons. Several non-pragmatic respondents prided themselves on their rejection of warnings by friends that they and their partners were not 'well matched' or 'from similar backgrounds'. Obviously these respondents would have made poor partners for lovers who talked about love in an almost businesslike, utilitarian manner.

The mere act of comparing several partners and choosing the most acceptable does not make a particular lover's approach pragmatic. Clearly, the erotic lover also compares – bodies, skin surfaces, hair colour and so forth. The ludic lover compares various alternative experiences, if only to choose which one to pursue first and which to leave until later. Even the storgic lover may have to choose between two possible partners, both of whom are long-time, familiar friends.

The difference is in the nature of the decision-making process. The storgic lover will have the greatest difficulty in choosing, and will probably 'let time tell' by waiting until the alternatives are reduced to one. The calculated weighting of alternatives in love is foreign to the storgic consciousness. The ludic lover will make an expedient and opportunistic choice aimed at enjoying *both* alternatives if possible. If one partner is available only on Saturday night, the other on both Friday and Saturday, he will automatically schedule the latter for a Friday-night date, the former for Saturday.

An erotic lover makes choices based more on feelings than on reasons, and will be hard put to choose in the absence of the partners concerned. An impulse, rather than a calculation, is the basis of choice. The erotic lover impressionistically compares the appearance and touch of potential partners with the ideal image in his mind, and chooses according to the power of his attraction. The erotic lover can therefore choose confidently only in the physical presence of the potential partner. He may make tentative choices based on impersonal data, for example by comparing photographs of alternative partners; but ultimately he makes the choice which is sensually most stimulating, and will probably find it impossible to explain this choice rationally. There are no specific qualities which he can list, and then 'score' each partner on. How does one rate a feeling of instant arousal, both sexual and psychic, provoked by one partner, against a feeling of deep inner contentment supplied by another? It is almost impossible even to describe these experiences, let alone give points to each!

The pragmatic lover, by contrast, can produce a list of distinct characteristics and rate each on a scale from high to low, or from advantageous to disadvantageous. Age, education, income, cooking ability, sexual technique, condition of health, religious or political affiliation – all can be listed and scored.

Some respondents were clearly torn between a pragmatic approach to love – reinforced not only by the warnings of friends and parents to 'be careful' and 'make a wise choice', but also by frequent magazine articles and self-tests ('Are you really compatible?') – and a more erotic conception of love, for which they also received constant reinforcement in literature and mass media. One of the convincing clues to whether such respondents were more pragmatic than otherwise was their use of mental lists to compare potential partners. When a lover begins to compute, mentally or on paper, which of several partners scores more points on a variety of specifications, then he is well into a pragmatic frame of mind.

Pragma as a Compound Love

Pragma is obviously a 'marrying kind' of love, even when marriage is not the result. Imagine my surprise when data processing of interviews indicated that pragma was a secondary combination, of which one component was ludus, the *least* marrying kind of love! Nevertheless, pragmatic respondents reported numerous instances of detachment, manipulation and cool-headed weighing of alternatives, and these are unmistakably typical of ludus. The

133

pragmatic lover is as self-controlled, as conscious of the substitutability of love partners, as deliberate in love, as the gallant ludic lover. The important difference is that the pragmatic lover wants to settle down in a single, satisfying love relationship rather than keep moving from one to another. In order to obtain a more permanent love, he is prepared to make concessions which a purely ludic lover would not make, but which come easily to a storgic lover. For example, he is willing to take time – perhaps even use expert advice – to work out sexual difficulties. He knows the marriage will be followed by a period of adjustment, and he will have the patience of a storgic lover to 'let time tell'. The pragmatic lover's emphasis on compatibility and the working out of differences through commitment and common interest derives from the storgic components of his love. But pragma is distinctly different from storge in its conscious, deliberate manipulation of compatibility. Instead of casually allowing companionship just to grow, the pragmatic lover tends to control the process with a calculating rationality more typical of ludus. Rather than slowly become accustomed to the partner as a purely storgic lover would do, he tries to 'hurry' storge by consciously choosing a partner with whom he will already feel at ease.

In comparison with storge, pragma is rather like the modern process of making wine. Nowadays many wine companies don't wait for the wine to mature naturally – they hasten the process by chemical additives, using science to help nature along. Pragma does much the same thing. Since there is a dearth of opportunities in modern urban life for a lover to grow up slowly with a potential storgic love-mate, the process is deliberately quickened by a ludic additive. The result is pragma.

The pragmatic lover acts as though he were thinking 'If I had had the opportunity to grow up naturally and slowly with a person whom I would now like to marry, what would she be like?' He looks for a woman with background and interests like his own. When he meets a stranger at the club or a dance, he is soon inquiring about her work, her background, her education. He is consciously taking note of her race, apparent social class and personal style.

If the pragmatic lover wishes to speed his search even

more, he can go to dating agencies and draw on thousands of potential choices. Not all customers of computer dating agencies are pragmatic, of course. The ludic lover can also use this means of meeting new partners, though many agencies try to discourage clients who are not serious about marriage. Even an erotic lover might try an agency, hoping to meet someone at the agency parties who will strike him with 'love at first sight'. But the kind of loving contemporary agencies can service most efficiently is pragma.

Storgic Ludus

What happens if a lover takes a pragmatic attitude towards finding a partner, but does not want a 'permanent' living arrangement or marriage? That is, he combines ludic detachment and control with storgic friendliness and familiarity, but declines to make a single lasting commitment. Such cases I call storgic ludus. Just as mania is the *compound* and ludic eros the *mixture* of ludus and eros, so *pragma is the compound* of ludus and storge, while *storgic ludus is the mixture.* When ludus and storge combine to form pragma, a compound love, the ludic disinterest in commitment disappears, along with the storgic lack of deliberate manipulation. Instead, there emerges a practical, almost scientific attitude to mate-selection which is not found in either ludus or storge. When storge and ludus merely *mix,* the disinterest in marriage typical of ludus remains. The lover then has a practical or convenient *affair.* Of course, not all affairs represent storgic ludus; we use 'affair' very loosely in everyday speech to indicate any short-term love relationship. A *storgic-ludic affair* is one in which two persons who are already somewhat accustomed to each other, perhaps as a result of working together, consciously decide to have a tactful, convenient love relationship. Such liaisons are marked by more concern for the ultimate fate of the partner than is typical of pure ludus; this is because the partners know they must maintain an acceptable relationship after the affair is over. This concern is drawn from the storgic component of familiarity and companionship. But the storgic-ludic affair is quite distinct from pure storge in its extremely conscious, manipulative handling of the liaison. The heart of this control process is discretion. A married boss and his secretary, for example, are discreet about who knows of their affair.

Convenience always dictates the action of the storgic-ludic lover. Pleasure, affection and reciprocity of feelings are sought and shown only when convenient in terms of the lover's more important commitments such as reputation, career and marriage. Ludic or ludic-erotic affairs need not be so discreet. Indeed, part of their satisfaction may derive from blatant thumbing of the nose at conventional morality. The patterns in a storgic-ludic affair, by contrast, share pragma's respect for conventional morality. A storgic-ludic lover would never wreck his own or his partner's marriage by becoming too involved or indiscreet.

The role of sexuality in a storgic-ludic affair is rather different from its role in pragmatic marriage. A convenient affair must include an early and satisfying sexual relationship, since there is little incentive to work out sexual difficulties over a period of time. In pragmatic love and marriage, however, there is a stronger motivation towards developing sexual techniques, consulting manuals and medical counsellors, and otherwise working out difficulties. The pragmatic lovers among my respondents showed as much interest in improvement of sexual technique as did the erotic lovers, while storgic-ludic respondents showed almost as little interest in sexual technique as ludic and manic respondents.

Storgic-ludic affairs can easily be distinguished from pragma (and from eros) by their initiators' lack of ideal imagining of the beloved. There is instead a ludic recognition of the substitutability of the partner: given the basic acceptability of a partner as a familiar, reasonably attractive person, one convenient affair is as good as another. There is no attempt to force the partner to show more love. The almost inevitable break-up takes place with good taste and practicality. The two partners will probably have to continue to relate to each other as friends of each other's spouse, as boss and employee, or whatever.

A university student gave me an interview report of a relationship with her coach which I eventually classified as a typical example of storgic ludus:

> We only saw each other at the pool, for quite a long time. He was always pleasant, but proper too – it was 'Miss Jones'

whether the team was there or not. Naturally I was flattered when he paid special attention to me, giving me hints on my style and so on. I admit I was just a little suspicious of his motives. He's single, and quite good looking – but I've never heard any gossip about him fooling around with students.

Ha, ha, that's a good question! 'How did we first acknowledge our interest in each other as possible lovers?' Well, he has a knack for saying what he wants without being obvious. For example, a little personal compliment thrown in the middle of instructions on my swimming technique. He let me know he thought I was pretty, and I sort of let on I liked his looks too. It was all very subtle, especially since most of the time other students were around. Then one night he asked me to stay for some extra pointers after the others left; it sounded very formal and teacher-like, and there was an important race the next day . . . but after a half hour of extra practice, he said I must be tired, would I enjoy going out to dinner with him? Nothing fancy, just a quiet place downtown. . . .

To be honest, I was hoping he was leading up to something. He was, but with the best of manners. After all, we would be going on as student and teacher for another term at least . . . After dinner we dropped by his place to pick up a record he had offered to loan me. Of course he invited me in to see his apartment, and I suggested he put the record on. We made love. I enjoyed it. He's very experienced and doesn't rush things.

Of course, my parents don't know about it, or anyone on the team. What's to know? We're not in love, we just enjoy each other. We never discuss our feelings or anything personal. It's always on a week night we get together . . . I imagine he has something else going on weekends but I've never bothered to ask. I've got a cute boyfriend and it might get serious. If it does, I'll tell my coach. I'm sure he won't mind – he doesn't even know what jealousy is. I won't ever tell my boyfriend though!

Pragma and 'Open Marriage'

A lover whose first choice in lovestyles is pragma, but who also feels a need for variety and excitement, may choose a pragmatic marriage with a compatible partner, then seek a 'supplementary income' of adventure outside the marriage. We have already discussed this pattern in Chapter Seven, and noted that generally such arrangements must be both

137

convenient and discreet. They must not threaten the basic security of the marriage, which is the pragmatic lover's first priority. So the outside affairs are usually of the storgic ludus rather than ludic eros variety.

In the film *A Touch of Class*, the husband is unfortunate in his choice of mistress. Her demands on him begin to jeopardise his domestic tranquillity. This provides considerable amusement for the audience – for example, when he uses the excuse for walking the family dog to respond to an urgent appeal from his mistress, then returns home without the dog, forgetting it at his mistress's apartment. But in this story, as in real life, when the chips are down, the pragmatic husband abandons his mistress for the safe, if dull, security of his marriage. At heart, the pragmatic lover likes to be able to calculate the odds on things working out. An ecstatic and unpredictable involvement with a jealous and demanding mistress or lover is too risky.

The conditions of a *complete* 'open marriage', in the sense used by the O'Neills (see page 115), are not achieved when the basic lovestyle is pragma. There is an element of hypocrisy, or what could more politely be called dissembling, in a pragmatic marriage with outside affairs; and the couple concerned therefore lose that possibility of growth which comes through the mutual sharing of adventures. Instead, each partner minds his own business in a live-and-let-live working arrangement. In the event of a crisis, a couple with such an 'arrangement' will temporarily bring matters out into the open in order to protect the marriage, then lapse into discreet tolerance once the crisis has passed. To use the investment analogy which so often applies to the pragmatic lovestyle, the couple do not accumulate and re-invest the dividends from outside affairs to increase the basic capital of their marriage. That kind of process requires the open rapport and honesty of ludic eros.

Lasting Relationships

Break-ups are rarer in pragma than in many other kinds of love because of the careful and deliberate calculation of the 'odds' that is made when choosing a mate. If failure does occur, it is usually due to irreconcilable incompatibility. Pragmatic lovers don't expect living together to be paradise, so a decline in intensity of feelings (which were never very intense to begin with) is not enough to lead to rejection of the partner. However, daily dissatisfaction with the behaviour and personality of the beloved, especially in practical matters of domestic life, is sufficient cause for an end to the relationship. Pragma is by no means devoid of emotion, but feelings are guided by rational consideration – quite the opposite of eros. Rational control over emotional expression is even more typical of the storgic-ludic affair. Yet this is still a kind of loving. Indeed, a discreet affair involving a total of only ten or twenty hours in private intimacy with the partner, with perhaps several weeks between each encounter, may be pleasantly remembered for months or years.

Respondents who reported storgic-ludic or pragmatic experiences were very similar in their attitude to love as essentially a convenient and useful relationship, but they assessed rather different qualities in the beloved when initiating the relationship. For the pragmatic lover, similar social background and a minimal age-gap were important considerations; but among the storgic-ludic lovers, many were separated by significant gaps in age and social status. It seems unlikely that a storgic-ludic affair would grow into pragmatic marriage. It is almost as if the lover, while assessing the partner, thought to himself: 'I like you and we get along well but we're from two different worlds. Let's have a friendly and discreet affair for a time, but marriage between us just wouldn't work in the long run.'

If a marriage were to grow out of a storgic-ludic relationship it would have the quality of a 'long-run affair of convenience'. There was one such relationship among my respondents. The couple concerned preferred to keep things 'legal' for business reasons, but each spouse was open-minded and permissive, and did not object to the other having affairs on the side. The husband took a pragmatic view of his marriage, considering it the 'best practical solution to having a home and family', but at the same time he had had five affairs in about ten years of marriage. His attitude to his wife was that she was his 'most important and longest lasting affair'. The wife didn't believe in marriage at all but had conceded its social and legal necessity for her husband.

Neither storgic-ludic nor pragmatic lovers are likely to

refer to themselves as having fallen in love. Rather, they had arranged a satisfying relationship. (Even the word 'affair' itself suggests organising something; it derives from the French word for 'business'!) Neither storgic-ludic or pragmatic lovers expect love to be life's most important experience. Often their occupations have priority over their love relationships. Obviously the two lovestyles differ in their attitude towards the 'seriousness' of love. In storgic ludus, seriousness extends only to discretion, while in pragma it extends to commitment in a responsible marriage as long as the partner is found compatible. A partner who began to interfere with the pragmatic lover's more important life activities, such as his career, would soon be dismissed.

Pragma's attitude to love is that 'it's safe enough to fall in love, if you're careful where you fall'. The pragmatic lover may wish to respond spontaneously to his feelings for his partner and marry soon after meeting her, but he knows that a reasonably long engagement is advisable if the marriage is to have the best chance of success. Nowadays he may choose to be really pragmatic about the decision. He may move in with the partner for a period of 'trial marriage', taking great care not to let accidental pregnancy upset a sensible and rational choice.

Pragma is a controversial lovestyle. Erich Fromm bitterly attacks the 'market mentality', accusing such lovers of being 'out for a bargain; the object should be desirable from the standpoint of its social value. ... Two persons thus fall in love when they feel they have found the best object available on the market, considering the limits of their own exchange values.' Fromm compares this kind of lover to a speculator in real estate. Early advocates of modern pragmatic love, such as Judge Lindsey and the philosopher Bertrand Russell, were attacked as immoralists; but today the argument that two people will make the best marriage when the sum total of happiness and other benefits which they can enjoy together exceeds the total which the two would enjoy separately, would seem reasonable to many lovers.

Nine

Agape and Storgic Eros – Dutiful Love

> For leaving special loves, thy mind
> Shall clasp the whole of humankind
> In large embrace.
>
> ('*Roman de la Rose*')

When Saint Paul wrote to the Corinthian members of the early Christian church telling them that love is patient and kind, that it is not jealous or boastful, nor arrogant or rude, that it does not insist on its own way, but believes all things and endures all things, the Greek word for love was *agape*. This concept of love implies a duty or obligation to care about the other person, whether you want to care or not, and whether the love is deserved or not. Agape is 'gift love', without ulterior motives and with no strings attached. It is completely altruistic and deeply compassionate.

The purely agapic lover may well hope for a reciprocation of his love, but agape does not act out of the expectation of, much less the demand for, such reciprocity. Distinterested love could not possibly be jealous; so it is worth noting that agape relates to the concept of God presented in the Old Testament, by Isaiah's 'suffering servant' (Isaiah 53), not to the 'jealous God' of the early tribal period of Hebrew religion. In the New Testament it is the love given to undeserving sinners by a God who dies for the sinner's salvation. Agape need not be Christian, of course. The concept of dutiful, unselfish love long pre-dates the Christian era and is found in many religions.

The truly agapic lover gives the kind of loving which the beloved needs, regardless of the benefits or difficulties involved for the lover. The greatest gift of such a lover may be to step out of the beloved's life altogether and allow her to love and be loved by someone else. The totally agapic lover does not use such unselfishness as a manipulative device, secretly hoping that when the beloved sees how devoted he is to her welfare, she will drop any other attachment and give herself to him alone. As Kierkegaard explained in *Purity of Heart is to Will One Thing*, the truly agapic lover cannot be 'double-minded'. He cannot love altruistically if he hopes it will bring him some reward in heaven or on earth. He must give his love with complete disregard for personal gain of any kind.

Perhaps not surprisingly, I have yet to interview any respondent involved in even a relatively short-term affiliative love relationship which I could classify without qualification as an example of agape. I *have* encountered brief agapic episodes in continuing love relationships. One of my respondents was a lover who, out of apparently unselfish and self-sacrificing concern for his beloved's happiness, disappeared from her life for several months so that she could pursue another partner. My respondent saw that his beloved was tormented and torn between two lovers and could never have chosen either for fear of deeply hurting the other. He resolved to take the hurt of choosing unto himself. Whether that was the best action for all concerned, no one but God could know, and indeed, when a human tries to act in a totally agapic way, he is almost attempting to be 'like God'. (That is why Christian theologians have generally argued that man cannot by his own efforts be truly loving [agapic] and that such loving is only possible through the gift of God's grace.)

However, my respondent's action fell short of pure agape because he went on being interested in how well his beloved was getting on with her new partner and could not help himself feeling a little pleased when they had a falling out. It is really difficult to be completely unselfish! Eventually, to my respondent's joy, his beloved dropped the other partner and, realising that my respondent's action had been motivated out of the deepest concern, chose him. Virtue had its reward after all. Of course the resulting affiliative love relationship was not agapic, though it had some agapic qualities. I eventually classified it as a mixture called storgic eros, which is closely related to agape and will be defined in more detail in a moment.

Agape is perhaps almost impossible as an *affiliative* love for mere mortals, since ideally it implies a universalistic concern embracing all mankind, not merely those people to whom one feels some special attachment. 'Thou shalt love

142

thy neighbour' means a duty to love whomever is at hand and in need of love. The stranger in the road whom we have never met before, and may never see again, is also our neighbour in agapic love. In direct contrast to eros, agape does not seek one perfect human beloved who becomes more important than all others.

Reason and obligation always overrule desire and emotion in agapic love as portrayed in literature. This quality of conscious control might make agape appear similar to ludus, but the purpose and means of control are quite different. Ludic love controls emotional investment in order to avoid commitment, whereas the fundamental motivation of agape *is* commitment. Agape has the objective of overcoming narcissism. There can be no selfish concern for one's own survival in agape, while in ludus, such concern is essential. The essence of agape is to be able to promise to love now and in the future, regardless of how or whether one's personal wishes may change. Although agape runs counter to what many believe to be our 'natural selfishness', and therefore requires great self-discipline, humility and self-sacrifice, it should not be concluded that agapic love is necessarily painful. Suffering will be an inevitable *part* of such love, the world being what it is, but action taken out of selfless love of another person can sometimes bring great satisfaction. Of course, it must not be done merely for the sake of the satisfaction – not even the satisfaction of 'doing the right thing'.

Many Christian theologians have argued that such exalted and selfless love is impossible for the ordinary mortal to attain. They claim that even the saints have achieved it only occasionally, and then only with the aid of divine grace. Some modern theologians have challenged this view. Reinhold Niebuhr, for example, has argued that during certain crises man can transcend natural selfishness and sacrifice himself without the aid of divine grace. And even if agape is not perfectly attainable, it is at least approachable, and so lifts our sights to more altruistic loving.

Some non-Christian analysts of love have adopted a version of agape as their own idealised definition of true love, and have argued that by great effort and discipline, ordinary persons can hope to achieve altruistic loving. Erich Fromm, for example, defines his 'productive love' in a manner very close to the central Christian concept of agape, arguing that the lover *must* love, out of duty. 'Thou shalt love', in Fromm, becomes the duty to love with care, knowledge, responsibility and respect, governed by will rather than emotion. Reason and duty, not desire and feeling, are central to Fromm's mature loving, which has its objective not in becoming lovable, but in loving others. Fromm wrestles with the conflict between his ideal of loving and the 'narcissim' of erotic love. He never, in my opinion, resolves the conflict:

> . . . love is exclusively an act of will and commitment, and therefore fundamentally it does not matter who the two persons are . . . We are all One – yet each one of us is a unique, unduplicable entity. Inasmuch as we are all one we can love everybody in the same way in the sense of brotherly love. But inasmuch as we are all also different, erotic love requires certain specific highly individual differences.[1]

This is as close as Fromm comes to dealing with the existence of two distinguishable kinds of loving, each of which has its merits. Because he prefers to consider his mature or productive love as the one true kind of loving, he is unable to leave his readers free to choose narcissistic forms such as eros as equally valid lovestyles.

Sociologist Pitirim Sorokin leads us to the same *cul-de-sac* by attempting to prove that his 'altruistic' love is the only valid kind. In *The Ways and Power of Love*, he defines the dimensions of such love as universalistic (loving all persons regardless of the lover's feelings or the beloved's merit), eternal, pure (unadulterated by ulterior or selfish motives), and adequate (providing fully for the beloved's needs).

Sexuality

One of the obstacles in the way of achieving pure agape seems to be man's sexuality. The literature of love portrays agape as a relatively non-sexualised form of loving. Where coition is discussed, it is usually considered to be a 'sacramental act', that is, an outward and visible symbol of an inward and spiritual gift. Agapic love views the body as the

1. *The Art of Loving.*

temple of the spirit, not to be profaned by lust. In its highest expression, agape should not seek sexual gratification at all.

An example of an attempt to achieve this goal can be found in the early Christian church, where unmarried men and women slept together in a practice called *agapetae*. They restrained themselves from all intimate contact, enjoying only the spiritual ecstasy of close proximity. They tested their faith by resisting the temptations of the flesh. Sufficient pregnancies resulted from this altruisitic practice to lead the Church Fathers to doubt the fortitude of many believers. The practice was forbidden. The Church concluded that it was better for Christians to marry. 'Better to marry than burn' St Paul put it.

As a concession to human frailty, the lofty concept of agape was compromised to permit a sexual relationship, but only within a marriage which is monogamous, and contracted for life. Even then, many Christian theologians frowned on sexual intercourse for any purpose other than procreation. To love one's own wife too ardently was the same as adultery, St Jerome warned. The Church in medieval times, and even later, placed severe limitations on sexual coition, forbidding it on Sundays, holy days, and numerous other occasions. Intercourse for sheer pleasure was unacceptable. It followed that prevention of procreation was opposed. Birth control and abortion were both excluded by traditional Christian agape.

Nowadays, not only birth control and abortion, but also homosexuality and many of the formerly forbidden positions in heterosexual intercourse, are increasingly accepted within love relationships. Consequently, lovestyles which emphasise feelings and enjoyment are more popular today than a lovestyle which demands dutiful self-sacrifice and onerous struggle with our selfish instincts. Outside religious writings we do not find many contemporary examples of agape in our literature of love. Yet the continued reprinting of Fromm's *The Art of Loving*, suggests that many people still respect the agapic ideal.

But is it only an ideal, which none but a few saints can be expected to achieve?

A small number of my respondents reported experiences of love which came fairly close to the ideals of agape. They reported the kind of sexual restraint, unselfish concern and dutiful self-sacrifice which has traditionally been considered typical of human altruism, and specifically of Christian agape. These respondents had an almost 'religious' attitude towards loving, not in the sense of following any specific religious creed, but in the original meaning of the term religion (from the Latin, *religio*, a binding or discipline, thus, a rule of life). This concept of love as a self-discipline, an art to be learned and practised, is not unique to Judaeo-Christian thought, of course.

What caused these respondents to fall short of perfect agape was a certain selfishness which seems almost essential if two people are to be more concerned about their relationship to each other than about any other relationship. It may be impossible, in affiliative loving, not to place the partner ahead – even if only slightly ahead – of all other persons in the lover's concern. Completely altruistic loving, such as that proposed by Pitirim Sorokin, probably would not satisfy the requirements of the pairing and mate-selection processes.

Obviously it is not enough to classify some experiences of love as 'almost agape'. What relationship do these experiences bear to the various identifiable lovestyles? A clue comes from the solution of similar problems in mania and pragma. It is possible to conceive of agape not as a primary type of love, but as a combination of more basic elements. In that case, near-agapic experiences would be alternative combinations of the same elements, similar to the cases of ludic eros and storgic ludus. But which elements are involved?

Analysis of the near-agapic respondents' reports indicated that they felt a good deal of intense intimacy on the psychological level, but without the physical preoccupation of eros. Instead of an ideal image of the appearance of the beloved, these respondents had a disembodied ideal of love relationship. They sought perfect love rather than a perfect beloved.

At the same time, these near-agapic lovers reported many

qualities typical of storge: an enduring patience and gentle affection, for example. Their sexual restraint seemed to be an extension of storgic attitudes to a more extreme self-discipline.

The element of which there is no evidence whatever in the near-agapic experiences, is ludus. Apparently no two love-styles could be more opposed in their definition of the appropriate attitudes and actions of a lover, than dutiful love and playful love. Thus it appeared that both agape and near-agape were likely to be combinations of eros and storge. The near-agapic respondents were therefore identified as examples of *storgic eros*.

The term storgic eros almost implies a contradiction in terms. How can one be storgic, in the gradual, gentle, affectionate sense of this lovestyle, and at the same time, immediate, intense and idealistic in the manner typical of eros? As it turns out, storgic-erotic lovers are themselves aware of this apparent contradiction. They experience the tension between the opposing expectations of eros and storge, in a manner similar to the experience of lovers in the ludic-erotic lovestyle. Storgic eros is a tightrope act.

According to my theory of agape, the contradictions between eros and storge would disappear, and a new, integrated conception of love take their place, if the components fully compounded to produce agape. Unfortunately, I have no real-life examples of agapic affiliative love to demonstrate this theory, and so it must remain just that – a theory. However, as we shall see, it proves to be a useful theory because it throws light on a number of ideas about agape found in theology and literature.

For example, Christian theologians have long struggled with the question of whether agape is an experience of loving limited to the deity, and perhaps a few superhuman persons to be called 'saints', or whether it is an ideal towards which all mortals should be expected to strive. Traditional Christian definitions of agape have included both the ideal of complete devotion to the act of loving, undiminished by any selfish considerations, and universal concern for all persons, not merely those one finds attractive or lovable. In short, the agapic lover is expected to be highly *intensive* and *extensive* at the same time.

But human love tends to get thinner as it is spread further.

147

A love which is limited to one person can become the focus of all one's emotions. It can become extremely intense – but at the sacrifice of universality. Or one can diffuse one's concern, affection and other emotions of love among an ever-widening circle of fellow human beings, but at the expense of intensity for any single person.

If we explain agape as a compound of eros and storge, we can conclude that, while it draws its intensity and power from eros, the exclusiveness and sensuality of that lovestyle disappear (just as the poisonous quality of sodium disappears in table salt). From storge come neighbourliness and sexual reticence, but the reliance on common activities and interests disappears. Emerging as a new quality in the compound, not found in either component, is the idea of love as a commanded obligation ('thou shalt') rather than either an intense attraction or a committed friendship.

Agape also differs from both eros and storge in its complete lack of jealous possessiveness. Eros and storge are selfish loves, seeking to preserve the mutuality of a satisfying relationship. Perfect agape, in theory at least, would be completely independent of any expectation of reciprocity.

Religion and Agape

Classifying agape as a compound rather than as a primary lovestyle may appear to some readers as 'demotion' for the love which has been the ideal of Christian doctrine for twenty centuries. But my theory could just as well be construed as a tribute to the sublimity of agape, inasmuch as it is described as a combination of the excellence of eros and storge without the narcissism of either. The unhappy record of Christian practice (in contrast to doctrine) over the centuries can be explained in terms of the difficulty of achieving the perfect compound. For most religious adherents, whether Christian or of other religions which idealise an unselfish, dutiful love, a mixture of eros and storge flawed with narcisissm has been the best that could be achieved.

The rarity of agape, in contrast to the prevalence of the other two compounds, mania and pragma, may be explained as a consequence of the social conditions which favour or hinder the development of each of these lovestyles. For many centuries the consideration of family, property and political power have favoured the pragmatic lovestyle; and, since the troubadour introduction of concepts of romantic love into European society in the eleventh century, social conditions favourable to mania have become increasingly predominant. These conditions seem to be associated with industrialism and urbanism. Evidence of this is the spread of romantic notions of love to the traditionally pragmatic oriental world as it becomes modernised.

The ambitions of the early Christian church to create a society which would favour the practice of agapic love were never realised. Neither the expected inauguration of the millenium nor the construction of the City of God on earth was achieved during the centuries when Christian doctrines of love prevailed over all others. Now the opportunity seems to have passed, perhaps for ever, as most Christians begin to realise that their view of love is likely to remain a minority position in the world. Of course, Christian theologians would have a different explanation for the failure of the agapic lovestyles – namely, the inherent selfishness of mankind, arising from 'original sin'.

History seems to support the concept of agape as a compound of eros and storge.[1] The Christian definition of agape owes more to St Augustine than to any other early Church Father, for it was he who converted St Paul's rather poetic concept into a systematic guide to everyday behaviour in a non-Christian world. St Augustine's thought clearly represents an effort to combine the intensity and passion of the pursuit of the beautiful (found in the Platonic idea of eros) with the compassion and universal brotherliness of the Gospel concept of love of one's neighbour as oneself. His concern to weld Platonic and neighbourly love into a single comprehensive norm of Christian action arose out of practical necessity – the bitter and potentially schismatic controversy with his theological rival, Pelagius. Somehow, the singular intensity of eros had to be linked to the grace of God, in order to remove the possibility of salvation of the human personality outside the Church. Otherwise, with the aid of eros, man might attempt to lift himself morally by his own bootstraps. Augustine rejected the possibility that eros alone could redeem man, seeing within it the fatal flaw of *hubris* (pride). At least partly because of his own life and

1. See, for example, K. S. Latourette, *A History of Christianity*.

conversion, Augustine insisted on the doctrines of original sin and total surrender to the grace of God.

Roman Catholic theological doctrine since Augustine has generally continued to emphasise the co-relationship and community of (erotic) intensity and passion with (storgic) friendship and neighbourliness in a single (agapic) love. Protestants have been more wary of intense extremes of love, distrusting both saints and passion. Thus, Protestant theologians have tended to make a sharp division between agape and eros, arguing that they are inevitably opposed. This position is clearest in Bishop Anders Nygren's *Agape and Eros.*

The theory of agape as a compound of eros and storge stands midway between the Catholic and Protestant conceptions, but at the same time provides agape with a distinctive trademark. Agape is the dutiful, altruistic lovestyle. Just as instant recognition of the ideal image marks the erotic lovestyle, and desperate forcing of emotions marks mania, so total selflessness identifies agape. 'You shall love even your enemy.' Sometimes the apparent self-sacrifice of mania may be mistaken for agape, but one has only to watch the manic lover after his disappointment to distinguish the two. There is never bitterness, recrimination or 'sorry second thought' in agape. Agape is not 'irritable or resentful' but 'bears all things', St Paul assures us. Agape could never be confused with the singular intensity of eros, but it does need to draw on this intensity. The patient companionship of the storgic component alone would never provide sufficient motivation to obey the call to love no matter what the cost. Storge may evoke great loving self-sacrifice for one's friends, but never for one's enemies.

Characteristics of Storgic Eros

Like ludic eros, storgic eros is a tightrope act, a constant balancing of potentially antagonistic forces. If the combination really 'jelled' and fell into place, it would become agape. But the 'pull' of agape in our society is far less than the pull of mania. It might be possible to construct a social order in which individuals combining erotic intensity with storgic friendliness could as easily slip into agape as lovers trying to combine erotic intensity with ludic detachment slip

150

into mania, but such a society has never existed in the Western world. It exists only as the Christian vision of paradise.

My storgic-erotic respondents were characterised by an initial attraction to the partner which was distinguishable from erotic 'first love' by the notable absence of physical symptoms of excitement. Unlike eros, the storgic-erotic respondents experienced little or no jealous feeling, and were surprisingly lacking in anxiety or concern for early reciprocation of their feelings. They seemed to find sufficient enjoyment in the act of loving another person to be initially indifferent to requital of love.

If a lasting relationship developed, the lover did become dependent on reciprocal feeling from the beloved, and thus fell short of an agapic ideal. Yet this mutual dependence was distinguishable both from erotic rapport, which is extremely upset by even a few days of separation from the partner, and from storgic 'accustomedness' or companionship, which is much less self-conscious about the relationship than is storgic-erotic love.

A Case History

One of the most interesting stories of storgic-erotic love was that of a couple living in common-law. Both were interviewed. Paul hired Ruth to live with him and his children as housekeeper and governess after his wife left him. Ruth brought two children of her own. Her husband had deserted her. For more than a year, Paul and Ruth shared the convenience of a single home, entirely without sexual contact or any expression of feelings inappropriate to a friendly employer-employee relationship.

Looking back on that year during their interview with me, Paul and Ruth admitted that physical attraction had probably existed to some extent between them, but it was held in check because Ruth very much hoped to return to her husband, and Paul respected this hope. It was in mutual play with their children that Paul and Ruth were best able to breach the formalities of employer and employee and attain a more intimate feeling. Finally, Paul invited Ruth out for dinner, the first occasion on which they had dated each other. That night on their return to the house, they did not go to their separate rooms.

Until their first sexual intimacy, 'mental communion' rather than sexual attraction was what each reported feeling for the other. Yet at the end of their first date, not to have slept together would have seemed (each told me) to be a violation of that mental communion, which they felt more strongly that evening than ever before. The absence of the children on this occasion heightened their togetherness, so that sexual union seemed consistent with the deep respect they felt for each other. Neither Paul nor Ruth can recall who first declared love of the other, nor even when they first felt themselves to be a 'couple' whose relationship to each other was more important than either's relationship with the estranged spouse. All this took place several years before I met and interviewed them and they had now achieved a settled, but not formally ratified, married life, which was accepted and approved by in-laws and neighbours.

The correlation between these two respondents' choices from my collection of opinions about love was remarkable. Each was interviewed separately; yet each selected almost the same mixture of typical eros and storge 'statements'. Nor did I have to rely on my data cards alone. A visit to Paul and Ruth's home left me deeply impressed with the powerful yet subdued and gentle warmth of their relationship to each other, which at the same time embraced all of the children and their guest. A quality of mental empathy (or what some would call spiritual communion) continued to distinguish their attachment to each other.

Mutual erotic lovers can be distinguished by the intimate rapport each obviously enjoys with the other, even in public. There is a constant flow of cues, gestures, touches, acknowledgements of each other. The intensity tends to leave the onlooker feeling somewhat excluded, and perhaps even envious or offended. Mutual storgic lovers, by contrast, seem to pay scarcely any direct attention to each other while together. Each goes about his own business, or works with the other in a friendly but task-oriented manner. They may even seem to 'take each other for granted'. Storgic-erotic lovers come midway between these two positions. The onlooker is aware and constantly reminded of the profound closeness of the lovers, but is not excluded by it. Rather, the lovers' rapport seems to embrace him as well. Mutual storgic lovers would simply include a third party into their activity, not into their relationship (of which they themselves seem hardly conscious). Storgic-erotic lovers are quite conscious of being lovers and embrace the onlooker within the context of their mutual love.

The opinions of the storgic-erotic respondents about the nature of true love conformed very closely to the definition of agape in Christian literature. These lovers were utterly opposed to any pretence or dalliance in love (such as exists in ludus), insisted on great honesty (balanced by consideration of the effects of such honesty), and were convinced of the necessity for commitment in love. In that the storgic-erotic lovers valued their partners in love more highly than they valued any other person, they fell short of achieving the entirely altruistic, universal quality of theoretical agapic love.

The storgic-erotic lover rarely idealises love; for him it is hard work and obligation. He therefore forms no ideal image of a partner. In this he resembles storge rather than eros. However, he does have definite preferences, especially as regards the personality of a partner, and in this he resembles eros more than storge. A pure agapic love would presumably feel obligated to love any person, whatever his merits or attractions, or lack of them, but storgic-erotic love falls short of this ideal too.

Returning to the colour analogy, the primaries, eros and ludus, have been considered to combine in two ways, to form two quite *opposite* secondary styles of loving: mania and ludic-eros. Eros and storge, on the other hand, seem to combine in two ways which produce rather *similar* secondaries, one being a more unified and integrated form of the other. Although there are quite important differences between the two, storgic eros appears to be an intermediate stage in the ultimate compounding of eros and storge into agape. More research is necessary to determine the exact social qualities of agape, and to determine whether humans can achieve such a kind of loving. Perhaps, like radium, it is most commonly found in a less perfect or pure form, the form I have called storgic eros. An 'ideal' form of agape would be eternally patient and entirely unselfish. Storgic eros has more human limitations.

Ten

The 'Tertiary' Lovestyles

And I thought how utterly futile everything was;
this was the second time in one night somebody had
told me they loved me and I didn't want it, I didn't
want it from either one of them and when you *did*
want it, you never got it.

(*Brian Glanville*
'*A Second Home*')

The world is filled with an amazing variety of complex experiences, but a child soon learns to distinguish between species of things. The device he uses is language. Some languages provide detailed specifications for things which other languages lump together. The Eskimos, for example, have numerous words for 'snow' because it is important for them to distinguish various kinds of snow. Even within a single language, people vary in their degree of differentiation of phenomena.

There may have been a time when one word, 'love', with a few general distinctions such as 'Christian', 'romantic' and 'Platonic', was sufficient for ordinary purposes, while theologians and philosophers disputed the more specific differences between types. But in modern, highly individuated cosmopolitan life, we need something more exact than the everyday phrase 'I love you'. Unfortunately for any simple theory of loving, the nine terms I have already introduced (three primaries and six secondaries) are not enough to account for the varieties of human experience. I must belabour you with terms for a third level of lovestyles beyond the primary and secondary; these I call *tertiary*. Actually, it is possible to continue the same process even further, and speak of a fourth or *quaternary* level, but just as colours which combine four other hues tend towards the same nondescript mud, so too with love.

Nine tertiary types of love are theoretically possible: manic eros, manic ludus, manic storge; agapic eros, agapic

154

ludus, agapic storge; pragmatic eros, pragmatic ludus, pragmatic storge. My techniques for distinguishing between lovestyles have not reached the level of sophistication to enable me to identify positively all of these tertiaries. In some cases, I suspect that the tertiary is only theoretically possible, and may not actually exist. A cross-breed of a man and a horse, or a woman and a fish, is imaginable, but science has yet to establish the existence of centaurs or mermaids. A cross-breed of agape and ludus is equally imaginable, but highly unlikely, due to the antagonistic qualities of these two types. Pragmatic eros is almost a contradiction in terms, but I have the impression from some interviews that it does exist. The only three tertiaries I am prepared to identify with certainty are those of mania. These require a less sophisticated level of analysis than do the others because mania is the most prevalent ideology of love in the modern world.

The combination of a *mixture* with a *primary* is not included in my concept of tertiary love because this is merely equivalent to lumping all three primaries together. For example, ludic eros is a mixture of its primaries in varying amounts, and may be more or less ludic or erotic. As a mixture, it always retains some proportion of the typical qualities of each primary, and no distinctive new qualities emerge as is the case in a compound. The combination of ludic eros with a storgic ingredient is quite possible. Most love relationships will include a little bit of each primary anyway. But the whole point of analysis is to identify the *main* components. If a love is a mixture of primaries we can understand it best – and thus find a mutual love most readily – if we reduce it to its two predominant primaries, or, in appropriate cases, to its one predominant primary.

When ludus and eros combine in mania, we have quite a different situation. Many of the qualities of mania are not found in either ludus or eros (as those of water are not found in hydrogen or oxygen); so the combination of mania with storge is not merely a lumping together of the three primaries in varying degrees. The same would be true of pragmatic eros or agapic ludus, if they exist. Pragma has a calculating, compatibility-seeking concept of mating which is not found in either ludus (which doesn't want to pair off anyway), or storge (which is not calculating), or storgic-ludus (which wants only a discreet affair). Thus, the com-

155

bination of pragma with eros (if it could be positively demonstrated) would combine a calculating, compatibility-seeking concept of pairing with the instant recognition of an ideal physical image and the profound psychological rapport which are typical of eros. If such lovers exist, my interview and data-analysis techniques have not yet succeeded in positively identifying them.

The gradient from eros to ludus via mania begins with relationships in which eros is pure or the dominant primary, with other ingredients considered irrelevant. From eros, we move to a stage of manic eros in which eros is still predominant but with some manic undertones. Then to a stage of manic eros in which mania seems more pervasive than eros. Then to mania itself, in which such basic erotic qualities as self-confident rapport have largely disappeared. Then to a form of manic ludus in which mania is predominant but with distinctive ludic aspects. Then to another form of manic ludus in which the ludic qualities are dominant, but with manic undertones. And finally we reach a stage in which ludus is the clearly dominant primary.

This gradient provides us with two of the tertiary loves, manic ludus and manic eros. The gradients from eros to storge (through agape) and from ludus to storge (through pragma) would each provide us with two more *theoretically* possible tertiaries, making a total of six so far. Three more are produced by crossing each compound secondary with its opposite primary: manic storge, agapic ludus and pragmatic eros. Thus, here are two kinds of tertiaries, those which are at the third level of combinations because they combine all three primaries (two of them being in the compound), and those which combine a primary with a compound of which the primary is also a part (but in a transformed aspect due to the emergence of new qualities in the compound). Manic ludus and manic eros have only ludus and eros as components, while manic storge has all three primaries. Remember the parallel with chemistry. Elements sometimes combine as radicals and together act in further combinations with other elements, but in a manner quite different from that in which either or both elements of the radical would when alone. Just as alchemy gave way to chemistry, it may turn out that the poet's alchemy of love will eventually give way to the sociologist's chemistry of love!

Manic Eros

Some of the men and women I interviewed were in various stages of love which could be located on the gradient from eros to mania. I called their experiences (as analysed at the time of each interview) examples of manic-erotic love. Manic eros appeared to be a transitional stage. Each lover's account of his relationship indicated that he was moving either towards a more stable eros or towards full-blown mania.

Some manic-erotic lovers appeared to be basically typical of eros in their relationship. They showed few or none of the predisposing factors (unhappy childhood, discontent with work, etc.) which would have suggested a tendency to mania. However, they were under some strain, often only temporary, which undermined their self-confidence and emotive rapport with the beloved. In some cases a short-term diminution in the beloved's response, or a temporary physical separation which forced such a diminution, had left the lover uncertain of the relationship. Where there was a threat from a rival or an intervening parent, greater uncertainty led to stronger manic qualities in the lover's responses to my sorting questions. In *manic* eros, preoccupation with the beloved increases and becomes more negative and anxious. This anxiety in turn invades the lover's other life-activities and undermines his contentment with work and friendships. The lover begins to show signs of desperation, and attempts to compel the beloved to show more reciprocal commitment. Instead of the absence of jealousy, or the self-confident ultimatum typical of the erotic lover, there are more and more frequent arguments, 'scenes', and attempts to hold on to the beloved by monopolising all his or her time. In the case of physical separation, the anxious lover begins demanding that the beloved return, or that he be allowed to join her, whatever the consequences. When the problems which originally induced the manic aspects are resolved, or even allayed, then the manic symptoms tend to disappear and the lover reports actions and thoughts about loving which are more purely typical of eros.

157

Other cases of manic eros were evidenced by lovers with predispositions towards mania. Such lovers were much less likely to attain erotic rapport even when the sources of their anxiety were removed. Instead, they showed a tendency to create new difficulties whenever old ones were resolved. In a few instances the manic-erotic lover had the good fortune to fix his exclusive attention on a beloved who was apparently self-confident, and reciprocally attracted. If this beloved turned out to be primarily erotic, he or she might be able to help the manic-erotic lover 'over the hump' towards eros. Most manic-erotic lovers with a predisposition to mania were not so lucky. They were struggling unaided towards an erotic self-confidence. Their relationships showed some erotic aspects: a tendency to believe in the sincerity of the beloved rather than doubt it, a reluctance to compel the beloved, a capacity for sensual and sexual rapport, and so on. But the successful expression of these primarily erotic qualities was repeatedly undermined by manic fears and anxieties, negative preoccupations with the beloved, and over-demanding reactions to the beloved's non-requital of attention. These manic-erotic lovers were acting like religious converts who wanted to believe, but somehow hadn't reached the certainty of conviction: 'I believe – help thou my unbelief.'

Manic-erotic lovers were distinguishable from more purely manic lovers (at the time of interview) by their more definite ideal image of the beloved they seek, and a greater correspondence between this image and the actual beloved. They were less likely to despise themselves, submit to any folly or abuse for the beloved, or remake themselves in an attempt to please the beloved. Of course, a lover who is moving towards mania will eventually show behaviour quite different from that of one who is moving towards eros. A diagnosis of manic eros is like a still photograph of a relationship which can be moving in either direction, and the outcome depends on the beloved's response as well as on the lover's resources.

When a typical erotic lover is temporarily unable to obtain the reciprocation and rapport – both physical and mental – which enable him to continue expressing the thoughts and actions of eros, it is by no means inevitable that he will slip into a manic-erotic condition. Mania is only one of several directions in which a lover may move away from eros. Much depends on the lover's methods of dealing with the temporary interruption. The lover may attempt to substitute remote forms of contact with the beloved for the immediate physical presence so essential to eros. The experience of respondents who attempted this solution would suggest that it usually leads to mania. Letters proved unsatisfactory and gave way to long-distance phone calls. These merely left the lover feeling more lonely when the phone was put down; so, the frequency of calls was increased. Soon the lover found his whole day pervaded with thoughts of the beloved: dramatisations of the past, anxious anticipation of the future, and the conjuring up of all manner of misfortunes. Such respondents were well on the road to mania.

Some respondents prevented a manic transition by either ludic or storgic stop-gaps. One erotic lover whose partner was absent for a sufficiently long time to provoke anxiety diverted his attention through temporary ludic-erotic affairs. To avoid the danger of involvement in these affairs he tried to conduct several at once, or in rapid succession. This solution is not always readily available, since it requires a supply of partners who approximate the lover's ideal image closely enough to arouse some of the intensity he feels for his absent beloved but cannot express, but not so closely as to undermine the ludic detachment he must maintain in the affair. Of course the lover must himself be attractive enough to hold the attention of such partners as long as he needs it.

Perhaps the solution of another respondent was more universally applicable. She concentrated on strengthening her storgic qualities by spending more time with mutual friends of herself and the absent beloved. Thus she was able to avoid writing sad and half-recriminating letters about how much she missed her partner, and instead sent news of evenings spent with their mutual friends. This news also had the effect of strengthening her absent partner's desire to return quickly, as she hoped he would. Manic effects can be avoided, then, if the erotic lover moves in either a ludic or storgic direction, temporarily combining either with eros.

Manic-erotic respondents who reported having previously experienced a fully manic relationship had sometimes been helped by new partners to avoid a second manic performance. In these cases the respondents described actions by the partner which went further, as expressions of affection and commitment, than the manic-erotic (and potentially manic) lover had expected. The very excess of devotion shown by the partner seemed to alleviate the latent anxiety of the manic-erotic lover and enable him or her to reciprocate with more risk-taking expressions of feeling.

Ironically, a manic-erotic lover who has never fully experienced the power and disaster of mania seems less likely to be helped by an overly affectionate and supportive partner. In cases of this type that I encountered, respondents remained constantly doubtful of themselves and fearful of responding to the partner's devotion by reciprocal risk-taking. Had such lovers previously experienced mania and survived it, they would have known that it is possible to take risks and survive, even though badly hurt. Though the ultimate outcome for these respondents remained unknown to me, it appeared that they would have to go all the way to mania in the reported relationship, survive it, and start again through manic eros towards eros, with a new partner.

One of the significant variables when comparing manic-erotic love with full-blown mania or successful eros is the expression of jealousy. As noted earlier, an erotic lover is most unlikely to express possessiveness through conflict, scenes and threats. Either he is confident and non-jealous, or else he takes an ultimatum position. The manic lover, by contrast, is constantly mounting guard on the partner, suspecting a rival in the partner's every acquaintance, demanding repeated proofs of fidelity, provoking arguments, and asking for an account of the partner's time not spent with the lover.

The manic-erotic lover has it both ways with jealousy: he feels possessive as a manic lover would, but tries to behave as an erotic lover would. Conversation with my manic-erotic respondents on this subject abounded with contradictions. They repeatedly expressed their certainty of the beloved's capacity to love them: 'I'm sure he'll grow to love me more; I can see it in him; it's just a matter of time.' But I often felt they were 'protesting too much', for they also reported numerous occasions of checking up on the beloved to find out what he was doing with his time, who else he was seeing, and so forth. Unlike a typical manic lover, however, the manic-erotic lover tries hard to disguise this jealousy as curiosity, or altruistic interest in the beloved's welfare. A manic lover believes unashamedly that jealousy is a proper aspect of loving – that the expression of jealousy is a proof of his love. The erotic lover tends to view jealousy as rather an immature emotion whenever it becomes possessive. Certainly one may be concerned with the fate of a beloved in whom one has a great investment of affection and rapport, but to express this concern in restrictions and suspicions is considered childish and untrusting. The manic-erotic lover would like to share the erotic lover's opinion about jealousy, but tends towards the manic lover's actions.

Manic-erotic lovers appear to go halfway to meet trouble and disappointment in love because they doubt their ability to achieve erotic rapport; but they don't actually create troubles and disappointments where none exist, as a manic lover would. The manic lover tends to despise himself, as Theodor Reik points out, but the manic-erotic lover merely doubts himself. In time, his form of loving is likely to be resolved towards a more self-confident eros (or a ludic or storgic variation of eros) if his luck is good and his partner helpful. Failing these fortunate circumstances, the manic-erotic lover is probably on his way to a self-tormenting manic obsession with the beloved.

Manic Ludus

Between mania and ludus there is a tertiary position which characterised a number of respondents in my interviews. These respondents combined the outwardly contradictory qualities of preoccupied, jealous love and detached, playful love. I call this condition manic ludus, though that is almost like speaking of cold fire.

The practice of ludic love requires conviction of self-sufficiency resting on feelings of vanity, and detachment from any single affiliative relationship. The successful ludic lover must really be able to think and act as if beloveds were relatively interchangeable, and the future supply sufficient for his needs. While a good deal of bluffing is incorporated into the gallant ludic lover's treatment of the partner, it is dangerous for him to kid himself. If he suffers from doubts about his attractiveness, or fears that he is getting too old or that the supply of substitutable partners is running out, then these anxieties are likely to undermine his ability to remain self-sufficient and detached from any single relationship. He will begin to show the preoccupation and possessiveness more typical of a manic lover. If conditions begin to verify his anxieties he may move so far towards manic obsession that he loses his ability to drop his current partner, especially if a new one has not already been secured.

The fully ludic lover is not afraid of being alone – 'between affairs' – while selecting a new partner. Nor is he reluctant to take the initiative in dropping any partner he no longer enjoys loving. When a would-be ludic lover begins to show anxiety about being without a partner, or attempts to hold on to a partner longer than he enjoys her because something else has not yet turned up, his lovestyle is probably manic ludus. Such a love has not moved to full mania so long as he continues to be willing to drop the partner and find someone new. A fully manic lover feels that life without his beloved is hardly worth living, and will take much abuse and torment rather than break off with her. A manic-ludic lover does not go to this extreme dependency, but he does lose the clear-cut ability to act independently of the partner in manipulating the relationship, and especially in terminating it. When the partner is coming on strong, the manic-ludic lover enjoys a revival of vanity and self-sufficiency, and it is then that he is most likely – especially if he sees an alternative available – to drop his partner. When the partner is herself showing signs of disinterest, a manic-ludic lover hangs on – just at the point where a fully ludic lover would immediately get the drop on his partner by acting first.

A typical manic-ludic case was that of a respondent I will call 'Jack'. He constantly alternated between complaints that his girlfriend Susan (not her real name) came on too strong, and equally annoyed complaints that she didn't show him enough love. At first it was quite difficult to comprehend this apparent contradiction. Finally it became clear. When Susan was showing more feeling for Jack than he felt for her, he felt himself at an advantage in the relationship and usually exploited his position by manipulating Susan into doing things she didn't want to do. This caused her to withdraw to some extent, leaving Jack to decide between dropping her or coming to terms with her. Instead of dealing with this crunch as a ludic lover ('there are plenty of other fish in the sea'), Jack became afraid of losing Susan, and especially fearful that she might drop him. He was not ready to look elsewhere. Indeed, he lacked the vanity and self-sufficiency to believe that he could easily find another partner. On the other hand, Jack was not predisposed to full mania. He was content with his work, had a pleasant circle of friends, considered his childhood fairly happy. He did not believe in one-and-only love and was not ready to marry. He could well imagine living without Susan – if a better person came along.

Jack was pleased by Susan's displays of affection because they restored his vanity and gave him more time to find a new partner, but he complained about them at the same time because they undermined his ludic detachment. He did not possess enough vanity and self-sufficiency to face a period with no girl at all while he looked for a substitute for Susan.

The manic-ludic lover is not the casual, easygoing playboy he *would like to be* and tries hard to be. On the other hand, he is not so self-despising or anxious for love as to become easily manic. His objective is fun, not commitment. There is simply a gap between his intentions and his ability to control his emotions completely. Unlike the manic respondents, the manic-ludic respondents were willing to break off a relationship, but not so confident of themselves as to be able to break at *any* time. Their anxiety about their ability to attract substitute partners makes manic-ludic lovers rather like tenants caught near the end of a lease with no new accommodation in sight; they are grateful for an extension in the present quarters even though they have already decided not to stay there permanently.

Manic Storge

Manic ludus and manic eros are transitional stages between distinguishable primaries and the compound of those primaries. They form a third level of love relationships. Manic storge is a tertiary in a different sense. It is a cross-breed of the compound of two primaries with the third primary. Two other cross-breeds of this kind are theoretically possible,

163

agapic ludus and pragmatic eros, but manic storge is the only one for which I have obtained positive evidence.

Storge is normally a quiet, companionate type of loving. The lover is typically from a large family, with happy memories of parental and sibling relationships. He is not only content with life, but has an unassuming trust in, or reliance on, the companionship and support of friends and neighbours around him. He becomes accustomed to his partner in a gradual process of acquaintanceship centred on shared interests and activities. Arguments may occur and problems arise, but storge shows no extremes of folly or ecstasy, and certainly no pervasive condition of anxiety or preoccupation with the relationship.

Some respondents I interviewed reported a history of a relationship whose overall pattern was unquestionably typical of storge, but at some time during this history there had been a sudden storm of emotions which shattered the unassuming unconsciousness of the lover and made him painfully, intensely aware of 'being in love'. The first instances of this condition which drew my attention (and indicated its existence) were taking place at the very time of my interview with one respondent. Later, I began looking for similar events in generally storgic relationships: perhaps a manic period had occurred long before and had been forgotten or repressed. Not all storgic relationships have had a manic period, of course. If a manic interval occurs, the lover may survive it (especially if in a mutually storgic relationship) with no lasting after-effects. A manic interval of more than brief duration, especially where the partner is not mutually storgic, can permanently alter a storgic relationship, or bring about its demise.

In an experience which can be classified, at the time of diagnosis, as manic storge, emotional charges will have built up between the lover and his partner. It may be that the partner is a different love-type; a manic or erotic partner, for example, may show increasing impatience and dissatisfaction with the way the storgic lover takes her for granted. Or the crisis may be precipitated by the arrival on the scene of a serious rival to the storgic lover, someone who offers the partner a more romantic and ecstatic (manic or erotic), or a more fun-filled and exciting (ludic), type of affiliative love. Whatever the cause, a point is reached at which the built up charges of unexpressed emotion are suddenly exploded. The storge lover is forced to become aware of the relationship, and to examine his feelings.

> I saw the quarrel had ... broken the outworks of youthful timidity, and enabled them to forsake the disguise of friendship, and confess themselves lovers.[1]

The new awareness of intense feelings for the partner may draw the lover nearer to rapport and commitment with the beloved, or it may so surprise and disconcert him that he becomes (at least temporarily) incapable of action. In instances where my respondents knew that the partner was enjoying new and more intense emotions with a rival, they were called upon to compete with the rival by showing similar feelings. Several of these respondents could not bring themselves openly and passionately to express their love and desire for the partner. Instead, they passively hoped the partner would 'get over her phase' and return to a more down-to-earth relationship with someone who 'really loved her and was not just out for excitement'. Unfortunately for these lovers, their partners did not always opt for the security of established storge over the promise of the newcomer's more eventful and fascinating lovestyle.

1. Emily Brontë, *Wuthering Heights*.

Eleven

Which is Your Favourite Lovestyle?

Pity me that the heart is slow to learn
What the swift mind beholds at every turn
Edna St Vincent Millay

Love is clearly a complicated experience. It is not easily simplified – and perhaps most of us prefer it that way! The purpose of this book is not to make love an instant process where we 'just add partner and serve', but many lovers might find life easier if they could sort out the different experiences of love, and decided which is their favourite lovestyle. Perhaps it would also help to know which is second best, in case you don't find the right partner to share your first preference.

For some readers, my detailed descriptions of the various lovestyles will provide the best means of sorting out past and present experiences of love. No doubt you have recognised yourself, or a beloved, or some of your friends, in the examples of various kinds of love I have described. But some of you may find the two self-tests in this chapter both helpful and interesting, even if they do no more than clarify or confirm your observations.

Many people enjoy self-tests like 'Known your own IQ' or 'How good a parent are you?' No one takes the results too seriously, because we know that such tests can never cover all the important details. On the other hand, a few simple categories can sometimes be more useful than a complicated diagnosis. In education, for example, several years of complex learning experience can be boiled down to a short list of grades, which enable another school, or an employer, or a parent, to compare one student's achievements with those of other students. No one supposes that all students with a B+ are the same kind of person, or even have the same abilities, but the grade is useful for some purposes.

The two tests in this chapter should be used with the

same sort of caution we would apply when comparing people according to school grades. The scores from my tests will no more decide whether you 'really love' someone than a school grade alone would make up an employer's mind about a job applicant. Yet you may find the test results helpful in the pursuit of your desired love-style.

The most beneficial and also the most risky use of the tests would be their completion by you and your beloved independently, followed by a comparison of the results. This should not be done too early in a relationship, any more than we should give a new-born babe a complete physical examination; but once your relationship has become stabilised and each partner's patterns of behaviour fairly well established, a diagnosis of the lovestyle or lovestyles involved could be mutually helpful.

Of course, there are some relationships where you know in advance that you and your partner are going to have sharply differing scores for the various lovestyles. If you're not ready to deal with that problem, you'd best keep the test to yourself. On the other hand, a comparison of the differences might be just the opportunity you need to make some point to your partner about the way your relationship is developing. Even a thoroughly ludic lover could use the tests, to remind a manic partner that he or she is getting too involved – and a manic lover could use the same scores to remind the ludic partner that he or she is taking love too lightly!

Differences in scores are not necessarily to our disadvantage in love. Some differences between lovers can be complementary, and actually strengthen a relationship. Suppose, for instance, that you value a partner who is good-looking above one who is good company. Your eros score will then be higher than your storge score. Suppose also that you are fortunate enough to have a partner who *is* good-looking, but that your partner has a higher score for storge than for eros, because he or she values your 'good company' over your good looks. In that case, you've gained the very useful information that conversation will do more to hold on to your partner than cosmetics.

If the tests indicate that you and your beloved hold strongly different views about the nature of love, and thus

167

prefer different lovestyles, the results can at least help you to discuss these differences reasonably, rather than argue about who is not loving 'enough'. One of the significant advantages of my theory of lovestyles is that it redirects our personal diagnosis of experiences of love away from quantitative comparisons and towards real differences in *styles* of loving.

Problems which are never talked about are not likely to be solved, and problems must be identified before they can be discussed. The tests may help you and your partner to locate the basic contradictions in your different lovestyles, and decide whether either of you can do anything about these differences. Remember that lovers can and do change their lovestyles, just as they can and do change their life-styles. You may decide that your partner is worth a change in your definition of a 'true love' relationship. Then again, you may not! In that case, you can break off because of differences in style, without rejecting the other person *as a person*.

The tests in this chapter can also be applied to past love relationships. After completing a test with your own answers, you can reply to the questions a second time with the answers you think your former partner would have given. This won't be as accurate as if the former partner had answered in person, but it may help you to diagnose the reasons why the relationship didn't work out (assuming you wanted it to – obviously those following a ludic lovestyle won't bother). Sometimes the realisation that the failure of a relationship was the result of irreconcilable differences of style can help you avoid blaming yourself or your former partner; and with a new awareness of what you are really looking for in a love relationship, you can approach your next opportunity with more confidence.

Test One – Twenty Questions About Your Love Relationship

The lovestyles described in the previous chapters were developed out of lengthy and detailed interviews. If such interviews could be compared to a complete physical checkup at your local hospital, then Test One is a sort of fifteen-minute checkup at your doctors office. Many import-

168

ant details have to be omitted, but the overall picture should be clear enough.

Because you have to score the test yourself, it is arranged in a simplified manner in which you may choose one, and only one, answer for each question. A few answers have no connection with any specific lovestyle and are included merely to round out the test; they have no score. Most answers have a score of one 'x'. Certain answers are especially significant, so a score of '2x' is indicated (This is similar to testing for TB, for instance: a cardiograph may not be a useful indicator at all, but a chest X-ray is particularly relevant.)

When the answer to a question is relevant to several different lovestyles, there is a score for each one of these. You must count *all* such scores. It is the overall pattern of final scores, not the individual answers, which will determine your favourite lovestyle(s). To use the medical analogy again, a bad cough may be indicative of a pneumonia, tuberculosis or bronchitis. Only after the doctor has made a number of tests will he be able to conclude which of the three (if any) you are suffering from. Please don't conclude from this analogy that I consider love something like a disease!

One problem with self-tests is that they can hardly make allowances for the passage of time. Your love relationship will have gone through several, and perhaps many, stages. These have to be collapsed into a short series of questions. This problem has been resolved by asking you to turn your mind back to the start of the relationship, and then live through it again in your mind, so that your answers become those you would have given then – not those you would give now with the benefit of hindsight.

By the way, it is quite possible to take this test without ever having been in an affiliative love relationship. You simply answer according to the way you would like to be in love. However, previous results from this self-test indicate that inexperienced lovers are unlikely to have made up their mind about which kinds of love experience they really want. This is not surprising – it would be equally difficult to choose the kind of work you like best, if you had never held a job – but it does mean that the results of the test are less likely to be clearcut. You will probably obtain almost equal scores on several different lovestyles. Only after some real experiences will your preference become clear.

Obviously there are no 'right' and 'wrong' answers in this test. And, of course, the eight basic lovestyles tested here may not be adequate to define all the delicate shadings of your experience. But you can fill in the missing details yourself, from the previous chapters.

Read the following instructions carefully before you do the test. Then relax and enjoy this quick checkup on the state of your lovestyles. Whatever the results, the diagnosis won't be fatal!

INSTRUCTIONS

1. The first six questions assume that the relationship is already several weeks old. Of course, it may be much further on than that. (If you are imagining a relationship, respond accordingly.) Question 4 asks you to use some hindsight about your orientation to the experience of love, but generally the questions ask you to respond as if you were feeling and acting in the present time. This might of course be the case, if you are diagnosing a current relationship. If not, try to avoid rewriting your past history in terms of what you discovered later in the relationship. For example, if you began by believing your partner was just right for you, but later decided otherwise, don't respond as if you always knew the relationship wouldn't work out.

2. VERY IMPORTANT: the rest can only be applied to *one* love relationship at a time. Remember that we are diagnosing an example of a lovestyle, not a kind of lover. Your lovestyle may differ considerably from one relationship to another, just as your lifestyle may change from time to time. If you want to compare several experiences, and perhaps discover whether you have a consistent preference for one lovestyle, you should complete the test in pencil, record the final score, erase your answers, and do the test again, once for each relationship. Of course, if your answers change, the diagnosis will change. For example, between your first and second relationships your attitude to jealousy or sex may have changed.

3. If you want to compare scores with your beloved, complete the test in pencil, and erase all markings completely

170

before showing the test to your partner. Do not discuss with your partner any individual questions or answers, or your final score, until after he or she has completed the test.

4. Obviously it is important to be honest with yourself.

Method of Answering

1. Read each statement and choose the *one* answer which best completes the statement to describe the relationship. Next, look across at the columns on the right. You will notice one or more scores of x or 2x on the same horizontal line as the answer you have selected.

2. Draw a circle around all the scores of x or 2x that correspond to your selected answer (that is, are on the same horizontal line).

3. Select one and only one answer for each question, and try not to skip any question.

EXAMPLE
Question 11 reads:

1. Our sexual relationship:
a must be ecstatic . . . (etc.)
b can be worked out . . . (etc.)
c may not work out . . . (etc.)
d should be enjoyable . . . (etc.)

After reading all the responses carefully and stopping to think of the way you feel, or felt at the time, or would feel (if imagining a relationship), you may decide that *c* comes closest to describing your feeling. You circle all the scores which are on the same horizontal line as *c*.

Instructions for totalling your scores will be found at the end of the test. Enjoy yourself – and try to be honest!

171

Twenty Questions About Your Love Relationship

	1	2	3	4	5	6	7	8
1. At the time this relationship begins, I think of myself as having had:								
a a happier childhood than most people.							x	
b an average childhood. (no score)								
c an unhappier childhood than most people.	x							
2. My feelings about my everyday life and work are:								
a I am really enjoying life and I have some good, close friends.		x	x				x	x
b My life is about as good as anyone's. (no score)								
c I feel something is missing, *or* I feel rather lonely.	x							
3. The other person in this relationship begins it as:								
a a complete stranger to me.	x	x	x	x				
b someone I am already acquainted with.						x	x	x
4. I realize (perhaps using a little hindsight) that as this relationship begins:								
a I am ready to enjoy any pleasant relationship that comes along, but I have no intention of 'getting serious' or 'settling down' with any one person.			x	x				
b I am rather anxious to be in love with someone (though I may also be a little afraid of love).	x							
c the idea of being in love hasn't even occurred to me. I am just getting to know this person as a friend.							2x	
d there is one type of 'looks' (physical appearance) that attracts me more than any other, and this person is 'my type'.		2x						

	1	2	3	4	5	6	7	8
e I am ready to 'settle down' with a partner who has a personality and background compatible with my own.						2x		
f I am already committed to someone else but I am prepared to have a relationship with this person 'on the side'.					2x			
g I feel that this person needs me (or needs my help).								2x
5. As I become involved with this person:								
a I soon become preoccupied with happy, hopeful thoughts (dreams, fantasies) that this is the person I have been looking for.		2x						
b I soon become preoccupied with anxious thoughts (concerns, worries) about the way the relationship will develop.	2x							
c I soon begin to analyse carefully whether this person would make a suitable, compatible mate.						2x		
d I go on with life more or less as usual, and don't give much thought to this relationship beyond the ordinary arrangements one needs to make. (no score)								
6. As we become more involved, I want to see this person:								
a every day, if at all possible	x	x						
b fairly often, when it is convenient for both of us.			x			x	x	
c when it is convenient for me, without taking too much of my time.				x	x			
d whenever my partner needs me.								x

173

	1	2	3	4	5	6	7	8
7. Now that we are 'involved' I feel that:								
a I can only be truly in love with this one person, who is more important to me than any other.	x	x				x	x	
b I like this person, but there are other people I could be (or am) involved with, who could be just as important.			2x	2x				
c I must help this person who needs me, but there are other people who also need my love.								x
d I am already committed to someone else, and I will have to be careful not to let this new relationship hurt the other person to whom I am committed.					2x			
8. If my partner in this relationship I am assessing wishes to be involved with other 'lovers' too:								
a I will do anything possible to prove that I can love my partner more than anyone else could, so that eventually my partner will love only me.	x							
b I will not compete for my partner's love: my partner will have to choose between me and anyone else.		x				x		
c It's fine with me, because I intend to be involved with other 'lovers' too.			x	x				
d It's fine with me, because I have a prior commitment to someone else anyway (for example, a spouse).					2x			
e I'll go on loving my partner anyway. In fact, if it seems that some other lover would be of								2x

174

	1	2	3	4	5	6	7	8
more good to my partner, then I will step aside.								
f I may not be happy but I won't ask my partner to make a choice. Time will tell, and eventually my partner will make a choice.							2x	

9. As my partner and I become more involved:

	1	2	3	4	5	6	7	8
a I am the first to say 'I love you'. I want to show that I am really serious.	x							
b I have to warn my partner not to get too involved, because I am not ready to commit myself to anyone. I've given fair warning.				2x				
c I tell my partner that I really enjoy this relationship, but there are also other love relationships I want to enjoy.			x					
d I become more and more aware of the ways my partner's body really fits 'my type' (and/or the ways it does not fit).		x						
e I feel that only after we have come to know each other really well, will we be sure of our love and able to make a commitment.						x	x	
f I am ready to help in any way I can, 'no strings attached'.								x
g I remind my beloved that I am already committed to someone else.				2x				

10. I want to have sexual intercourse:

	1	2	3	4	5	6	7	8
a very soon after we begin seeing each other – within the first few encounters or 'dates'.		2x	2x					
b only after we have come to know each other well and feel some commitment to each other.						x	2x	
c when it is enjoyable, without interfering with my other love relationships.				x	x			

	1	2	3	4	5	6	7	8
d perhaps not at all, and certainly not early on. Sex is basically for the purpose of procreation.								x
11. Our sexual relationship:								
a must be ecstatic and compatible almost from the start, or I am likely to decide we are not suited to each other.		2x	x					
b can be worked out as we go along. We can learn to have good sex even if we don't 'turn each other on'.						2x	x	
c may not work out, but I'll go on loving just as much (and perhaps 'hope for the best').	x							x
d should be enjoyable or 'fun' but not become serious or overly emotional.					x	x		
12. I express my feeling for my partner:								
a as often and intensely as possible, even if my feelings are not reciprocated, in the hope that eventually I will persuade my partner to love me.	2x							
b as openly and honestly as possible, but not more intensely than my partner's feelings are expressed to me. Our feelings should be just about mutual; I don't want to get 'ahead' of my partner.			x					
c as openly and intensely as I feel, without much consideration of whether my partner will reciprocate or feel the same way for me.		x						x
d in quiet, restrained, and sensible ways, as I would with a close friend.						x	x	
e in polite, sophisticated ways which do not embarrass or over-commit either one of us.				x				

176

	1	2	3	4	5	6	7	8
f freely, when in private with my partner, but only discreetly when observed by others who may not approve.					2x			
13. I will reveal my deepest thoughts to my partner:								
a early in the relationship and often as it goes on, even when such honesty might hurt our relationship. I want my partner to know me really well.	x	x						x
b only when necessary to prevent my partner from getting the wrong idea and becoming too involved. Most of the time I hope we can be pleasant without baring our souls.			2x		x			
c gradually, over a long period of time, as we grow more accustomed and trusting with each other and feel committed.						x	x	
d rarely or never. I expect my partner to respect my privacy.				2x				
14. If there is trouble ahead in our relationship it will:								
a probably develop because my partner does not meet my rather demanding expectations. I will simply have to explain that a mistake has been made.		x	x			x		
b probably develop because my partner becomes too serious, involved, argumentative, or jealous, so that the relationship is no longer fun for us.				x	x			
c probably prove to be a test of our real friendship and patience. If we are meant for each other, things will work out.							x	
d be my opportunity to show how I can go on loving my partner no matter what happens. No trouble will prove greater than my love.	x							x

	1	2	3	4	5	6	7	8
15. I will want to discuss our future plans together with my partner:								
a early in the relationship, so that I can show my partner how serious I am, and, hopefully, obtain my partner's commitment to our future together.	x							
b as we become more committed to each other, to make sure we agree on such basic matters as money, children, etc.						2x		
c very little. It will really be up to my partner to decide in the future how much I am needed or can be of help.								x
d very little, because life should be taken as it comes. As long as we really care about each other, the future will take care of itself.						x		
e very little or not at all, because our relationship does not have a 'future'. Each of us will eventually go our own way.			x	x	x			
16. If our love is 'for real' it should last:								
a forever (my lifetime).	x	x						
b as long as I enjoy it. If our relationship ceases to be pleasant I will break off (even if my partner doesn't want to).				2x	x			
c as long as we both enjoy it. I expect that whoever loses interest first will let the other down gently so that each of us can find other relationships.			2x					
d as long as we are compatible with each other and want to go on living together.						2x		
e as long as we remain friends, even if we cease to be lovers.							x	
f as long as my partner needs me, whether I need my partner or not.								2x

	1	2	3	4	5	6	7	8
17. As our relationship develops, fights and arguments happen between us:								
a quite often. My partner often says or does things that hurt me, or seems to take advantage of my love.	x							
b occasionally, because we may disagree, but I try to work things out rationally.						x		
c occasionally, but we are basically good friends, so fights and arguments are not likely to break us up.							x	
d rarely, because once we started to fight or argue a lot, it would be time for me to break off.			x	x	x			
e rarely, because unless we are so close to each other in our bodies and minds that important disagreements do not arise, I would be convinced that this was not the beloved I seek and I would look again.		x						
f rarely, because I don't make any demands of my partner. I will suffer patiently and in silence if necessary.								x
18. The opinion of others, such as friends and parents, about our relationship:								
a is not important to me. If I know my love is real I don't care what the whole world thinks.	x	x						
b is important to me because my partner should be able to get along well with my friends and fit into my social life.						x	x	
c is not important to me, because it is my duty to love, regardless of what others may think.								x
d is important to me, if our relationship interferes with other obligations which have a prior claim on me.					x			

179

	1	2	3	4	5	6	7	8
e is only important to the extent that these opinions make our relationship difficult or unpleasant, in which case it would be simpler to find another partner.			x	x				

19. If my partner should lose interest in me:

	1	2	3	4	5	6	7	8
a I will hang on and keep trying. I'd never be the first to give up.	2x							
b I simply look elsewhere for a new partner. Anyway, it is more likely that I will lose interest first.				x				
c I will take this in my stride and look for someone new.			x					
d I will try to remain friends, and perhaps later start in again, unless I've found someone new.		x					x	
e I will talk things over with my partner to find out what's not working and if possible mend the problem. But if we are basically incompatible I will look again.						x		
f I will feel that my duty is done, but if I am needed again later I'll always be available.								2x

20. If we ever do break up, 'getting over it' will take me:

	1	2	3	4	5	6	7	8
a a long time. I would be really hurt.	x							
b a long time, but I would try to understand and remain a friend.							x	
c very little time. There are other fish in the sea.				2x				
d not so long, if I could find someone new who came close to meeting my expectations.		x				x		
e very little time. I expect to be in and out of love a number of times.			x					
f very little time, as I would still have the other person I am involved with (or married to).				2x				
g perhaps a little time, because I'm only human, but I will try to be								x

180

unselfish and realize that my
partner must be free to live his or
her own life with no demands
from me.
(Are you still answering *honestly*?)

SCORING

1. Go back to question 1. Looking only at column 1,
count the number of scores (x or 2x) which you have circled
in this column. Each 2x is counted as two x's, of course.
Keep counting scores in column 1 until you have reached
question 20, and then, in the box below for column 1, enter
the total number of x's you have circled in column 1 for the
whole test.

2. Repeat this process for the circled scores in each of the
remaining columns. You will have a score for each box
below, ranging from 0 (lowest possible score) to 22 (highest
possible score).

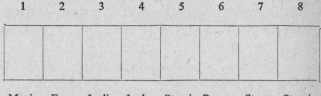

1	2	3	4	5	6	7	8
Mania	Eros	Ludic Eros	Ludus	Storgic Ludus	Pragma	Storge	Storgic Eros

INTERPRETING YOUR SCORES

Each numbered column in the test represented one lovestyle, and these are now indicated by the final score boxes.
(The columns were not labelled in the test itself, to avoid
prejudicing your answers!) Interpretation of your scores
depends more on the *general pattern* than on any single
score. One high grade on an arithmetic test doesn't make
you a mathematician! Since there are no right or wrong
answers in the test, it's obvious that no particular pattern of
scores is more desirable than any other. The results simply

181

indicate your relative preference for various styles of loving, during the relationship in question. If you complete the test again using a different relationship you may obtain a quite different pattern of scores.

If one box contains a score well above all the others, then the corresponding lovestyle is or was clearly your preference during the relationship you have diagnosed. It is important not that this score be above any particular number, but that it be three or four points ahead of all the others – a case of the person of average height looking like a giant among pigmies and a pigmy among giants. Thus a score of 12, with no other score above 7 or 8, is a significant indicator of your preferred lovestyle, but a score of 15 would not be as significant, if there were one or two other scores of 12 or 13. The way the test is set up (with forced choices) makes it likely that a really high score, such as 17 or 18, will be well ahead of the next highest score. Maximum scores of 22 are very rare: such a score would represent a 'perfect' example of the type of love indicated, which is as unlikely as a 'perfect' Christian or a 'perfect' Republican. The highest score I have seen on this test was 19 in mania, and it was a very manic relationship indeed!

It is obvious that very low scores, under 3 or 4, indicate that the corresponding lovestyles were not to your liking, at least during the relationship you have analysed.

Problems of interpretation arise when there are several scores all about equal, with no lovestyle score standing head-and-shoulders above the others. The best way to help you interpret such patterns is to consider a few examples.

9-10-3-2-2-6-6-2 These were the scores of a young man who claimed to have kept trying to work out a relationship in a pragmatic way, but who kept 'losing his cool'. We can see why. There is evidence, indeed, of pragmatic elements, with a score of 6 in box 6 (pragma) and a supporting score of 6 in box 7 (storge, one of the basic components of pragma). But the secret is out with the scores in boxes 1 and 2! He was suffering from too much intensity about this relationship. The 9 in mania and 10 in eros indicate a manic-erotic tendency. If this lover had a lower score in mania, with the same high score in eros, he might have succeeded, as this would have indicated strong erotic self-confidence.

But the about-equal scores in mania and eros indicate an anxious rather than a self-assured intensity.

0-4-7-8-7-3-1-4 These were the scores of a self-sufficient young woman, who claimed she knew how to handle her love affairs without getting hurt. The scores bear her out. She shows no manic tendencies whatever, and very little storge and pragma. Obviously she prefers relationships which are pleasant and noncommittal. Her highest score is in ludus (box 4), with supporting scores in ludic eros and storgic ludus, both of which involve many of the same attitudes and actions as the ludic lovestyle.

6-3-0-0-4-11-8-3 These scores, of a divorced woman of 50 years of age, indicate a preference for a pragmatic relationship; and the fact that another score comes fairly close is not a problem because it is in a related lovestyle, storge (Box 7). There is no basic conflict between the two highest scores.

It was, in fact, one of the intentions of this test to show up the overlap between related lovestyles. Circling some scores in the test necessarily involves circling others – remember, a cough can be a symptom of several different conditions.

When your test reveals relatively high scores in several *different* and apparently *contradictory* lovestyles, however, how are these to be interpreted? For example:

8-11-4-1-1-6-11-4 These were the scores of an inexperienced teenage lover. This respondent just hadn't made up his mind about which lovestyle he preferred. On one question he chose an answer indicating a jealous approach, then, on another, a devil-may-care attitude. He hadn't decided whether he really wanted – and missed – the woman in question, or not. Such scores are also likely when you attempt to analyse a love relationship too soon after an unhappy ending, or at a moment of crisis. Later, when you can stand back and look at the experience more objectively, a meaningful pattern will emerge.

2-7-10-5-5-7-10-2 These were the scores of a young woman in her first 'serious' love relationship, and still very undecided between two conflicting lovestyles, eros and pragma. She wanted a partner who fulfilled both her ideal image of physical beauty and her conception of a compatible companion. Unfortunately her partner didn't quite fulfill either of these goals. Where the pattern of scores indicates preferences for two different lovestyles which are not in neighbouring boxes, it is probably that the lover is torn between contradictory expectations in love. When a neighbouring box for either of these high scores is also fairly high, the pattern is confirmed. This woman has one tendency towards eros, indicated by boxes 2 and 3 (eros and ludic eros), and another towards pragma, indicated by boxes 5, 6 and 7. Ludic elements of manipulation and self-sufficiency make her less than fully erotic. If she was really erotic, box 2 would be at least 10, and box 3 would be 7 or lower. The same ludic tendencies make her less than convincingly storgic. While there is a score of 10 in storge, it is the overall pattern which counts, and its 'slope' is back towards pragma and storgic ludus, not towards storgic eros. In other words, the elements of conscious manipulation and 'realism' typical of the pragmatic lovestyle are much more evident in her attitude than the altruism of a dutiful lovestyle.

Difficult-to-interpret scores, where there are two 'peaks' as in the example above, often make more sense when thought of as the profile of a mountain range. You are more likely to pay attention to the *related* scores which form the 'slopes' of the peaks. Remember, the eight columns do not represent eight entities with no relationship to each other, but rather, a series of structurally related lovestyles – the 'love-spectrum; where each lovestyle 'shades into' the next one.

Sometimes the scores prove meaningless, because the lover has not been willing or able to answer honestly. A sour-grapes attitude, lingering feelings of hurt, or even the optimism of a new affair, can cause you to rewrite the history of a past relationship. Some lovers, like those in the film *The Way We Were*, keep the good memories and forget the rest.

You will find more information to help you interpret your Test One scores in Chapter Twelve. Test Two below may also throw more light on your preference in lovestyles.

In Test Two, you can compare the overall profile of a love relationship you have experienced (or are experiencing, or can imagine experiencing) with thumbnail sketches of eight of the most familiar and recognisable lovestyles. No doubt your experience will not exactly correspond with any of the profiles portrayed here, but it will probably come much closer to some than others.

Of course, you must remain aware of the limitations of such shortcut summaries. A sheep is still a sheep if its wool is black, but not if its hair is wiry. It is the distinctive characteristics we look for when classifying a species, and the same is true of lovestyles. Of course, no single characteristic is conclusive, for poodles also have woolly hair. It is the overall pattern which makes a profile. In the lovestyles portrayed here, the profile has been constructed from the most regular features observed in the experiences of love reported by my respondents. A feature has to occur at least 75% of the time before it is included in the profile. For instance, over 90% of the reports of erotic lovestyles included a belief (at the time) that the lover's childhood had been a happy one. One hundred percent of these lovers reported an ideal image of the physical appearance of the sought partner. Such an ideal image is to eros as woolly hair is to a sheep: non-erotic experiences may include it, but the eros lovestyle *must* include it.

As in Test One, keep in mind that love relationships, not lovers, are profiled here. The same lover may cast a different silhouette when in love with a different partner. Also, the profile is a still photograph of a moving process. Over time, a relationship may change in profile, just like the profile of a mountain or a human face.

INSTRUCTIONS

Simply read each profile in detail and compare its overall pattern with the attitudes and events of the love relationship you are analysing. For maximum precision, you should read the profiles of related lovestyles; for instance, eros and mania, if intensity seems to be a crucial aspect of the relationship. Obviously, in that case, a moment's thought will soon rule out some other profiles, such as ludus.

For the sake of simplicity, the profiles refer to the lover as male, but of course they apply equally to female lovers, and to both heterosexual and homosexual relationships.

Eros

The typical erotic lover

believes his childhood was a happy one, feels he had a warm relationship with parents and siblings. He is content with his life and work and feels self-fulfilled;

is ready for love and for the risks it will involve, but is not anxiously searching;

knows definitely what physical type attracts him most and is quite demanding in his specifications for an ideal beloved;

begins with a partner who is a strange at the first encounter, and who evokes instant approval and excitement;

is soon preoccupied with pleasant, hopeful thoughts about the beloved and their life together;

is eager to see his beloved at least daily, with many contacts arranged quite informally;

feels no anxious anticipation of problems, but if there are warning signs they are noted and acted upon to avoid troubles;

continues to feel strong physical attraction and expresses it both verbally and tactilely;

seeks a deep, pervasive rapport with the partner as quickly as possible. He is open and honest, strives for sincerity;

shares development and control of the relationship with partner;

elicits reciprocal feelings from the beloved but does not demand them. He enjoys intense emotions;

may be exclusive but is not possessive or fearful of rivals;

seeks early sexual rapport, enjoys sexual variety and artful technique;

considers love to be life's most important activity but will not abase or abuse himself for the sake of love.

Ludus

The typical ludic lover

believes his childhood was 'average'. He has 'no complaints'. Life now is OK, though perhaps somewhat frustrating;

is not ready to commit himself to anyone in a love relationship ('not ready to settle down');

likes a variety of different physical types and can switch easily from one type to another;

begins with a stranger who has a physical appearance within the lover's wide 'acceptable' range; may rise to a challenge, but refuses to become overly excited about any one partner;

goes on with his life as usual after meeting his beloved; does not 'fall in love'. He has no intention of including partner in plans for future life;

avoids seeing his partner too often, and may use formal means to avoid getting 'too involved' ('Don't call me until next week');

may be anxious about the future with a partner who is too intense. He will worry about how to remain free to break off, and will warn the beloved 'not to get in too deep';

continues to remain casual and in control of his emotions; tries to help partner retain self-control too;

limits rapport to the pleasant diverting aspects of the relationship. Feels that insincerity and lies may be justified by the rules of the game;

expects the partner to control herself and play the game for mutual enjoyment. Avoids intense emotions;

is not exclusive or possessive, may encourage other (rival) relationships; seeks sexual enjoyment with good technique, but for fun, not emotional rapport;

thinks love is not as important as work or some other activities.

Storge

The typical storgic lover

comes from a happy, secure family background, often from a large family. He feels that life is good, and dependable, and that he can rely on his friends;

187

is ready if love comes along but is not looking. He expects that true love will not be very exciting, but likes friendship;

has no conscious definition of a favoured physical type: it's more important to 'get to know' the partner first;

goes on with life as usual after becoming aware of 'love', but may plan more activities with partner;

does not become preoccupied with the beloved, but begins to enjoy their common activities more;

feels no anxious anticipation of the future, since 'time will tell';

continues to remain relaxed because there are no strong emotions to control. He recoils from any excess of emotion shown by partner; prefers to talk about and do things they share as interests, rather than to express direct feelings for each other. He also avoids conscious manipulation of the partner's feelings;

is quietly possessive but not jealous or fearful of rivals until a real threat to the relationship occurs;

is shy about intense physical contact or sex, preferring non-genital expressions of affection: after declaring commitment for each other, sexual difficulties (if any) will be worked out;

considers love an important aspect of life, but as an extension of friendship, not as a goal in itself. Love is the basis of society and family.

Mania

The typical manic lover

feels his childhood was unhappy, feels he had a difficult relationship with his parents. He is not content with life, probably has few friends and feels lonely;

is anxious to fall in love, yet expects love to be difficult and probably painful;

is uncertain what type attracts him, and is often looking for a combination of contradictory qualities. He may even dislike the first appearance of his partner;

begins with a stranger, in a first encounter in which his feelings are mixed;

soon becomes (often to his surprise) intensely preoccupied

188

with thoughts of his partner and need for the partner's love;

begins to imagine the future together with considerable anxiety and much wishful thinking. He tends to ignore warning signs of trouble ahead;

wants to see the partner at least daily, and is easily upset by delays and postponements;

will create problems if there are none, to intensify feelings;

periodically tries to calm and control his own intense feelings, but 'can't help himself';

experiences a loss of control over his feelings and the direction of the relationship;

tries to force the partner to show more affection and commitment;

is unable to break off the relationship himself;

becomes extremely possessive and is constantly on guard over partner;

becomes sexually frustrated and unable to enjoy intimacy;

becomes convinced that life without the partner's love is hardly worth living. He will abase and abuse himself in the hope of winning the partner's love.

Pragma

The typical pragmatic lover

shows no particular childhood pattern or attitude;

feels he can master life and achieve goals through his own efforts. He has a 'practical' outlook;

is looking for a compatible mate;

knows exactly what type(s) will be suitable, but tends to define these by biographic qualities (race, job, education, etc.) rather than physical appearance. The top priority goes to those with qualities most compatible with his own biographic data;

begins with a partner who is familiar, or encountered at work or in a place where people 'like himself' are easily met;

goes on with life as usual while incorporating the partner into his activities; meets the partner's friends (the better to compare him or her with other eligible prospects);

carefully notes warning signs of future trouble (incompatibility). He will drop a partner who doesn't 'measure up';

restrains mutual discussion and expression of feelings to a 'sensible' level, avoiding extremes. He wants to get to know the partner well over a period of time;

expects the partner to reciprocate feelings, but will change partners rather than force reciprocation;

is possessive about a highly suitable candidate but avoids jealous conflict or 'scenes', and will probably seek a new partner if the present one is unfaithful;

considers sexual compatibility important, but something that can be worked out through mutual effort and, if necessary, expert assistance;

believes a loving mate-relationship is desirable for a happy life, but not essential, and that no particular love partner is worth sacrificing too much for.

Storgic eros

The typical storgic-erotic lover

feels that his childhood was meaningful, whether happy or not, and that he 'learned from it';

is fairly content with life and has 'come to terms with himself';

feels that loving is a duty of the mature person, whether or not one finds love in return;

has no favoured type, and feels everyone is worthy of love;

begins with a partner who is at hand, familiar, and in need of being loved;

begins love not with pairing or commitment in mind, but the duty to respond to the need for love;

sees the partner when activity brings them together or when the partner expresses need;

believes in the power of mature unselfish love to resolve any problems that might arise;

controls his own feelings, not to restrain himself or manipulate the partner, but the better to meet the partner's needs;

strives for honest, open rapport based on trust. He is happy if the beloved reciprocates but does not depend on reciprocation;

does not feel jealous or possessive of the beloved or fearful of rivals; may even step aside in favour of a rival who seems more likely to meet the partner's needs.

he continues with the relationship as long as the partner wishes, and would not break it off to spare his own feelings;

never tries to compel the partner to reciprocate or show love. He never demands commitment from partner;

usually places little emphasis on sexual intimacy, preferring gentle warmth of feelings which may be communicated by tactile gestures;

believes love is the central purpose and meaning of human existence, and the means of fulfilling himself.

Ludic eros

The typical ludic-erotic lover

believes that he had an average or happy childhood, or, if unhappy, he is 'over it' now;

is quite content with life and feels able to cope with his problems and fulfil himself;

enjoys being in a love relationship, even several at once. He likes 'getting experience';

is attracted to several different, though usually related, types, often with an order of preference. He is not too demanding;

usually begins with a stranger as a partner. He meets people easily;

enjoys love but is not obsessed with thoughts of any one beloved. Fits love relationships comfortably into his daily lifestyle;

maintains a fine balance between casual detachment of feelings for any beloved and warm attentiveness to the beloved he is with;

enjoys each relationship for what it offers, taking risks in showing his own intense feelings when they occur and accepting intensity from a beloved, while all the time remaining open-eyed to the problems of each relationship;

feels care and concern for each beloved and tries to avoid hurting the partner. He tries to help the partner not to get 'too involved' with him;

191

shows intense feelings in such a way as to indicate that they are not exclusively felt for that partner;

is not jealous or possessive and may even encourage partner in other love relationships;

aims for sincerity and rapport with partner while each remains 'free';

does not demand or compel reciprocity and can end the relationship when it is no longer enjoyable;

enjoys sex and is willing to work to improve it over a short run;

believes loving is fun but not all-important.

Storgic ludus

The typical storgic-ludic lover

shows no particular childhood pattern;

is self-reliant, but shows no particular attitude towards contentment with life;

is usually already experienced in love relationships but feels no special need to be in love;

has no definite preference in either physical or biographic types of partner, other than a general taste for partners who are socially acceptable within the lover's own lifestyle;

begins with a partner who is familiar at work or in personal life, or is married to a friend;

goes on with life as usual (perhaps deliberately more so). He behaves discreetly with the partner when they meet at work (or with spouse present) and expects reciprocal discretion;

expects to continue the work or personal contact outside the love relationship (which is not necessarily secret) and after the love affair is ended;

enjoys being with the partner as lover at mutually convenient times, and may enjoy subtle or secret signs in the presence of (unknowing) others;

carefully notes warning signs of trouble ahead and acts to avoid it, though 'brinkmanship' may be fun;

may be intense with the partner in private, but in public restrains expression of feeling and expects partner to do likewise;

breaks off when relationship ceases to be enjoyable;

is not jealous or possessive. He does not want the partner to divorce, if married, in order to marry him;

is more concerned with considerate discretion than with sincerity;

enjoys sexual intimacy, though this may be only a minor part of the relationship;

probably believes that this kind of love is just 'a love affair'. He is likely to have some other concept of lasting love.

Twelve

Mixing and Matching Lovestyles

> The whole trouble is that I love you and that you
> don't love me. I keep trying to discover the meaning
> of this judgement on me . . . I look at myself, I go over
> our whole life together and everything I know about
> myself, and I can't find the beginning, and I can't re-
> member what it is I did and how brought this mis-
> fortune on myself.
>
> (*Boris Pasternak*
> '*Doctor Zhivago*')

The French proverbial saying that 'in every love, one person
loves and the other allows himself to be loved' may be too
cynical, but I am convinced that the most common problem
in love is the difficulty of achieving true mutuality.

In the stereotyped and simple view of love, the question
of mutuality is usually quantified: 'Do you love me as much
as I love you?' In the more sophisticated 'love-spectrum'
analysis of love, which depicts different but equally valid
lovestyles, the question 'how much love?' becomes sub-
ordinate to the question 'what kind of love?' To use a
market analogy, you would not be satisfied to exchange an
equal number of francs for pounds or dollars until you had
first determined a fair rate of exchange between the two
currencies. It may turn out that you should receive twice as
many francs for your number of pounds. For example, a
lover who insists that he loves you very much is not speaking in the same currency as you, if *he* means 'at the moment'
and *you* mean 'for the rest of my life'. Your lover's currency
is ludus, and yours is storge.

A daily phone call may constitute desirable contact to an
erotic lover, and a necessary reassurance to a manic lover,
but it is likely to prove a nuisance to a ludic lover. In calculating the contribution of such calls to the mutuality of
love, it is more important to consider each lover's valuation
of the calls than the number of them. In short, it is not

194

enough to be assured by your partner, 'I love you, after my fashion'. You want to be loved after *your* fashion.

Once lovers have established that they are negotiating in the same, or exchangeable, currencies, then they can try to measure which one loves the most. If the fashion of each is eros, then you may wish to consider who best fulfils the ideal image of the other. If the mutual lovestyle is pragma, each may happily compete in satisfying the other's shopping list of desirable qualities in a lover. Even in mutual mania, lovers could dispute which is the more ready to sacrifice everything, including life itself, for the other.

I leave calculations of this sort to lovers themselves, as I know of no way to measure the quantity of a given lovestyle. How much red is more truly red than how much red? Eros as a lovestyle seems distinguishable only in comparison with other lovestyles. To say that a lover is 'more' or 'less' erotic in his or her relationship, means that the relationship is, more or less, sharply distinguishable from, say, ludus or storge. If two lovers are both erotic, the amount to which each one loves in an erotic fashion can be measured only by comparing each to some other lovestyle. Whether one of them loves with a greater *amount of eros* than the other, is something my theory can't measure.

Thus, in the pages that follow, the term 'mutuality' means a *mutual definition of lovestyles*, not a situation where lovers love each other with equal amounts of love. As we shall see, this does not necessarily require that each lover should have the *same* lovestyle as his or her beloved. It means, rather, that the lovestyles must be reciprocal. To use the market analogy again, there must be some way of exchanging from one to the other. Or, to use the analogy of language, we can enjoy a conversation despite the fact that I always speak English and you always speak French, providing each of us understands the other's language, and agrees on the translation of all important words.

Obviously, within my definition, the simplest mutual love will be the one where both partners share the same lovestyle. There is no need for 'exchange' or 'translation'. If our style of loving is eros, for example, then 'I love you' means 'you turn me on' – for both of us.

Mutual love is not necessarily happy love. Mutual mania,

for example, is tantamount to reciprocal torture. Although it seems rare, I have interviewed one couple who thrived on mutual mania. Each partner used the psychological torture instruments of jealousy and repeated demands for love, to make life delightfully miserable for the other. 'Why did you take so long to get home?' 'I got caught in the traffic – and by the way, why was the phone busy all day? Did you have it off the hook?'

Mutual love is not necessarily long-lasting love. Two lovers who each define the relationship as ludus will have fun while it lasts, then go cheerfully on to the next affair. Matched storgic lovers are most likely to have the longest relationship. Each will leave it up to the partner or the passage of time to make decisions, and in their gentle patience and forbearance they will slip through the years hardly noticing that they have grown old together.

Perhaps a matched pair of erotic lovers would seem the ideal to many readers. Two beautiful people turning each other on, sharing every thought, enjoying blissful sex and warm tactile contact! Alas, it may be because such love is so difficult in real life that it suffers so many misfortunes in literature. Eros is the most demanding of lovestyles, the most expectant and intense. Like two forest fires meeting, two erotic lovers seem to burn up their combined resources. If the ideal physical image of each lover remains fixed, then the passage of years that would have drawn storgic lovers closer together drives erotic lovers further apart: each breaks away in search of a younger partner who will refresh the ideal.

Matching Lovestyles

Because of the great variety of lovestyles available in modern society, very few lovers are likely to pursue one lovestyle throughout the whole of their lives. Most modern lovers go through a 'love career': just as your lifestyle is likely to change as you move from job to job, so your preference in lovestyles is likely to change from one relationship to another. Even within a single love relationship lasting a number of years, the favoured lovestyle of each partner may change. An initial stage of intense romance (in the mania-eros range of the spectrum) may give way to a playful period of open marriage (in the ludic range), succeeded by quiet companionship (of the storgic kind).

One of the problems of mutuality, then, is to find a reciprocal combination of lovestyles which will endure for the length of time desired. Suppose you and your partner have each completed Test One in Chapter Eleven, and found that the overall pattern of your scores was similar. This would indicate that you are a mutually matched couple *at the present time*, but it is no assurance that you will be, several years hence.

If you are mutually matched in the ludic range (boxes 3, 4 and 5 in Test One), anything beyond the near future will hardly matter. Each of you apparently agrees that a love relationship should be good fun while it lasts and should last no longer than it is good fun. Problems may arise in your reciprocal definitions of how and when the relationship should end. For instance, your highest score may be in ludic eros (box 3), which emphasises more consideration for the partner, or in storgic ludus (box 5), which emphasises more discretion (consideration for your *other* partner, or spouse). Your partner's score, by contrast, may be highest in ludus (box 4): he or she may be prepared to break off without warning, and let you 'sink or swim'. If such differences exist in your preferred lovestyles, they can spoil what would otherwise be a pleasant and memorable affair. You could make the relationship more *mutual* (in my definition) by clarifying and if possible eliminating these differences in styles of loving.

One simple method for bringing your definition of a relationship closer to that of your partner, is to examine in detail the choices each of you made in the twenty questions of Test One. In the above example, the key difference may have occurred in question 16, on the duration of the relationship. An agreement in advance to 'let the partner down gently' would make this a more *mutually* ludic relationship.

The same general principle applies, whatever the pattern of preferred lovestyles in your Test One scores. If both you and your partner obtained high scores in eros (box 2), and you tend to fulfil each other's ideal image, then the relationship is reasonably mutual at present. But what of the future, when one of you may lose his good looks before the other?

197

A glance at the rest of your scores will indicate whether you will survive this crisis. For example, if you both have reasonably high scores in the pragma-storge range (boxes 6, 7 and 8) then you will be able to alloy your eros lovestyle with companionship and unselfishness as the years pass. But if one of you has the next highest score in ludic eros (box 3), with supporting scores in ludus (box 4) and even storgic ludus (box 5), while the other has low scores in these boxes but high scores in pragma and storge, then trouble lies ahead. As you lose your beauty, your partner is likely to look elsewhere; while you will want to hang on to your partner, substituting his or her good company for vanishing good looks.

A further technique to help you predict the eventual direction of your present love relationship(s) would be the repeated use of Test One, for each love relationship you have experienced thus far in your love career. The stable or shifting patterns of the test scores will give you some indication of the preferences you have developed among various lovestyles.

For instance, a steadily mounting score in the pragma lovestyle would indicate that you are really ready to 'settle down'. If your partner showed a similar pattern, and each of you finds the other a compatible character, then you are likely to enjoy a mutual, lasting and satisfying relationship. Of course, many lovers throughout history have made the same sort of observations impressionistically, by looking at a potential partner's 'track record' in love. All Test One does is to make this process of assessing the partner more systematic.

Your first problem in matching lovestyles with your partner may be convincing him or her that such questions should be consciously analysed. Perhaps your partner still prefers the age-old impressionistic method. In my opinion, this is similar to the attitude which for centuries prevented dissection of the dead to improve the health of the living! Fortunately for modern medicine, some doctors decided that human life was too sacred for its health and preservation to be left to chance and circumstance. The health of your love life might also benefit from dissection of your past relationships, and a gentle but systematic diagnosis of your current relationships.

The objective of an analysis is not merely to apply a label. To be told that a person has pneumonia, not merely a common cold, is only useful if we know something about pneumonia. In the same way, it is only useful to know that you or your partner 'has a higher score for storge than any other lovestyle' if this is translated into specific attitudes and feelings. Does this score mean that the lover is less likely to be jealous, or that he is more modest about sex, or that he puts a higher value on companionship than on expressions of feeling?

A really 'close match' between lovers would be one where not only the final scores in Test One, but also the individual choices in each of the twenty questions, tended to correspond. Such lovers would be speaking both the same language of love to each other, and the same dialect. But whatever the scores, it is my hope that you may find a discussion of your individual answers, not only to Test One but also to many of the other questions raised in this book, useful in achieving a truly mutual definition of your shared lovestyles.

Mixing Lovestyles

When two people speak different languages and cannot translate from one to the other, there are bound to be, at best, misunderstandings, and at worst, misery. It is obvious from the profiles of love in Test Two (Chapter Eleven) that a relationship one lover sees as 'true love' might not qualify as love at all for someone else. The choices of answers in Test One vary widely. Look again, for example, at the immense differences of opinion in questions 10, 11, 12 or 16. Every one of these possible opinions has been selected by some actual lovers. Test One has been used with hundreds of students, members of church groups, and even mature people taking 'Creative Divorce' courses. Each individual's final scores were posted (anonymously) for all to see. What always amazed such groups was the infinite variety of patterns. There seems to be at least one lover for any combination of answers you could select in Test One – even the most contradictory selections.

Obviously there is nothing to be gained by arguing that one set of answers, one definition of love, is the only true and correct position. Since many lovers are faced with the prospect of never finding a partner who is a 'perfect match', one may have to settle for 'mixing' instead.

Which lovestyles mix most successfully? Generally speaking, the further apart any two lovestyles are on the love-spectrum, the greater the difficulty of 'translating' one style to the other. Think of our colours again: blue is quite unlike orange, violet bears no relation to yellow, and red could not be more different from green – they just don't have 'ingredients' in common. So a ludic lover and an agapic partner may as well forget about reaching a mutual definition of true love. A manic lover with a storgic partner is scarcely more suitable. A lover preferring an eros love-style won't see eye to eye with a pragmatic lover. But a ludic-erotic (reddish-blue) lover has a good chance of coming to terms with an erotic (red) mate, and a storgic (yellow) lover will find much in common with a pragmatic (green) partner.

As with every general rule, there are possible exceptions or qualifications to the rule about proximity of lovestyles on the love-spectrum. Mania and ludus are near each other, but a manic lover will never achieve mutual love with a ludic partner. This is because mania, of all the compounds, is the one whose qualities are most strikingly unlike those of its components. However, there is a strange kind of mutual attraction between mania and ludus which makes their proximity not entirely misleading. A manic lover's intensity in love is increased by difficulties, and no one is likely to make things as difficult for him as a ludic partner; and although the ludic lover may be overwhelmed by the manic lover's intensity, his vanity is much expanded by this ardent devotion. As I noted in Chapter Three, a ludic lover may be loth to break off with a manic partner whose attentions are so flattering. In spite of the fact that ludic and manic lovers will never achieve a mutual definition of love, it seems that these two types do mix with each other a good deal. And since each serves as something of a foil or complement for the other, a mania-ludus partnership, while it lasts, might be considered a 'success' in love after all.

Two other lovestyles which are located near each other on the love-spectrum, but seem strikingly unmixable are eros and agape. To some extent this question is more theoretical

200

than real, since I have already indicated the dearth of agapic relationships among affiliative lovers; but where one person's preferred lovestyle is eros, and another *tends towards* agape, a basic incompatibility would seem probable. Eros is exclusive, agape is universal; eros is sensuous, agape is indifferent to beauty; eros is motivated by attraction, agape is driven by duty. Some writers have insisted that eros and agape are poles apart. Others have suggested that, under appropriate social conditions, these two types could merge to become one. Since this book is more concerned with love relationships than with philosophy, we will not go into the problem more deeply here.

The compatibility of some lovestyles is indicated by the scores for various answers in Test One (Chapter Eleven). You will have noticed that some answers provide 'x' scores in several columns. This means that several lovestyles share the same opinion on that particular question. In fact, ludic eros and eros have six opinions in common out of 93 in the test (not counting no-score items). Ludus shares seven opinions with ludic eros, and seven with storgic ludus (but not the same seven). The greatest overlap, and thus the best potential mixture, is between storge and pragma, which share eight answers of the 93 in the test.

When two lovestyles are 'poles apart' on the love-spectrum, this does not mean that a relationship between two such people could not happen. An agapic lover would still care about a ludic partner – and the ludic partner would probably have unsurpassed opportunities to manipulate and exploit a long-suffering agapic lover. But a *mutual* relationship is highly improbable, as they would find so little to agree on, in terms of the appropriate attitudes and actions of a lover.

A storgic lover might well find common interests and activities to share with a manic partner, despite the inevitable differences which would arise over such issues as intensity of feelings, verbal reassurances of love, and frequency of contact. Indeed, a storgic partner might function as a sort of brother or sister, relaxing and reassuring the manic lover until the causes of mania disappear and the lover settles into a quiet friendship. On the other hand, the storgic lover may be caught up in the manic lovestyle, and enter a manic storgic phase.

Fortunate circumstances may permit some unusual mixing of otherwise contradictory lovestyles. One of the most interesting examples I have encountered, involves two gay men. Barry is a balding forty-year-old professional man who makes up in charm and sophistication what he lacks in looks. His preference is eros, and for more than a decade he searched in vain for his ideal: the young 'tall blond Scandinavian' type. He could hardly have made a worse choice. (But of course erotic lovers do not 'choose' their ideal; their attraction to a particular type is generally irrational and inexplicable, though quite real). Not only had Barry little to offer in exchange, so far as looks were concerned; he had also selected a type which happens to be in great demand in North America (where he lives) among both gay males and heterosexual women.

But Barry was lucky. He met Alan, a strikingly handsome Norwegian new in town and looking for friends. Alan grew up in a small town. He had the shy manners and simple tastes of a rural background. Thus he was turned off by the over urbane gay men he met in North America. Typical of rural people, Alan's preferred lovestyle was storge. He had, and still has, no sense whatever of an ideal type of physical appearance to which he is attracted. Alan likes quiet times, gentleness, and consideration; he distrusts excitement and adventure.

Alan was exactly the ideal physical type Barry was looking for, and Barry had exactly the manners and personality which made Alan feel wanted and secure; but Alan's definition of a valid love relationship clearly differed from Barry's. Fortunately for Barry, however, he had learned from previous heartbreaks not to drive away a potential partner with the intensity of his erotic lovestyle: he struggled to mask his attraction to Alan, and treat him as a friend.

One accidental event helped Barry restrain himself. He met Alan in a swimming-pool shower room, so he saw him nude on the first encounter and did not need to worry whether Alan's body would or would not conform to the ideal type he sought. He was able to postpone going to bed with Alan much longer than is usual in cases of erotic attraction, both heterosexual and homosexual. Negative remarks by Alan about gay men who rushed to bed, helped hold Barry back.

Barry also used a method as old as Ovid's advice to lovers

in the first century: 'So I suggest that just before zero hour on the night in question, you pop into some other woman. It does not matter who she is: just find someone to take the edge off your appetite.' (By the way, Ovid was not a male chauvinist – he offered the same advice to women!) So Barry quietly carried on ludic affairs with other men, while pursuing his erotic ideal in Alan.

Alan was so pleased and mystified by Barry's patient and considerate approach, that it was he who made the first move, declaring his love both verbally and physically. This gave Alan a new trust in himself and a great deal of confidence in Barry. Perhaps you might say the confidence was misplaced, because Barry deceived Alan into thinking that their mutual lovestyle was matched storge, when it was really a mix with eros, carefully masked. In any event, these two unlikely partners in love have been together a long time, and of course the real story came out long ago.

A Dilemma in Lovestyles

The difficulty of mixing different lovestyles is not easily resolved by one partner masking his real preference until a reciprocally satisfying relationship is achieved. Cyrano de Bergerac, in the famous play of that name, masked his passionate love for Roxane behind a facade of big-brother solicitude for many years. He was never able to reveal his true feelings or win from his beloved a mutual return of the love he felt for her.

Sometimes accident and good fortune may close the gap between divergent lovestyles, as in the case of Barry and Alan. Occasionally, two lovers can achieve a mutually satisfying mix of two opposing lovestyles, by beginning with a single shared lovestyle, then moving in separate directions on the love-spectrum while somehow holding the relationship together.

Such a mixture seems to be the case with Gay Talese (American author of *Honor Thy Father*) and his wife Nan. An *Esquire* article in December 1973 informed its readers that the Taleses 'have a dilemma'. In terms of lovestyles, they do indeed; for they are united by the shared lovestyle with which they began, but if they loved each other exclusively in that style, they would probably end up separating.

Obviously Philip Nobile's fascinating article does not supply all the necessary data for an adequate analysis of the Talese marriage, but it does permit a general interpretation. Gay's love for Nan apparently began as eros. In Nan, he found a woman close to his ideal image, so that even in her absence he fantasises about her body. He says she has never failed to turn him on. Nan's love for Gay also began as eros: 'it was love at first sight', and Nan continues to find Gay physically and intellectually attractive. It might therefore appear that this couple could enjoy a mutually erotic relationship, exclusively fulfilling each other's ideals.

But Gay's choice in lovestyle is not limited to eros. He says he needs the beauty of other women, in pleasant relationships which he enjoys without anxiety or jealousy. Clearly he practises ludic eros as a second lovestyle. Typical of that lovestyle, his plural relationships are open and honest. If they weren't before the *Esquire* article they certainly are now.

Nan's erotic lovestyle is firmly based on poise and self-confidence. She shows little of the possessiveness and anxiety of mania. However, Nan's quiet family and Catholic background somewhat predispose her towards secure companionate love in the storgic style, and it is this that has enabled her to cope with Gay's playful behaviour with other women. Nan has alloyed eros with storge, and thus avoided the pitfalls of manic eros and mania.

The Talese marriage is not a free-for-all; it has its ground rules. These appear to be implicit, rather than consciously negotiated, but they are evident all the same. Gay's approach seems superficially hypocritical, because he is unwilling to allow Nan the same pluralistic freedom that he enjoys. But Nan does not regard Gay as a two-timing husband. She defends his behaviour against the jibes and accusations of her friends. She does, however, have her limits – as her reaction to one of Gay's affairs, with a Roman actress, demonstrated. That woman was too threatening, and Nan, to Gay's amazement, threw a jealous scene.

If this marriage could be analysed as a contract or working agreement, its terms would run something like this: Gay agrees to give Nan all the devotion, companionship, sexual gratification and admiration any woman could expect, providing (1) that he is permitted to devote his *surplus* time and energy (which is apparently considerable) to pleasant affairs with other women, and (2) that he does not become involved with any woman who is too much like the ideal which Nan fulfils. In exchange, Nan agrees not to demand Gay's 'surplus' energy and time in love, and agrees to remain faithful to him, because she is already fully satisfied with what he does give her. She reserves her right, however, to indicate which women threaten to become her substitute (by coming too close to Gay's ideal image), and to insist that Gay drop such women.

This is an amazing – and many will say impossible – contract for two lovers to keep over a period of time. The secret of its success thus far is its counterbalance. The lovers meet at eros, but Gay leans towards ludic eros, while Nan leans towards storgic eros. If Gay tried to persuade Nan to adopt the same lovestyle he practises, by having her own affairs, both lovers would be unhappy. If Nan tried to convert Gay to her position, it also appears that both would be dissatisfied. Like most delicately balanced arrangements, there are tensions constantly pulling at the Talese 'contract'. Nan's friends apparently interfere, to undermine the unselfishness and trust characteristic of Nan's storgic-erotic love. Gay's ludic-erotic style is always in danger of collapsing into mania. There are signs that he could become a jealous husband policing his wife if she showed much interest in other men.

Ironically, Nan's storgic-erotic style could even drift towards agape, making her resigned, long-suffering, a martyr to her husband's indiscretions. This would not only destroy her erotic union with Gay, but also his enjoyment of her as his ideal woman. The Taleses are held together by erotic joy, sensuality and intense trust. Yet their fragile union would be shattered if either one of them insisted on the other adopting a single, shared lovestyle. Their mutuality in eros is a cement, not a foundation. It holds the marriage together, but if both were to adopt a fully erotic exclusiveness, Nan could not tolerate Gay's pluralism, and Gay could not tolerate Nan's tolerance. In love, a dilemma can become a solution!

Meeting Halfway

The Talese marriage demonstrates the possibility of compromise between two conflicting approaches to love – the playful husband and the faithful wife. Whether implicit or explicit, ground rules are an important basis for such compromises.

For example, one ludic-erotic husband I came across reached a working agreement with his wife, who was typical of manic eros. This consisted of a 'boy's night out' for the husband, while the wife joined a social group, so as to avoid feeling 'left alone'. The wife agreed to avoid moping or sulking while her husband prepared to go out. This was not easy: watching him shave, preen his hair, and 'dress to kill' was difficult when she knew this courting behaviour was not intended for her. She found that the best solution was to go out early for dinner with members of her social group. Her husband, for his part, agreed always to return home before dawn, so that when his wife awoke in the morning she would not be reminded of the previous night's events.

There is usually some vestigial tension in such arrangements. The partners can attempt to cope with it by reminding themselves and each other of the ground rules. In Malraux's *Man's Fate*, Kyo has agreed to his wife's infidelity, but on difficult terms in this case, because he permits May to tell him about her adventures. Kyo finds it nearly impossible to disguise his uneasiness: 'what agonised him, was that he was suddenly separated from her, not by hatred . . . not by jealousy . . . but by a feeling that had no name.'

Sometimes compromises break down. Attempts to mask or disguise one's true feelings are undermined by nagging fears. Concessions granted to a partner's preferred lovestyle at the expense of one's own, begin to cost more in emotional distress than the relationship is worth. Going halfway turns into going too far, and each lover pulls back to his own lovestyle.

Timing

The difficulty of mixing and matching certain lovestyles and working out ground rules for compromise is not merely a matter of different *definitions* of true love. The problem lies at a deep level of interpersonal intimacy. There is a marked difference in the *pacing* of various types of love, the rate at which they cover the ground of human involvement.

For example, the pacing may be measured by reciprocity periods. This refers to the time which lovers typical of a certain lovestyle consider appropriate for a response to any given expression of such love. It is like the time between a shout into a canyon and the return of the echo. In storge, reciprocity periods of a considerable length are acceptable. A letter may not require a reply for days, or even weeks, while in eros a delay of more than one or two days would justify (in the lover's view) a second letter, or a telegram or telephone call. The ludic lover will be equally impatient, but for different reasons. He is often on the move from one partner to another. If reciprocation of his outgoing communications of love (as he defines it), in the form of compliments, favours, or whatever, is not quickly forthcoming, he will soon be out of reach of the last partner and concentrating on the new one. The erotic lover requires short reciprocity periods because the take-off into ecstasy demands intensification of contact, a telescoping of the stages of an encounter which a storgic lover would find overwhelmingly hurried.

Ground rules are more difficult to apply when the rapid pace of development of a love relationship requires a high degree of synchronisation of needs and gratifications. Just as modern jet planes are less forgiving of pilot error than slow-moving propellor planes, so eros is less forgiving of miscalculations than are ludus and (especially) storge. The erotic lover puzzles other types by allowing 'such little things to become so important', but this is because a fast-moving vehicle is turned off its intended path by even the slightest error in navigation. The shortest reciprocity periods occur in mania. The manic lover must always settle things *now*. Problems can never be postponed to the morning – the argument must continue long into the night.

Manic love can even involve a *negative* reciprocity period. The lover's impatience is so great that he sends out new messages before the answers to earlier ones can possibly return. New pleas pile up on returning 'echoes', so the air is soon filled with a chaos of messages: 'Where were you last night?', then, before the partner has time to answer, 'Why haven't you told me you love me for several days now?' Most partners will soon give up trying to synchronise their expressions of love with such a turbulent obsession. Paradoxically, this lends intense power to the experience of mania as a self-redefining and self-transforming process. Perhaps the lover becomes more 'in love with love' than with a particular person, but he may also discover for the first time his ability to transcend himself. Since a manic lover is usually unwilling to tolerate any working agreements or ground rules which compromise his intense, but obsessive devotion, mania is almost self-terminating. Fortunately, most experiences do not terminate the lover!

Torn Between Two Lovestyles

Some lovers who complete Test One (Chapter Eleven) will have a pattern of scores which peaks in two distinct and conflicting lovestyles, with 'slopes' of high scores around each peak. The pattern I have seen most frequently is that which peaks in both eros and pragma. As I noted in Chapter Nine, there is no convincing evidence yet for a compound lovestyle which could be labelled 'Pragmatic eros' but it is theoretically possible. What *is* evident is that some lovers experience an agonising struggle to meet the demands of both eros and pragma.

Our society is in transition from a long era in which pragmatic considerations prevailed in choices of love and marriage, to a new age in which beauty and sensuality are more commonplace. There is less need for pragmatic concern with family inheritances, property, and similar matters, in the welfare state. At the same time, better nutrition, medical and dental care accessible to everyone, and cosmetic surgery when necessary, have improved the chances that a modern lover will be good-looking.

Yet it is still a fortunate person who can find both the ideal physical image and the ideal pragmatic choice in the same partner. To ask that the same person should fulfil a physical description which might occur once in a thousand people (which would be very good odds indeed) and at the same time be of the preferred vocation, religion, ethnic group, or whatever, is asking a lot. The problem is that our present social values are conditioning us to look for both these ideals.

A typical pattern for a lover torn between an erotic ideal image and a pragmatic shopping list, is vacillation between partners who exemplify one ideal and those who provide the other. Such a lover may first choose a partner who seems 'beautiful' (by the lover's definition) but who lacks the desired qualifications in education, vocation, or whatever. Finally these practical shortcomings become too obvious and the lover bursts out 'How can you be so stupid?' or 'Aren't you ever going to get a decent job?' Thinking there must be somebody better out there somewhere, the lover starts searching again.

In due course our optimistic lover may meet a partner who fulfils the pragmatic requirements, but alas, does not 'turn him on'. Deciding that 'beauty is only skin deep', the lover tries a pragmatic lovestyle. After a time, the flaws in the partner's physical appearance (when compared to the lover's erotic ideal) nag their way to the surface. And so the pendulum swings back again to an impractical but ecstatic eros.

Students have often asked me whether it is possible to combine all lovestyles – or at least the primaries – into a sort of 'white love', just as white light consists of the whole spectrum of colours. It seems not. Admittedly, since the lovestyles are so confused and intermingled in the mass media which influence our conceptions of love today, it is unlikely that any modern lover will be a pure example of any one type. The classification of types was not *perfect* for any respondent. There was always some characteristic in a manic report more typical of storge, something in a pragmatic report more typical of eros. Yet even where '57 varieties' are combined, there is still the possibility of classification by elimination. Just as the most mongrel dog does not include every breed (he can't be typical of both the dachshund and the greyhound at once), so each respondent's report was less typical of certain types than others. Thus, the most hybrid love can always be reduced to two primaries which are more relevant than any others.

A Career of Lovestyles

In medieval Europe, and in Russia even into the nineteenth century, most people had no control over their working lives. They were compelled by law to remain in the same vocation as their parents. Even after these laws were abolished, many working people entered one job in their youth, and stuck to it for a lifetime.

Today the notion is vanishing forever of the 'fifty-year' man retiring with his gold watch, or of the schoolteacher remaining in the same classroom all of her adult life. It is generally recognised that the self-fulfilled adult should follow a career development process. Women's liberation groups are insisting that the same career opportunities must be open to both sexes. Older people are insisting that they should not be automatically retired while they are still capable of being useful.

Something of the same process has been taking place in love experiences. The idea of a single lifetime monogamous union, entered into in youth and terminated only by death, has given way to 'alternatives to marriage'. Women are insisting on the same opportunities as men for a variety of love experiences. Older people argue that they are still able to enjoy romance and the excitement of newly falling in love.

The idea of a 'love career' will become as familiar in the coming decades as the idea of a vocational career has already become. Once the idea has become popular we shall turn to the models of 'great lovers' of the past, from Casanova to Edith Piaf, to learn how to live a great love career.

'You'd have had to give Edith's guys numbers to keep them straight. Even she got them all confused. She forgot what order they came in. ... The silly thing was that she could never decide which was the best.' Thus did Piaf's half-sister Simone describe a love career which rivalled Piaf's success as a singer and entertainer. Each time Edith Piaf fell in love, 'it was always for the first time, and for life'. From mania to eros to ludic eros to storgic eros, Piaf tried love-styles the way she tried new songs, hurling herself whole-heartedly into each rendition. At the end, she was still enjoying a devoted and profoundly happy relationship. She was exhausted at 48, but insisted: 'Je ne regrette rien.'

Lord Bertrand Russell, accomplished in so many endeavours, also achieved a rare success in his love career. Writing of his life towards the end of his 97 years, Russell declared:

> I have sought love, first, because it brings ecstasy – ecstasy so great that I would often have sacrificed all the rest of life for a few hours of this joy. I have sought it, next, because it relieves loneliness . . . I have sought it, finally, because in the union of love I have seen, in mystic miniature, the prefiguring vision of the heaven that saints and poets have imagined. That is what I sought, and though it might seem too good for human life, this is what, at last, I have found.

It might indeed seem too good to be true: Lord Russell's love career included several marriages and affairs. He found everything he wanted – finally – when he was 79 years of age!

As in any great career, the sheer stamina of the great lover impresses us. One cannot help but sadly contrast the love career of Russell with that of his first wife, Alys, who never recovered from her break-up with Russell. She wrote fifty years later:

> I was neither wise enough nor courageous enough to prevent this one disaster from shattering my capacity for happiness and my zest for life.

The Range of Choice

Modern lovers can take their pick from the whole gamut of lovestyles, and they are constantly reminded by the mass media that alternatives are available. A full range of ludic styles is made possible not only by the permissiveness of modern urban life, but by the enabling technology – the pill, penicillin and abortion. Mania is no longer deplored as a melancholic illness or youthful insolence. Instead, it is glamorised as a sentimental tragedy, a romantic way to suffer and even die. Eros has become badly muddled with sex, but in recent years the emphasis on physical health and beauty, body language, tactile contact, interpersonal encounter and sensitivity, have all contributed to wider interest in the style of loving which emphasises these qualities over practical considerations of marriage. Meanwhile, storgic-ludic affairs are becoming an accepted part of urban life. Ludic eros is facilitated by occupational and residential mobility, and rapid transport between major urban centres. Casanova spent a lifetime travelling Europe to meet a few dozen suitable partners. I have interviewed respondents who have conducted a score of ludic, ludic-erotic, and storgic-ludic relationships, averaging between two and six months each, within a single decade.

The nature of pragma has changed, from its traditional approach – the arrangement of youthful love-matches by parents or other elders – to self-application through computer dating agencies; but the pragmatic approach to love is still popular. Perhaps storge and agape are the only two types which have suffered a setback in modern society. Storge is more difficult when few people live near each other or go to the same schools or organisations together for more than a few years. In an age of instant everything, storge seems too slow. Meanwhile, efforts to achieve the agapic ideal have all but disappeared from ordinary life. Even those who still sing its praises on Sunday morning feel that love should be enjoyment rather than self-denial during the rest of the week.

Chances for Lasting Mutuality

In modern pluralistic society the chances of mutual love remaining mutual are probably much lower than in past centuries. Rural, slow-changing societies tended to favour storge and pragma over all other types of love. Ludus was generally disapproved of as socially irresponsible promiscuity which would undermine the family. Eros and mania were suspect because they roused youth to 'unrealistic' expectations and provoked young lovers into rebellion against their worldly-wise parents. They also engendered individualist ethics which were in opposition to the moral authority of church and state.

A society in which storge is a prevailing definition of love offers no great problems in terms of mutuality. Young people do not then expect love to be exciting, but rather a process of gradually becoming accustomed to someone. Pragma is often correlated in such societies; where the young people do not grow up together, their parents or a matchmaker can

212

arrange 'a sensible match'. In either event, the young people are likely to share the same or similar definitions of true love in terms of compatibility, sexual fidelity, and degree of commitment to the relationship. They may not be attached to each other with the same degree of affection and commitment, but at least their definitions of love are mutual. With time, they are more likely to grow to love each other 'about the same amount' than they would be if one of them considered true love to be something quite different, such as mania, eros or ludus.

Considering all the complications of mixing and matching lovestyles, it is little wonder that many lovers hesitate to believe in the possibility of enduring mutuality. We have learned to solve the problems of control, timing and synchronisation necessary to land a man on the moon, but the problems of balancing two lovers in orbit around a common nucleus of intimate experience baffle us today more than ever before.

Thirteen

The 'Love-Story' Influence

Some people would never have fallen in love if they had never heard of 'love'.

(*de La Rochefoucauld*)

Contrary to the popular song, loving does not come naturally. We learn to love. A man and a woman raised from birth in complete isolation from other human beings might still be able to engage in sexual intercourse when brought together, but their actions, guided only by instinct, would seem more like those of animals than of people. Primitive societies still exist in which kissing is unknown, foreplay minimal, and the sex act complete in a few minutes. Loving and making love are products of human civilisation.

Life would be complicated enough if each civilisation provided a single, consistent pattern of ideas and behaviour for loving. We would still have to cope with cross-cultural misunderstandings. But even within the Anglo-Saxon branch of Western culture there exists a confusing welter of definitions of love. We are exposed every day to songs, novels, films, television programmes and other sources which influence us towards different and often diametrically opposed conceptions of the true nature of love.

Songs

Should we believe that love and marriage go together like a horse and carriage, or that saying 'I love you' is stupid? Will love be unmistakable and forever, or a pleasant interlude after which we'll get along the way we got along before we met? Is falling in love a time to get ready for heartaches, a promise that even the bad times will be good, or an invitation to build your world around the beloved?

When we don't ignore the lyrics entirely, we usually cope with the conflicting conceptions of love in popular songs by selecting those appropriate to the mood of the moment. As

David Horton and S. I. Hayakawa have demonstrated,[1] popular lyrics suggest a cycle of loving which moves from expectation, through courtship, to disenchantment and recovery, and thus to new anticipations. Lovers employ phrases from songs to express their sentiments, adopt favourite lyrics as 'our song', and dance closer or look meaningfully at each other when appropriate lyrics are in the air.

The theory of lovestyles suggests a new way of analysing and classifying popular song lyrics. Most songs express the ideology of one or another type of love, though some actually mix two different and conflicting types. By comparing the explicit or implied experiences and ideas referred to in lyrics with the behaviour and ideas typical of each of the major profiles of love in Test Two, it is usually not difficult to recognise which kind of love any given song is about. By making such an analysis, we may more readily discover which lovestyle we prefer, and which we dislike. Conversely, we begin to notice how certain popular songs may help to condition us towards one lovestyle and away from another. For example, I found respondents who could hardly bear to hear certain songs which were associated with disappointment in love, while other songs were much listened to because they had an optimistic outlook.

There are numerous examples of popular song lyrics which express – in some cases we might even say *promote* – manic attitudes to love. The words of manic love-songs warn us that falling in love will bring pain and trouble. It is almost as if the lover should anticipate (and perhaps masochistically enjoy?) such pain. Let the heartaches start! So what if love will make me unhappy! The 'lover' assumed to be singing the song invites his partner to abuse him, make a fool of him, twist him around her finger, just as long as she will allow him to love her. I know I'm a fool to fall in love again but I can't help it! Life is nothing to me without you, and you are everything to me.

Of course, many manic love-songs depict the lover pleading and begging with the partner to show a little more love. After all, who could love you as much as I do? How could you love anyone else when I want to give you all of myself? And after the manic love is over, there are songs the disap-

1. See Bibliography.

pointed lover can turn to which express – and possibly encourage – a despairing pessimism about love. The lover is
afraid to look backward, or else asks himself where he went
wrong, and assures himself that he will never be so foolish
again. Thus, the full cycle outlined by Horton and Hayakawa is covered by a variety of manic songs. But mania is
only one kind of loving; other lovestyles have their songs
too, in similar cycles.

The ludic or ludic-erotic lover can identify with songs
which remind him that love is only a game in which people
meet, have some fun, say goodbye without bitterness or
hang-ups, and go on to meet someone else. The ludic lover
can assure his partner, through song, that he managed well
enough without her before they met, and that he'll get along
after they've parted. A more considerate ludic-erotic lover
can urge his partner to take a little time off from her earnest
search for perfect love and simply enjoy a few good times.
Then he'll let her go, and she can return to her search. There
are even songs for the storgic-ludic lover who tells his partner that they'll have to be careful not to let her husband find
out about their little affair.

Preparing for Love

Suppose you were in line for promotion from a clerical to
executive position in your office. In order to persuade your
superiors that you were suitable for promotion, you might
begin acting more like the executive type. You could
become more punctual than most clerks, even coming in
early. You could make bright suggestions about changes in
procedure, fraternise with some of the executives, and show
a concern for the company's future.

Many popular love-songs involve the same sort of anticipation of the role of lover. They offer us models of the ways
a lover should act, talk, and think. Even before we meet a
person to love, we are being prepared (a less polite word
would be 'brainwashed') for one or another lovestyle. However, just as different executives may provide us with
different models to emulate in our office, popular love-
songs confuse us by advocating different lovestyles.

Those of us who are 'looking for love' may hear a song
like 'Strangers in the night' or 'Some enchanted evening'.

216

Our hopes aroused, we look around the party, dance, or bar, thinking that perhaps this will be the night. Stendhal once observed that a person anticipating love can pin hopes on the most fragile cues. A smile, a few kind words, a pleasant dance with a stranger, and our fantasies are running wild. At the same time, another song may caution us to get hold of ourselves. 'There you go, falling in love again!' 'Don't you know it's just another way to catch a cold?' But then a song like 'You make me feel brand new' is played on the juke box, and our hopes rise again.

With full-page advertisements in magazines, a mid-western American record company recently announced a set of four records of popular love-songs which a lover could use to court a partner. They were arranged in four stages: Seduction, Foreplay, Passion, and Climax. For $20 you could buy 'the complete conquest'.

I purchased these records and tried them. The result was complete chaos. Whoever put the selections together was amazingly insensitive to the conflicting lovestyles included. Imagine cuddling up with your partner to the words and music of 'Can't take my eyes off you' (a perfect example of eros) followed by 'Something stupid' (a very ludic song)! How could 'You don't have to say you love me' be combined with 'If ever I would leave you'? Listening to these love-songs, a would-be seducer is plunged into eternal togetherness ('Eternity' by Vicki Carr) then blasted apart by playboy callousness ('Rules of the road' by Tony Bennett).

The same problem occurs, of course, when a juke box or radio programme spills out discordant songs. The mood you were carefully establishing with your partner is suddenly shattered. 'Let's not dance this one,' you say, and hope the interruption won't last long.

Lovesongs and Lovestyles

The sudden, ecstatic recognition of the ideal image of the beloved, which is sought in the eros lovestyle, is celebrated in numerous popular songs. Such songs may encourage listeners to attempt eros when they lack the necessary preconditions (such as self-confidence) to achieve success. The result is likely to be mania. Eventually our hopes are dashed, but the love-songs are prepared for this too, and

217

provide us with models of the rejected lover. 'Goodbye . . . this is where our story ends . . .', if we take a noble view; or 'I got along without ya before I met ya', if we try to bluff our way out.

The gentle, gradual companionship of the purer forms of storge offers less dramatic material for the song writer, but examples do exist. These songs ask when the lover first fell in love, for he hardly noticed it; he simply grew more accustomed to his partner as time went by. Some songs seem to encourage a storgic attitude to love, urging the listener not to try to hurry love, but to let it grow slowly. Since storge was a more common approach to love in the past, the old favourite songs are more likely to celebrate typically storgic attitudes than are modern pop tunes. The old songs speak of taking walks together, kissing shyly, falling in love with the little girl down the street who's been a neighbour for so long and thus involving the whole family in the love relationship. Modern songs are more likely to dwell on the intensification of a storgic relationship into something more manic or erotic. I used to care about you as a friend and we could just enjoy each other's company, such songs observe, but now I feel something stronger, and I don't understand it.

As one of the prevailing conceptions of love in past centuries, pragma is also more likely to be expressed in old favourites than in modern hit-parade lyrics. Love, these old songs say, is down-to-earth practical things like a good home, nice children, some pleasant times together as we grow older. But modern songs sometimes strike a pragmatic note too, urging the lover to be sensible, work things out rather than give up too soon, keep a cool head and assess the relationship carefully to be sure the love is real. Perhaps the revival of thoroughly pragmatic love-songs will occur when a successful computer-dating agency commissions lyricists to write songs! A modern pragmatic love-song would urge the lover to accent the positive, eliminate the negative, calculate the odds, improve his chances with a UNIVAC computer, compare his partner's social data with his shopping list, and never hesitate to let the experts help him find a happy, lasting love.

In *Love in the Western World*, Denis de Rougemont argues that the most pervasive theme in the Western novel over the past three centuries has been passionate adulterous love, a theme which owes its origin to the romantic tales of earlier centuries, of which the archetypical example is the story of Tristan and Iseult.

It is true that the tale of Tristan and Iseult contains many of the elements repeatedly found in succeeding centuries of romantic fiction. The knight Tristan is cured of apparently mortal wounds by Iseult, a lovely princess. Tristan cannot marry her because duty requires him to bring Iseult to his king, Mark, with whom her marriage has been arranged. But by accident Tristan and Iseult drink a magic potion which makes them passionate lovers – and also tragic lovers. 'Passion and Joy and Anguish without End, and Death' is their fate. While King Mark grows to love Iseult tenderly and warmly – and legally – Iseult and Tristan indulge their secret desires. Mark is too kind to notice, but his barons betray the secret and the king, still unconvinced, reluctantly banishes Tristan. Undeterred, Tristan and Iseult continue a secret liaison. After a while they are exposed by undeniable evidence and Mark wrathfully sentences both to death. They escape, and after numerous adventures Tristan does the noble thing and restores Iseult to her forgiving husband. Tristan departs and eventually marries a foreign princess, but he cannot bring himself to consummate the marriage. His heart is still with Iseult, whose heart is also with him. The two lovers never do reunite in life, but are joined in death.

I have generally avoided the term 'romantic' in my classification, because of its vagueness in relation to specific lovestyles. Stories of 'romantic' love can in fact involve several different approaches, varying from quite ludic adventurism to thoroughly manic self-torment. However, de Rougemont is correct in noting the antipathy of romance (whether ludic, erotic or manic) to any conception of love which emphasises either duty or quiet companionship. Whatever the other elements of the romantic story, we can count on its placing true love *against* the call of duty, whether that duty be to the king, the husband or parents of the beloved, the Church, or whatever. Most important for de Rougemont, romantic love stands in opposition to the duty that arises from marriage.

Romantic tradition is also at odds with the ideal of companionate love, developing slowly between neighbours or acquaintances. Romance must be sudden, magical, adventuresome and dramatic. Indeed, romantic passion overrules any obligations binding one to companions and friends, and legitimises almost any violation of ordinary social mores or codes of behaviour in the name of love.

In terms of my classification, romantic love has no element of storge or agape, or of any other storgic derivative such as pragma. Even a discreet storgic-ludic affair is not what most persons would understand by the term 'romance'. The most common romantic theme is tragic love, and often, self-destruction. 'What stirs the lyric poets to their finest flights of fancy,' says de Rougemont, 'is . . . not the satisfaction of love, but its passion. And passion means suffering. . . . Happy love has no history.'

In his analysis of love as portrayed by Pasternak's *Doctor Zhivago*, de Rougemont reiterates that there is 'but a single novel in all our literature', the romantic Tristan theme. Certainly this theme is repeated innumerable times in Western literature, from *Romeo and Juliet* to *West Side Story*, from *Of Human Bondage* to *Love Story*. But even allowing for de Rougemont's poetic licence, is it reasonable to consider this the only theme, or even the single major theme, of Western love-literature? I think not. An application of the theory of lovestyles to examples of literature demonstrates the existence of a wide variety – indeed, a confusing Babel – of loves in fiction, though de Rougemont might be correct if he said the *majority* of examples are Tristanian.

The type of love exemplified by any fictional character can be assessed in much the same way as that of a living respondent being interviewed, providing sufficient detail on the acts and thoughts of the lover is contained in the novel. To demonstrate how the notion of lovestyles can provide new insights into the fictional portrayal of love, I will apply the same process of analysis (though not in as much detail) to a Tristanian love story that I would to a living respondent's experience. Then I will turn to non-Tristanian examples.

The love of Philip for Mildred in Somerset Maugham's *Of Human Bondage* is an interesting case because it is highly detailed and essentially autobiographical. Maugham said of it '. . . the emotions are my own'.

Philip had an unhappy childhood, 'led the solitary life of an only child', and as a youth 'felt the misery of his own life'. At the time of his first encounter with Mildred he is discontent and 'sometimes so lonely he could not read' because of his 'bitter wretchedness'. These are precisely the typical pre-conditions of mania, much more so than of any other lovestyle.

Mildred is not Philip's first love. He has had a ludic affair with Miss Wilkinson, 'a chance for adventure' and a 'game'. After this encounter he is still in great need of love. When he meets Mildred as a perfect stranger, she has no strong initial attraction for him; indeed, he finds her unattractive, but he 'could not get her out of his mind'. Again these are all typical of a manic lovestyle.

Philip 'knew the best thing he could do was to cease coming to the tea shop'. But he can't help himself; he is losing any ability to terminate the relationship. He makes futile attempts to restrict discussion of his feelings and to avoid any overt show of affection which would put him in Mildred's power. 'He clenched his teeth to prevent himself from uttering a syllable'; 'It was with the greatest difficulty he could prevent himself from seizing her hand . . .'

No erotic lover would make such attempts at self-control, unless temporarily masking his intensity for a storgic beloved, in order to win her – and this was clearly not Philip's situation. No accomplished ludic lover would fail in these attempts at self-control. A storgic or pragmatic lover would consider the whole pattern of behaviour little short of madness. That Philip should neglect his work, be so eager to see her that he uses a cab he can ill afford, and finally humiliate himself completely with a plea of pity because of his bad foot, simply convinces us of the overpowering obsession of his manic lovestyle. He becomes insanely jealous, spies on Mildred and is 'always on the verge of a quarrel'. It is little wonder that Maugham wrote years later:

The book did for me what I wanted, and when it was issued to the world ... I found myself free from the pains and unhappy recollections that had tormented me.

Of Human Bondage is about another love too, the brotherly-sisterly relationship between Philip and Sally Athelny which eventually leads to marriage. This storgic, happy love serves as a literary background for the more dramatic torment of a manic lovestyle. Nor was *Of Human Bondage* all that Somerset Maugham had to say of love. Far from it. His numerous stories depict a great variety of types of affiliative relationship, ranging from the ludic to the pragmatic to the erotic. For example, in *The Painted Veil* he draws a portrait of Charlie Townshend's ludic attitude to Kitty (contrasted to his pragmatic attitude to his wife, Dorothy).

There are numerous novels and novelists one could cite in order to take issue with de Rougemont's claim of a single major love-theme in fiction. D. H. Lawrence, Graham Greene, Lawrence Durrell and C. P. Snow have portrayed almost every type of love. Even an agapic note occasionally creeps in, as in John Steinbeck's *Burning Bright*, which concludes:

I know ... that every man is father to all children and every child must have all men as father. This is not a little piece of property, registered and fenced and separated. Mordeen! This is THE CHILD.

Perhaps it might be argued that the authors I have referred to are modern, with post-Freudian literary conceptions of love, and therefore more sophisticated psychologically. Yet we need only turn to Fielding, Cleland, Casanova, Laclos, Flaubert, Standhal, Tolstoy and many more, to find conceptions of love which are not Tristanian.

The greatness of Tolstoy's novels is universally acclaimed, and certainly one of the measures of this greatness is his acute perception and portrayal of complex, intimate human relationships. It would be interesting to construct a catalogue of all the lovestyles portrayed in Tolstoy's writings, but it would require whole volumes just to analyse the characters and love relationships in his major novels. However, we can apply our lovestyles theory fairly easily to his short stories. One of the most interesting is 'A Happy Married Life'. The nature of true love in Tolstoy's writings varies with the stages of his own life. When he was converted to Christianity at about the age of fifty, his personal life – and in particular his warm relationship with his wife – was deeply embittered. 'A Happy Married Life' predates this unhappy period. In fact, Tolstoy's notes indicate that the idea for the story is derived from his own youth, based on his love for a girl eight years younger than himself to whom he nearly became engaged.

In 'A Happy Married Life', Masha, a girl of seventeen, has not seen Sergei, a friend of her recently deceased father, for more than six years. Prior to that period, however, he was a familiar figure in Masha's childhood life. Sergei now returns to Masha's village. He is thirty-six. His relationship to Masha in the earlier period was like that of an older brother, but Masha recalls that her mother (also dead) once mentioned Sergei as a potential husband.

Sergei, for his part, remains the older-brother figure. 'Keep yourself busy and don't allow yourself to mope,' he advises with slight condescension as he prepares to leave the village. His voice seems to Masha 'very cold and matter of fact', a hint that she would like it some other way. Sergei, too, seems to have new thoughts. Across his face flits a suggestion of attentiveness and sadness, as if he wishes life could somehow be rearranged.

Months later Sergei returns again to live in Masha's village for the summer. It soon becomes apparent that Sergei feels more intensely about Masha than a brother-figure of thirty-six should feel about a girl of seventeen. He is aware of this. In response to a hint, he says he is 'not the kind of husband you dream of . . . wouldn't it be a misfortune for you if you were to tie yourself up to an old man . . .?'

'Not a misfortune,' Masha disagrees, but 'perhaps a mistake'. She likes Sergei because he is constantly interesting. She misses him, whenever he is gone more than a few days, because she has no life of her own, while Sergei seems busy with the world: 'At that time none of my thoughts, none of my feelings, were my own – they were all his, but had suddenly become mine.' A manic phase has disrupted the placid tedium of Masha's youth and she begins to experience both the obsession and the self-transcending qualities of mania.

Some of the typical social supports which would have steered most Russian village girls away from mania are lacking in Masha's case. She has lost both parents. Her older sister manages the household and supervises the servants. Masha has had little opportunity to develop responsibility. Sergei, meanwhile, shows the greatest self-control in expressing his obviously growing physical attraction to Masha. He laughs indifferently when others compliment Masha's beauty; but Tolstoy leaves no doubt that the laugh is a painful mask.

Since Tolstoy tells his story in the first person, using Masha's voice, he cannot reveal Sergei's thoughts to us except as Masha experiences them. Thus, Tolstoy falls back on the device of having Masha overhear Sergei thinking out loud when he thinks himself alone and unobserved. When he discovers that Masha has overheard him mooning about her, he is much embarrassed. For a moment his love, now full of appreciation of Masha's youthful beauty, shines on his face, but he gets a grip on his emotions and reverts to the older-brother role.

'Why is he pretending?' Masha worries. The symptoms of mania are pushing her storgic familiarity with Sergei further into the background. She begins to believe that Sergei loves her but that he is fearful of admitting it because of their difference in ages. She becomes more preoccupied with thoughts of him and spends a sleepless night, seeing 'an early sunrise for the first time in my life'. Sergei decides that he must leave the village before he becomes so intensely attracted to Masha that the power of eros overwhelms both the older framework of storgic affection and his more recent, ludic-like self-restraint. He is experienced enough to know that the struggle between attraction and control could easily pull him into despairing, melancholic love.

Masha demands an explanation of Sergei's imminent departure, and he, for some reason, chooses to say that he is afraid she would not take him seriously. This caution (which rings suspiciously of ludus rather than eros or storge) manipulates Masha into making the first (and most risky) declaration of love. He will pay for this cunning later, when Masha has caught up with him in worldly wisdom.

Tolstoy has a variety of options open to him in completing the story. He could have followed a familiar romantic tradition and portrayed Sergei as restraining his involvement and manipulating Masha more, thus keeping her in a manic dependency. Masha would have returned the favour, of course, by making life painful with jealousy of, and obsessive attention to, Sergei. But Tolstoy takes a different road. He sees Sergei's self-control as unselfish, disinterested goodness rather than as calculating detachment. Of course, the fact that Tolstoy is telling us his feelings for a girl in his youth no doubt prejudicies his interpretation! He begins to portray Sergei as basically storgic with a newly developed and newly admitted erotic attraction to Masha. The suspected ludic qualities disappear from Sergei's behaviour and he becomes a model example of storgic-erotic love.

At first there is merely the conscious recognition, on Masha's part, of the power which *being loved* gives the beloved over her lover. This is true, of course, only when the type of love shown by the lover is dutiful. Had Sergei been ludic, Masha would have had no power over him. 'I do not know whether it was he or I who had changed, but now I felt myself absolutely his equal,' Masha tells us. Later, she says disenchantedly of her wedding, 'And this is all I have received from this moment of which I expected so much?' She has become bored and restless again: Sergei is not enough to keep her life interesting.

But Masha is no longer the simple village girl. She has won power over a man, and now she is ready to manipulate him. The balance of power in the marriage shifts to her. They go to Moscow and St Petersberg, where her rustic charm and beauty soon turn everyone's head. She realises that she can have power over many men. A ludic consciousness becomes apparent in Masha's style of loving.

For Sergei, loving Masha is enough. He is tired of the big city life. 'You're my whole life. Everything seems good to me only because you're here – because I need you.' Masha cheerfully exploits this need: 'I had accomplished what I wanted – his composure was gone.' The small-town beauty has become a big-city bitch, who 'found it pleasant to be considered in these circles not only his equal but his superior, a thing which enabled me to give him more lavishly and voluntarily of my love. ....' This last exquisite

225

rationalisation, placed in Masha's mouth by Tolstoy, demonstrates why this author is so rightly regarded as a deep-sighted student of human emotions. Masha excuses her ludic gamesmanship in the name of storgic respect!

Sergei is not deceived. He warns Masha not to seek a stormy, excited life, and mocks her 'self-sacrifice' for his sake: 'You ... *sacrifice* [he stressed the word] ... and so do I. What could be prettier? A contest as to who is more magnanimous. What other happy married life is there?'

Frustrated from achieving a mutually storgic-erotic relationship with Masha, Sergei retreats to his former storgic attachment to her, sublimates his erotic intensity, and transfers 'his former tenderness and gaiety to the baby'.

As Tolstoy portrays Masha, she is unable to go the whole way to ludic behaviour. When an opportunity arises for an affair during a holiday trip, she runs back to Sergei. Contrast this behaviour with that of the more ludic Madame Bovary, whose reaction to her first affair is celebrated: 'I have a lover! I have a lover.' In Masha's case, the earlier mania, though no longer manifest, seems occasionally latent. She asks Sergei if he doesn't feel the same 'melancholy pleasure, as though you wanted the impossible'.

Again, a point is reached in the story at which Tolstoy could have taken the Tristanian route. Masha could have fallen in love with a young man, abandoned Sergei, become pregnant, then been abandoned in turn by her new lover, and so on, in the traditional romantic style. But recall that at the time of writing the story Tolstoy was still a happily married man. So, he closes his story with Masha sublimating her potential manic tendencies by loving her children more intensely. At last she and Sergei find common cause.

The mixture of eros and storge in Sergei's first love for Masha has been transformed by bitter experience into a storgic-erotic mixture which comes close to agape in its unselfishness; but Sergei feels he has lost something priceless in the metamorphosis of his lovestyle:

> Every time has its own form of love [Sergei says] ... there were terrible nights when I could not sleep so I broke and destroyed the love that had tormented me ... I found peace and I still love you, but in another way ... I grieve over the love that is dead. Love remains, but it is not what it once was ... love itself has undergone some illness. ...

Limited to the one one word 'love' Tolstoy can only hint at a distinction of its kinds; he can never firmly pin it down. With my somewhat clinical terminology, we can see Sergei's dilemma a little more clearly. He is aware of the danger that the erotic component in his relationship with Masha will turn manic as his confidence is lost in the face of Masha's ludic challenge. His only escape is to 'destroy' the erotic component, that is, to repress its sexual intensity in a combination with storge.

Don Juan

If manic love has cropped up again and again in different guises since Tristan and Iseult (or since Dido and Aeneas, if we wish to go back to ancient literature), so also has ludic love had its varying portraits. Indeed, a single legendary figure has been the subject: Don Juan. There are numerous fictional Don Juans, the creations of de Molina, Molière, Mozart and Shaw, to say nothing of the portraits by film artists such as Ingmar Bergman and John Barrymore.

Don Juan makes his first appearance in our literature in *The Trickster of Seville* by Tirso de Molina in 1630. He is already the diametric opposite of Tristan, that legendary romantic idol of long-suffering servitude for the adored Lady. This Don Juan is a faithless and devious lover, but he is not yet a great ludic champion – he conquers only four women!

He is a rebel against both the tradition of romantic love and that of the church-approved 'arranged marriage'. No star-crossed love for him; and the promise of marriage is merely to trick the gullible. He rejects any kind of involvement with his women. He doesn't even hate them – which raises doubts about those psychologists who have argued that he was 'really' a repressed homosexual. This first Don Juan simply uses women as a means to riskful adventure. Even as the first story ends with his being dragged into Hell, he shouts defiance at authority and morality.

Molière's Don Juan (in *Le Festin de Pier*, 1665) is more self-consciously liberated. He mocks those who make a virtue of faithfulness (which Kierkegaard was later to agree was a poor substitute for love), and wonders how any normal person could deliberately deny himself all the beautiful people one misses in a monogamous marriage. The noble gallantry of a Casanova is still lacking, for he has no scruples against lying to seduce a woman. 'I love you, Charlotte,' he assures a woman he has only just met, and uses the promise of marriage to gain her favours.

In Mozart's operatic masterpiece, Don Juan emerges for the first time as a credible, fully rounded human personality. Part of the explanation may be the fact that the Abbé Lorenzo da Ponte, who wrote the libretto, was a personal acquaintance of Jacques Casanova. The two visited Mozart together, and Casanova was at the première of *Don Giovanni* in Prague in 1787. There is also a variant of the second act among Casanova's papers. Another important factor probably affecting Mozart's portrayal was the emergence in the same century of a new literature of romantic love. Richardson had created that laughable and ineffectual seducer, Robert Lovelace; Laclos had shocked Europe with the cynical manipulations of the Count de Valmont; while Fielding, in his *Tom Jones,* had brought his sincere playboy through incredible adventures to success. Mozart thus had a much wider range of characterisations to choose from than Molière had had, and his Don Juan becomes reasonable, delightfully scandalous and improbably courageous – all the while remaining the earlier figure of unrepentant rebellion. His conquests have grown from four to thousands; in Spain alone, one thousand and three. He is an expert in promiscuous behaviour. Fat girls in winter, thin ones in summer.

In the next century, Sören Kierkegaard makes the legendary Don Juan the model for his *Diary of a Seducer*, 'What was impulse has now become method'; his seducer is patient and systematic.

> I am an aesthete, an eroticist, one who has understood the nature and meaning of love ... and only makes the private reservation that no love affair should last more than six months at the most, and that every erotic relationship should cease as soon as one has had the ultimate enjoyment.

Kierkegaard uses 'erotic' to intend sensuality, not the relationship I have called eros. His Don Juan has become a modern professional, what Robert Meister calls 'an engineer of consent' in love. Eventually he will emerge in the twentieth century as the expert sent on special missions of seduction, as in Ingmar Bergman's film *The Sty in the Devil's Eye* (1955). But how many will recognise the immortal figure of Don Juan in the James Bond series? He is still there, the expert manipulator of sensual attraction who retains a domineering indifference to the women whose love he exploits.

In the recent American movie, *Shampoo*, Warren Beatty portrays one of the most ambivalent, self-doubting Don Juans yet to appear. He may be the stud of Beverly Hills, but from time to time we catch glimpses of an underlying mania. He even lets one former girlfriend leave him literally high and dry at the film's finale. Beatty plays a Don Juan who is half-embarrassed by his ludic conquests, and occasionally on the verge of quitting his game to 'settle down'. Don Juan has travelled a long way from the callous deceiver to the reluctant stud!

Love in the Cinema

Film may be regarded as an electric 'extension' of the novel, as Marshall McLuhan points out, so we can expect from that medium much the same variety of lovestyles. A careful analysis of the portrayal of affiliative love relationships in a film, using the same approach as in an interview, would produce a range of conceptions of the nature of love. But this field of research is almost untouched, and the work of another volume. Here I will consider only a few films as examples, choosing two which almost every reader is likely to have viewed, and several that are less well known.

The Sound of Music: The impression left after viewing *The Sound of Music* of what constitutes proper behaviour in love is almost diametrically opposite to that created by the novel and film *Doctor Zhivago*. The latter is thoroughly Tristanian, as de Rougemont observes. But whereas Zhivago is immobilised, and finally destroyed, by political forces in a battle in which love has disabled and burdened him rather than given him an advantage, Captain Von Trapp and Maria in *The Sound of Music* are emboldened and aided on all sides, through their love, to defeat the Nazis at their home, the concert hall, the convent. Nature, in the form of forest and winter, provides the Tristanian handicaps in *Doctor*

Zhivago, but is friendly in *The Sound of Music*, and offers escape – through the mountains. Zhivago is torn – like Tristan – between two women, and loses both. The Captain makes a choice and wins happiness.

Maria's relationship with the Captain – our focus of analysis at this point – begins in an agapic form, as an expression of religious duty, not as affiliative love. Her role at the Von Trapp home is counterpoised to that of the Countess, a stereotype of ludus. The dramatic interest in this film is of the simplest order, directed at the lowest common denominator in the audience. A conflict between two women representing the same or related types of love would provide greater sophistication, but here the authors want a black and white contrast, hence the apposition of ludus and agape.

Maria's agapic love is not a stable, fully fused compound of storge and eros. She is uncertain of her religious vocation, and a little too full of optimism and joyfulness for convent life (as the first songs tell us), but there is no question of her reliable, companionate storgic qualities. Soon after she begins working with the Von Trapp children the storge-eros compound comes unstuck as Maria's religious agape gives way to affiliative love. The Countess is first to notice this – even before Maria. She senses that the Captain and Maria share a mutual but latent erotic (*not* sexual!) attraction, and tries to head it off by suggesting a party in her own honour.

Since Maria's relationship to the Captain has become potentially affiliative and falls short of universal, selfless religious dedication, we should probably speak now of storgic eros rather than agape. The storgic element in Maria's storge-eros combination is expressed in her relationship with the children, but the eros component quickly becomes dominant over the companionship aspect in her relationship to the Captain. The turning point comes at the party, when the Captain replaces his son in the dance with Maria on the terrace. For the first time there is a tactile expression of Maria's erotic attraction – from which she immediately retreats – and a hint of the Captain's probable reciprocation brings the Countess to urgent action. She closets herself with Maria, to bring to her consciousness the attraction she (Maria) has hitherto felt without being able to express it. Maria needs no more counsel than this to return to the convent.

230

At this point the story could have taken the usual Tristanian route. The Mother Superior could have reminded Maria of her religious vocation. Maria could have pined in solitude and dedicated her life to self-sacrifice, while the Captain married the Countess, soon realised his lack of love for her, suffered for want of Maria, and so forth. Such a tragic outcome might have been quite popular, as Segal's *Love Story* has demonstrated.

Instead, Maria encounters the most improbable singing eros in her Mother Superior. Dare to dream, urges this life-loving woman. Climb every mountain till you find that dream. It's not a hopeless dream, as in the song 'The Impossible Dream' from *Man of La Mancha*. Love *can* win happiness, with some help from one's friends, in this case the Von Trapp children. Maria returns for the first intimate encounter with the Captain. The Countess packs her bags. From this point, love conquers Nazis, mountains and all.

The Sound of Music, analysed according to its lovestyles, proves to be a testimony of faith in the power of eros (quite free of manic obsession, and victorious over ludic competition) to achieve profound happiness in everyday life. Here is no fairy tale, the film tells us, but a real family. They didn't have to defy reason and morality to win ecstatic love. The highest ideals of family, religion and politics were respected, but love also had its reward.

The Graduate: During the Sixties, young people asserted the supremacy of love. 'All you need is love', sang the Beatles. 'Make love not war', urged the posters. An unusual example of the supremacy of love appears in *The Graduate*, a film that had millions of young people standing in lines outside the cinemas.

The Graduate turns upside down the Tristanian myth, and in particular, the *Romeo and Juliet* version of that myth. Its story is the improbable and wildly amusing victory of manic love over powerful social opposition. The unhappy endings of Romeo and Juliet themes, from Shakespeare's original to the Broadway version in *West Side Story*, come to a complete reversal in *The Graduate*. Admittedly the happy ending for mania did not become a new trend. A year or two later, *Love Story* demonstrated that most people still prefer a manic experience to end in tragedy.

The hero of *The Graduate* Benjamin, returns to his affluent parents' Los Angeles home after graduating from college. He finds himself utterly out of touch with his parents' generation, but he has not yet achieved his own liberation. He is part of that sizeable college group who are aware that everyone is doing it nowadays, but who haven't yet made it with a girl themselves. He pretends to be experienced, but Mrs Robinson, the wife of his father's business partner, is not deceived.

Mrs Robinson seduces Benjamin, and a series of assignations ensues. Benjamin frantically tries to introduce some emotion into the relationship, but Mrs Robinson wants only sexual release. A most cynical Donna Juanita, she remains firmly dominant. Her daughter Elaine returns home from college. Elaine's childhood friendship with Benjamin is rekindled and bursts into a manic obsession on Benjamin's part.

Mrs Robinson is incensed at the loss of her sex partner and gives Benjamin an outraged warning: she will reveal all to Elaine if Benjamin doesn't leave her daughter alone. Poor Benjamin collapses into total manic lack of control. He rushes to tell Elaine the truth himself, hoping this gesture will bring absolution. But Elaine, far from appreciative, is stunned and repelled. Equally alienated from her promiscuous mother, she returns to college.

Benjamin follows her there and devotes his days to attempting a reconciliation. Just as she seems ready to forgive, the Robinsons hear of his campaign and intervene. Elaine has been dating a socially respectable medical student. Her parents insist that she marry him. Benjamin learns of the plot and sets out to rescue Elaine. He arrives at the church in a state of wild anxiety, literally shrieking with manic emotion. Elaine, just that moment married, suddenly realises that her future lies with Benjamin, and abandons husband and family on the altar steps. The young lovers escape the enraged parents by bolting the church doors with a cross, and just barely catch a passing bus.

The enormous popularity of this film with young people, especially college students, was readily accountable. Parents, social morality, the business establishment ('plastics'), marriage and religion are all flouted and surmounted. Even the traditional concession to morality, made by an arrival 'Just in the nick of time', is lacking. Benjamin arrives *after* Elaine has spoken her vows. These rebellious young students succeed where Tristan and Iseult, Romeo and Juliet, Zhivago and Lara, and countless others have failed.

Mania, an ideology of love which has so often in our literature expressed the futile rebellion of the young against parental authority and social morality, is used here to affirm that the present young generation will succeed nevertheless in catching the bus that most of *them* missed.

Love Story: Erich Segal's novel, and the film made from it, certainly struck a respondent chord in contemporary feelings about love. The tears it caused to flow would suggest that there are still many who believe, with Hemingway and Shakespeare, that true love must often be unhappy.

The theme is not new – it is merely a sophistication of the Tristan theme by eliminating adultery. We are bored by love conflicts centred on adultery. It scarcely interests us as an excuse for divorce, let alone a formula for schmaltz in romantic fiction. Yet suffering love continues to hold greater fascination than pleasant love. We are ever ready to take 'amorous Death to be our paramour'. This is a tradition deeply rooted in our culture. In the ninth century, the Arab poet Ibn al Ahnaf sighed:

Oh what glance has torn my heart away, its arrow
    left my body wounded.
If only my princess would send another such, that I
    should have to lament these wounds once more.[1]

Three centuries later the troubadours of southern France entertained the courts with 'tales of love and woe'. Still later, readers of Richardson's serialised novels wept, and church bells were rung when the latest chapter reported the tragic death of the heroine. *Love Story* has a long ancestry.

All the classic earmarks of mania are present: the opposition of the parents (right out of *Romeo and Juliet*), the clash of social backgrounds, the poverty, the emphasis on 'noble' emotions to the exclusion of baser motives. (There is surprisingly little *sex* for a popular contemporary movie!) Most characteristic of mania – stemming all the way back to

1. Peter Dronke, *Medieval Latin and The Rise of the European Love Lyric.*

233

the ancient Greek *theia mania* – is the baffling, inexplicable intervention of relentless fate. This time it takes the form of leukemia. In great manic love stories the flaw must always be beyond the lovers' control. Mania is 'stronger than us'. A magic potion, a star-cross'd destiny, an unavoidable journey, a tragic accident, a fatal Caesarean childbirth, or an incurable disease – these are the stuff of mania.

The fatal flaw must be no one's fault. It is not the lack of something which might be made up, it is 'in the nature of things'. It is beyond the reach of doctor, or marriage counsellor, or well-intentioned Friar, or repentant parent. In an age when people are all too familiar with forces bigger than themselves and far beyond their control – nuclear power, economic dislocation and political corruption – there is still some surety in Fate. Perhaps there is consolation too. If the rich, the beautiful, and the brilliant aren't able to find happiness in love for more than a few years, perhaps the rest of us don't have to feel so bad.

Happy Love

There are, fortunately, fiction writers and film makers who believe in the possibility of happy love. There is space here to deal with only a few examples.

Le Bonheur (Happiness) is the story of a young mechanic living in a southern French village. As the film opens we find him blissfully married. He and his family are going into the woods for a picnic. Flashbacks show that this couple are a joy to each other in bed and out. Eros is clearly their mutual lovestyle.

Then a pretty telegraphist moves to town. The mechanic quite cheerfully falls in love with her and is requited, except that the girl doesn't want to ruin his happy marriage. The mechanic assures her she need not worry. He feels so much rapport with his wife that he explains his new love to her. There is a delightful analogy – that of different fruit trees in an orchard, each to be enjoyed for its own kind of fruit.

The film leaves the reaction of the wife undefined: she wanders into the woods and drowns, but whether it is an accident or suicide is unclear. The mechanic is grief-stricken but *not* guilt-laden. After a period away from the unhappy scenes of the village he returns. The telegraphist is still there. Old acquaintance is renewed, first by her expression of sympathy for his loss, then by mutual attraction. The film ends as it began, with the mechanic and his family going off to the woods for a happy picnic. The wife, of course, has changed!

Most of the people I talked to who had seen this film felt it somehow immoral that a love which was portrayed as both intense *and sincere* could be replaced by another which was both intense *and sincere*. They felt that either the first relationship could not have been as intense and joyful as the mechanic felt it to be or else the second relationship could not have been equal to the first. In any event, the mechanic did not 'deserve' two chances at happiness in love.

The analysis of this film in terms of lovestyles would be that the mechanic, in his relationship with the telegraphist, alters his lovestyle from eros to ludic eros. The quality of ludic eros is that it really can be both intense and sincere. As a ludic-erotic lover, the mechanic could intensely, happily love both his wife and the telegraphist. However, his wife did not accept this change in lovestyles, and the marriage relationship therefore lost its mutuality. But whatever the cause of her fate, the mechanic is as happy in love as before.

The Immoralist: This Italian film, by Pietro Germi, argues that one may simultaneously enjoy several happy love relationships, though they may prove rather exhausting.

Masini, a happy married man with three children, has a comfortable pragmatic relationship with his wife. However, he also has a common-law wife and two sons in a relationship started ten years after the legal marriage. The second woman, Adele, is aware of his first wife and family, but the reverse is not true.

Masini has worked hard to fulfil his obligations to both families. Adele is not jealous of his wife; nor does his wife suspect Masini's infidelity. Adele's relationship with Masini is portrayed as more erotic, but there is no apparent manic element. Of course Masini must work hard to earn enough – and to arrange his time – to please two families. Christmas Day is a masterpiece of organization!

Then into Masini's already over-extended schedule steps Marisa, an exciting and lovely eighteen-year-old, who doesn't know about Adele but does want Masini to leave his wife for her. Masini refuses, but manages to hold on to Marisa, fitting her in when he can, pacifying her manic possessiveness with promises.

Finally, the effort kills him. Playing so many simultaneous love relationships is too much for an ageing man. Everyone comes to the funeral and meets everyone else. They all forgive him, and admit that he loved each as best he could.

Masini is a kind of marrying Casanova who insisted on filling his life to the brim with as much experience of love as he could manage, and then some. We are left with the assurance, when he momentarily comes to life in his coffin to speak to the film audience, that it has been a good life.

Homosexual Love in the Arts

Until recently, both scientific studies and fictional portraits of the homosexual experience of love tended to be based on a limited sample of gay people – those who sought therapy, got into difficulty with the law, or otherwise became *unhappily* visible to society. Intimate homosexual relationships were widely assumed to be specifically *sexual* relationships, to the extent that numerous studies, and even some dictionaries, defined the term *love* to exclude homosexuals. Love was 'an attraction between the *opposite* sexes'.

A homosexual literature of love has existed since ancient times, but a conspiracy of silence and censorship has restricted awareness of this literature to a ghetto-like homosexual subculture. Much of the fiction and biography of homosexual love was purged of its alleged perversion by successive generations of translators and editors. Authors themselves often censored their works, or prevented their publication during their lifetimes. For instance, the original manuscript of Walt Whitman's famous love poem, 'Once I Pass'd Through a Populous City' contains male pronouns. The celebrated novelist E. M. Forster forbade the publication of *Maurice* until after his death.

In a detailed historical review of literature containing these and other examples, an editorial in *College English* (an official American journal of the National Council of Teachers of English) declares that 'homosexual literature is

236

written, read, criticised and taught within a generally hostile environment.'[1]

The opportunity to view a sensitive and realistic depiction of gay love relationship in *films* did not occur until the present decade.

If Tristanian torment and manic melancholy have been the most popular themes in heterosexual love fiction and films, this has been all the more true of gay love. Unless the story was set in some remote age and culture (as for example in Mary Renault's novels of ancient Greek life), the fictional portrait of a gay love relationship was limited to a narrow choice of orientations. It might be a lonely struggle against social reproach, as in Radclyffe Hall's *The Well of Loneliness*. It might be an occasion for amusement at the pathetic caricature of intimacy invoked by gay affection, as in *Boys in the Band*. In any case, it seemed impossible that any reasonable person could *want* to be homosexually in love.

Sunday Bloody Sunday: This was probably the first popular film to depict a homosexual love relationship explicitly (including bed shots of two men together). It neither mocks or moralises, and the homosexual character is deliberately atypical. What could be less of a stereotyped gay figure than a middle-aged, sympathetic doctor who is still devotedly Jewish?

The story concerns a young bisexual sculptor who is involved with two lovers – the Jewish doctor, and a divorced professional woman. We have already seen how difficult it is to find mutual, lasting relationships amidst the plethora of lovestyles available, but the problem is clearly intensified when the choice is not limited to relationships with the opposite sex. The film does come to grips with the problem of over-simplified definitions of love – but it offers no new solutions for lovers.

The doctor has a life-long yearning for profound, rapportive love of the kind I call eros – and seems no closer to finding this ideal, though he has learned to resign himself to living without it. The divorcée tries to maintain a ludic detachment but is constantly in danger of slipping into manic tears, preoccupation and possessiveness. She cannot believe

1. Louie Crew and Rictor Norton, 'The Homophobic Imagination . . .'

237

that half a loaf is better than none. The young sculptor does his best to give something of himself to each lover, yet retain his own identity; but he finally leaves for America. He lacks the maturity to play two ludic-erotic roles sufficiently well to satisfy his lovers' emotional needs while at the same time sparing some energy for his art.

Sunday Bloody Sunday highlights the problems of a generation facing over-choice in love. Not only does each person have to understand, and make selections among heterosexual lovestyles of quite different kinds; he or she now has much greater opportunity to experience homosexual and bisexual love. It has been difficult enough in the past to choose between one lovestyle with one person of the opposite sex, and another with another *also* of the opposite sex. Now that the beloveds can so easily be of *different* sexes, the potential combinations and permutations of loving may overwhelm us. It is to be hoped that the analysis of lovestyles in these chapters will explain and help us to survive those dilemmas which now confront us in our own love-lives as much as in the 'love-stories' of our day!

Fourteen

Loving and Living

> If two people who have been strangers, as all of us are,
> suddenly let the wall between them break down, and
> feel one, this moment of oneness is one of the most
> exhilarating, most exciting experiences in life.
>
> (*Erich Fromm*)

The idea of love, reports the American Institute for Philosophical Research, 'proved to be the most difficult . . . so far subjected to dialectical analysis'.[1]

> [It is] more difficult than the idea of freedom and much
> more difficult than the ideas of progress, justice and happiness. One measure of its difficulty is the wide variety of
> meanings of the term as it is used in the literature of the
> subject . . . another is the thinness of the thread of common
> meaning that runs through all these uses of the term.

The Institute engaged a team of researchers who ultimately produced a work of almost 500 pages simply to establish a systematic relationship between the idea of love – or more accurately, the many, varying and conflicting ideas of love – and other basic, related concepts of human thought such as benevolence, desire, judgment, sexuality and friendship. This analysis is one of the very few existing which does not assume that one or another of the competing definitions of love is more true than the others. But the extremely complex and abstract results of this research, though a brilliant contribution to the discipline of philosophy, will be of little help to the ordinary lover looking for a workable, everyday definition of loving.

As this book has, I hope, demonstrated, this 'everyday definition of loving' is not so easy to come by. Each of us faces several difficult tasks in translating the definition of love into the act of loving.

First, you need a clear understanding of your own

1. Robert Hazo, *The Idea of Love*.

definition of love, your own preferred *lovestyle*. This, we have noted, may vary from relationship to relationship. It is no more possible to define a single appropriate lovestyle for all occasions than it is to define the well-dressed person for all occasions.

Your second task is to estimate each *partner's* lovestyle. Again, we have noted that such estimates may have to be brought up to date from time to time, as the relationship develops. Maintaining a truly *mutual* definition of lovestyles with a beloved, over a period of time, may prove no easier than grappling a moving lifeboat to a moving liner on a storm-tossed sea.

The task is still not complete, for thus far you have merely made your analysis. Now you must act. But which specific actions, in which order, are most appropriate for the particular lovestyle you have chosen? In this book we have been able to consider only the general categories of such actions – the obsession and jealousy of mania, the urgency of eros, the playfulness of ludus, the companionship of storge, the benevolence of agape. Some examples have been given for each lovestyle, but they clearly fall short of your needs for everyday acts of loving.

Nor is the opportunity for action yours alone. You must also decide how best to respond to the initiatives taken by your beloved. And some partners will give you precious little time to stop and contemplate the best response!

The act of loving looks so challenging that it might seem surprising that so many willingly attempt it. But we are not left free to choose whether to love. Throughout the long centuries of Christendom, vast and powerful social institutions persuaded, and at times literally compelled, ordinary people to act according to the dictates of 'love'. Of course, at that time, the lovestyles in fashion were those of agape in religion and pragma in marriage.

Since the rise of the romantic notion in our society, a new compulsion has driven us to seek the experience of love. In literature, songs, and film, we are constantly reminded that success in love is at least as essential as success in education or business. You are nobody until somebody loves you. You must find someone to love. Even those who have already achieved a substantial basis for personal happiness through wealth and fame frequently tell us in their autobiographies

240

of their determined pursuit of a satisfying love relationship.

In the springtime of life most of us are optimists about love, as we are about other things, such as fame and fortune. At twenty we are convinced that we shall become rich and celebrated. By thirty most of us have learned to live within a more modest income. So too with love. Many compromise on youthful hopes and settle for less than passionate bliss. Later, some ecstatic experience may tempt us one last time, but this also fizzles and dies.

How many of us have the stamina of an Edith Piaf or a Bertrand Russell to go on searching and trying out relationships, again and again, in the hope that, despite discouraging odds, we may finally achieve our desired lovestyle? How many people, in the twilight of their lives, ask why they, with so many assets, talents, and 'things to offer', should have gone unloved, or only partly and inadequately loved while some poor, untutored, and unbeautiful person has known the incomparable happiness of a mutual and lasting love?

We are persons with a high degree of self-awareness, compared to former generations. We have countless material, social and psychological advantages not available to our forebears. We can expect to live nearly double the lifetime of our great-grandparents. Yet our cities are crowds of lonely and alienated people. We are nations of strangers! For most of us, love seems to be the last great adventure, the last open frontier to explore. But happiness in love seems more remote than ever. Is happy, mutual, lasting love becoming an impossible dream?

Of course many writers on love would argue that our dilemma is the consequence of our attitude to love. They would insist that the appropriate act of loving is giving, not seeking. But in many of the lovestyles we have examined, seeking often eclipses giving. Eros, ludus, pragma and mania are all lovestyles with objectives, and means of assessing whether or not a particular partner fulfils those objectives.

We are not interested in loving just anyone, or in having just anyone love us. Thus we find it extremely difficult to accept the advice of the advocate of unselfish agape, whether it be St Paul or Erich Fromm. When the film *Carnal Knowledge* poses the question of which to choose – loving without being loved in return, or being loved without loving in

241

return – we may reluctantly opt for the active role of loving without a return, but we can't be happy with it.

When I review the love careers of my many respondents, as well as those of acquaintances and colleagues – and add my own frequent disappointments in love – I have to conclude that happiness in love is a rare experience. It's certainly not our human birthright!

Yet our century has been marked by the most daring experiments in defining and achieving the human 'birthright'. We not only proclaim the human right to good health, useful work, privacy, and even clean air – we dare to reorganise human institutions to make the attainment of these conditions possible. Even in the few decades since the Second World War, the change in social attitudes towards our planet and its ecology, the responsibilities of government and business, the rights of young people – to name but a few examples – has been so staggering as to justify the term 'revolution'.

Compared to our advances in other areas, our understanding of love is desperately obsolete. My analysis of lovestyles is not even the *outline* of a new science of love, much less a finished product. Scores of important questions remained to be researched, and the methods of study require refinement. We know little about the distribution of lovestyles among various segments of the population. What are the most common sequences of lovestyle in a love career? How do education, religion and the mass media affect our choice of lovestyles?

But the ordinary reader of this book will not be willing or able to await the eventual 'revolution' in living and loving which may become possible when social science finally answers these and other similar questions. You are already faced with the bewildering choice among lovestyles, the choice between various sexual orientations, the choice among an increasing number of 'alternatives to marriage'.

In short, you are probably looking for happiness in love, *now*. Despite all the difficulties and hazards, you have decided that this dream is worth dreaming. In that case, my advice is to *study love*. Luck may play its part, but you can improve your chances through careful study. It is my experience that love, like art and music, is not diminished by a greater understanding of its structure and its styles.

If 'learning is doing' in other endeavours, how much more so in love! The study of love must become the act of loving. The risks are worth taking. As one wit put it, you'll never get out of this life alive anyway. No amount of objective data, or vicarious information about love from literature and the arts, could have led me to the theory of lovestyles presented here if I had not also experienced a considerable variety of love relationships. Nothing in this book will be useful to you unless you too are actively involved in the experience of love. It is in the everyday acts of loving and living that the insights offered in this book may become meaningful to you.

Appendix

How I carried out the research

The analysis of love relationships used in this book is based on the method of ideal types first developed by Max Weber and subsequently applied to love and marriage by such sociologists as Robert Winch and John F. Cuber.

Everyone uses a simplified form of 'ideal type' thinking almost every day. For instance, you notice that there are several types or breeds of dogs. Even though every dog has four legs, two ears, a mouth, and so forth, you don't have to be an expert to distinguish a poodle from a terrier or a beagle from a greyhound. A dog breeder will of course define the various types of breeds of dogs more carefully than the amateur. He can distinguish breeds which the amateur could scarcely tell apart. He can point to ways in which a particular dog fulfils or falls short of the 'ideal' of a perfect specimen of its pedigree breed. The important thing to recognise is that the 'breed' or 'type' is an *ideal*. No dog may absolutely fulfil the ideal specifications; nevertheless the breeder knows what to look for[1].

A typology is simply a set of related types in a systematic classification – breeds of dogs, varieties of flowers, species of mammals, and so on. *Lovestyles* is a typology of loves. There may be no 'perfect' eros love relationship, but my typology tells us what to look for in distinguishing an erotic relationship from one that is manic or storgic.

The advantages of ideal types are obvious, but there are dangers too. Ideal types tend to generalise and oversimplify reality. It may be convenient to talk about poodles as if all poodles are essentially alike; but any child will remind you that this is not so, if one pet poodle is lost and you attempt to replace it with another.

Throughout this book I have used terms such as 'manic ⸱r' or 'erotic love' or 'pragmatic lovestyle'. These are the

⸱ a detailed explanation of ideal types, see John C. McKinney,
⸱ive Typology.

244

same sort of generalisation as 'poodles'. To be completely accurate, I should say of each relationship that its style, at the time of observation, included ideas and behaviour which I have chosen, for purposes of contrast and comparison with other styles of loving, to lump together under one general label which I call eros, mania, storge, or whatever. This sort of verbal accuracy would produce a dreadfully unreadable book, but the use of shorter, more readable phrases like 'a manic lover' should not mislead you into thinking that there is such a thing as a purely manic lover. A poodle may always be a poodle, but people can change from one lovestyle to another.

The idea of different lovestyles is not new. Plato, Ovid, Capellanus (twelfth century), Burton (1621), Stendhal (1830), Finck (1887), Anders Nygren, Theodor Reik, Denis de Rougemont, Pitirim Sorkokin, and Erich Fromm are but a few of the authors who have examined different types of love. One of the first systematic approaches in sociology was developed by Llewelyn Gross in 1944.

I began sorting out the various styles of loving by collecting thousands of different statements about love and lovers from fictional and non-fictional literature. Each was recorded on a separate file card. These cards were then cross-classified according to topics such as jealousy and fidelity, sexuality and intensity, and so forth. I was looking for the way certain ideas about love are connected to other ideas.

For example, some authors speak of love as a duty, a promise, a *Thou Shalt*. I noticed that this idea of love tended to go along with the idea that love is universal, rather than attracted to one person. Authors such as St Paul, Erich Fromm and Kierkegaard argue for a dutiful, universal love, and tend to reject the idea that love is a feeling or emotion, especially if outside rational control.

Thus certain ideas about love tend to 'cluster together' in each author's definition, just as a certain cluster of ideas about shape, size, snout, tail and skin comes to mind when I speak of a dachshund. There are many species of dogs, but how many species are there of love? Eventually I settled for just six distinct species. If this doesn't seem like many, remember that most people still speak of love as if there was only one true kind, and all the rest were counterfeit!

245

There are a number of ways of telling one species of dog from another – height, head shape, hair, and so forth. I settled on twenty ways of telling each of my six types of love from the others. These are listed in Table 1, below. The six types of love were called love of beauty (eros), obsessive love (mania), game love (ludus), companionate love (storge), altruistic love (agape) and realistic love (pragma). The names in parentheses are the names I eventually gave each type; but, as you will see in Table 1, their original descriptions are not the same as the final results presented in this book.

The lovestyles described in Table 1 are drawn from literature, not from real life. The problem was rather analagous to drawing six species of animals, using only verbal descriptions. Our fictional and non-fictional literature of love inevitably contains some distortions, which were eventually corrected when I interviewed real lovers. For example, eros is described as a more fickle love in Table 1 than I found it to be in real relationships.

My next step was to make certain that the idea of six different species of love made sense to other people. I asked a few professional friends to sort sixty different descriptive statements about love into six species. I did not show them my descriptions or sorting in Table 1. After each friend completed his or her sorting, I compared it to my own, and to each other friend's sorting. It was as if we were trying to agree on the descriptions of some hypothetical animals such as dragons, mermaids and centaurs, since I still had no proof that any of the species of love actually existed.

Some of the sixty statements proved quite useless: there was no agreement on their meaning of 'love'. These were discarded. Some statements were sorted together into one species by one person, but combined in a different way by another. Fortunately, there were some ideas which generally got sorted together into a single species by each sorter, or at worst, got sorted into two or three similar species. I retained these more definite ideas about love and used thirty of them to make Table 2.

Table 2 consists of thirty statements about the nature of love. Each is obviously a matter of personal opinion, because, as you will notice, some statements directly contradict others. Alongside the statements is a list of the

246

Table 1. Six lovestyles drawn from literature

Criterion	Almost always present	Usually present	Sometimes present	Rarely present	Almost never present
1. Lover feels physical shock symptoms – loss of appetite, faster heartbeat, lack of sleep, etc. – all involuntary.	mania	eros		storge, agape	pragma, ludus
2. Lover feels overpowering physical, sexual attraction.	eros	mania	pragma, ludus	storge	agape
3. Lover feels emotional pain long after relationship over.	mania	agape	storge	eros, pragma	ludus
4. Lover's attention compulsively focused on beloved, distracted from normal activities.	mania	eros	ludus	pragma	agape, storge
5. Power of lover's emotions seems to overwhelm his reason and will or self-control.	mania, eros		storge		pragma, ludus, agape
6. Lover believes purpose and meaning of his life now depends on continued relation with beloved.	mania	storge	agape	pragma	ludus, eros
7. Lover becomes ready to mutilate his personality, take abuse and even remake self for the beloved.	mania		eros, storge, agape	pragma	ludus
8. Lover seeks profound personal knowledge and rapport with beloved.	agape	storge	pragma	eros	ludus, mania

Table 1. Six lovestyles drawn from literature—continued

Criterion	Almost always present	Usually present	Sometimes present	Rarely present	Almost never present
9. Intensity of lover's emotions seems increased by barriers, conflicts, lovers' quarrels, etc.	mania		storge	eros	pragma agape ludus
10. Lover is extremely jealous, possessive, fearful of rivals.	mania		eros pragma storge	ludus	agape
11. Lover believes he can be almost immediately certain of the validity of this experience as love.	mania	eros	pragma		agape ludus storge
12. Lover believes in complete 'honesty' – tell all, share every experience – no manipulation.	mania agape	pragma	storge	eros	ludus
13. Lover believes relationship brings its own morality; anything can be justified in the name of this love.	mania agape	ludus	eros	storge	pragma
14. Lover weighs and measures socio-cultural data about beloved to assess compatible backgrounds.	pragma	storage	ludus	eros	mania agape
15. Relationship is continued as long as mutually enjoyable (not much longer than that).	ludus storge	pragma	eros	agape	mania

248

No.	Statement					
16.	Lover manages his involvement so as to avoid overcommitment or emotional pain.	ludus	pragma agape	storge	eros	mania
17.	Reciprocity (mutuality) is essential for continued loving.	pragma	storge		eros	ludus mania agape ludus eros
18.	Lover believes love to be a serious, committed relationship with responsibility for fate of beloved.	agape mania	storge	pragma		
19.	Lover believes love is predestined, meant to be.	mania		eros storge		agape ludus pragma ludus
20.	Lover believes love to be life's most important activity. True love overcomes all.	mania agape		storge	eros pragma	

species of love into which my friends tended to sort each statement. Sometimes there is general agreement that a statement belongs in only one species. Sometimes a statement may describe as many as three related species; but it is still useful, because it does not apply to the remaining species. Dogs, ducks and dragons walk, but only ducks fly. Eros, ludus, and pragma may all 'play the field' (statement 18), but only ludus would rather 'drop than be dropped' (statement 17).

Table 2 could be used as a research instrument. I could ask anyone to read each statement, and locate it on a five-point scale ranging from strong agreement to strong disagreement. You can try it, if you wish. The columns on the right will tell you which lovestyles your opinions tend to agree with.) However, when I tried this 'opinion sorting' on a large number of ordinary people who had not thought about love analytically, I found a great deal of contradiction among their opinions. Certain statements were agreeable to almost everyone. Statements which expressed directly contradictory ideas about love were selected by the same person. Many lovers wanted to eat their cake and have it too. They wanted a 'unique other half' for whom their attraction would never tire, but they also wanted a compatibility that would rely on friendship rather than feelings.

It became obvious that asking lovers for their opinions about love was not going to help identify the different species of love, or lovestyles. No doubt this is the reason why so many opinion surveys and self-tests ('What kind of lover are you?') do not work well for actual lovers. In love, as in most things, it's difficult to be both 'fish and fowl' at the same time, but most of us wish we could be!

My next step was to construct a method of interviewing actual people in love, not about their opinions, but about their own experiences of love. However, since I wanted to develop a systematic description of different species of love, I needed a method which would enable me to compare one love experience with another. As any lover knows, this is no easy task. Eventually I devised a method I call the Love Story Card Sort.

This method consists of about 1,500 cards organised into 170 sets. Each card contains a brief description of an event, idea or emotion which might possibly occur in a love relationship. Related events are grouped into a set. Thus the whole card sort constitutes an omnibus love story – everybody's love story rolled into one. The task of each individual respondent is to select those cards which tell his or her own love story, and ignore the rest.

Despite the fact that every lover's experience is in some respects unique, it is ultimately composed of ideas, feelings and situations which are provided by our basic human nature and our social culture. The possible number of combinations of these facts is very great, but the basic components themselves are remarkably few in number. Any novelist knows how difficult it is to come up with an 'original' love story, because most of the common plots have already been used again and again. The same is true of most love experiences.

In the Love Story Card Sort, each question, or incomplete sentence, is presented on a green card and the selection of 'answers' are on individual white cards. The respondent is 'I' and the beloved, to preserve anonymity, is called 'X'. There are different sets of cards for male and female respondents. The omnibus love story has many possible endings – marriage, engagement, break-up, or continuation – and each is provided for by appropriate sets of cards.

A respondent begins with the first set:

GREEN CARD: At the time my story begins, just before X and I started going out together, I was . . .
WHITE CARDS: 1. on vacation (choose another card for regular work). 2. a student. 3. working in a factory (etc.; 10 cards in all).

If you were telling me about your experience of love, you would simply select from the white set the card which most correctly answers the statement on the green card. Since all the cards have been pre-coded, it is easy for me to record your selections. When no white card is suitable, you can tell me what happened and I will record this, and transfer it to a code later. A few examples will give you a little of the

Table 2. Thirty statements about love and the related lovestyles

Statement number	Exact statement used in Card-Sort	Related Lovestyles		
1.	Lasting love must be based on a decision of the mind or will, not a feeling or emotion.	Agape		
2.	When two people are truly in love, sex becomes a pure and beautiful way of showing their love and they never do it simply for pleasure.	Agape		
3.	Each lover must find his 'other half', the soul to match his own and make his life complete	Agape	Mania	
4.	True lovers must share every secret, and hide nothing from each other, even though telling may hurt their love.	Agape	Mania	
5.	If your love is true, you can overcome every obstacle. Love will find a way.	Agape	Mania	
6.	If necessary, lovers should take strong action, even threats of violence or suicide, to prove how deeply they love.		Mania	
7.	If you find your one true love, and it fails, life is no longer worth living.		Mania	
8.	In true love, you feel a strong, unexplainable attraction. If it isn't there, or it goes away after a while, there's nothing you can do to make yourself feel in love with the other person.		Mania	Eros
9.	True lovers 'just can't get enough of each other'. They will never tire of making love with each other.		Mania	Eros
10.	True lovers always enjoy the touch, smell and voice of each other.		Mania	Eros

252

	Mania	Eros	Ludus	Pragma	Storge
11. Love is stronger than us; it cannot be denied or resisted, even when the person involved is already married to someone else.	Mania	Eros			
12. Two people can love each other truly, even when they know they have only a short time before they must part, never to meet again.		Eros	Ludus		
13. No one expects a lover to mean sincerely everything he or she says while in love.		Eros	Ludus		
14. There's nothing wrong with pretending you are in love, as long as you do the other person no harm.		Eros	Ludus		
15. Two people who would never make good friends could still be truly in love with each other.		Eros	Ludus		
16. It is possible to fall in and out of love quite a few times without getting badly hurt.			Ludus		
17. If a break-up is coming anyway, it is better to drop the other person than be dropped.			Ludus		
18. There's nothing wrong with playing the field, and having your choice from several persons who love you.		Eros	Ludus	Pragma	
19. It can be very annoying to have someone fall in love with you when all you want from him or her is some good times together.		Eros	Ludus	Pragma	
20. The best cure for heartache is to find someone new.			Ludus	Pragma	
21. There are other things in life just as important as finding true love.			Ludus	Pragma	Storge
22. There may be good reasons for people to marry even when both know that they are *not* in love.				Pragma	Storge
23. Lovers should be prepared for a certain amount of letdown and disappointment after marriage.				Pragma	Storge

253

Table 2. Thirty statements about love and the related lovestyles—continued

Statement number	Exact statement used in Card-Sort	Related Lovestyles		
24.	Love between people of similar background and common interests is the only kind likely to last long.		Pragma	Storge
25.	The need for someone you have grown accustomed to depending on can grow into true love.		Pragma	Storge
26.	It's more important to find someone you'll always enjoy being with than to find someone good-looking and exciting.	Agape	Pragma	Storge
27.	The test of time is the only sure way to know if your love is real.	Agape	Pragma	Storge
28.	Physical (sexual) attraction is not an important part of love.	Agape		Storge
29.	True love ripens slowly out of friendship; it does not happen suddenly or dramatically.	Agape		Storge
30.	True lovers respect and admire each other, and each feels that the other is somehow the 'better' person.	Agape Mania		Storge

254

flavour of an interview. Early in the story you are asked to tell me something about your parents:

Set 5
GREEN CARD [If raised by *both* parents] While I was growing up, my parents, or the adults who raised me, were . . .
WHITE CARDS: a. still very much in love, and quite openly affectionate (kissing, holding hands, etc.). b. happily married and affectionate, but not usually in front of other people or their children. c. well suited to each other, but not affectionate except for a routine kiss, etc. d. not happily married because one of them was much more in love than the other. e. no longer in love, and probably just making the best they could of married life. f. unhappily married, and often arguing, backbiting, and pulling each other apart. g. very unhappy with each other and they separated or divorced. h. other (specify) [*h* is a blank card].

The white cards in this set are arranged and coded in a pattern from happy to unhappy marriage. Remember that they are shuffled before being handed to the respondent, so that the order itself is not apparent when you sort the cards.

Once the origin of the relationship has been described, you begin to move into the events of getting to know your partner. Obviously you will not be able to describe everything that happened, so the Love Story Card Sort concentrates on the types of experience which sociologist William Goode calls 'strain points'. These are the times when you are most likely to be conscious of 'how the relationship is going'. For example, Set 55:

Set 55
GREEN CARD: On our first date, the closest we got to being intimate was . . .
WHITE CARDS: a. just being together; we never actually touched. b. holding hands. c. one good-night or parting kiss. d. kissing several times. e. cuddling, holding each other close, embracing while clothed. f. close body contact unclothed, without sexual intercourse. g. we spent the night together in the same bed but did not make love. h. making love 'all the way'. i. other (specify).

The white cards are shuffled to a random order before you see them, so no choice seems more appropriate than another. There are no 'correct' answers in the interview, other than those which most accurately tell your own story. The cards are not meant to put words into your mouth, but to help you recollect and recount a series of events in a manner which I can systematically record. You are welcome at any time to use the blank card, which reads 'other' (i. in set 55) and fill in your own words.

The Love Story Card Sort is clearly more flexible than a printed questionnaire. Sets can be moved to a different order in the story, to fit your own experience. You can become 'involved' in the telling of your story. Indeed, many of my respondents have remarked, on seeing some particular card: 'Hey, that's exactly what happened', or 'How did you know I would do that?' The Card Sort also provides for a variety of different plots and themes in love relationships, including love triangles, where you or your partner are involved with more than one person at the same time.

All respondents answer most of the questions up to Set 96, variations depending on special cases like triangles. By this point they have reported, through their selections among about 1,000 cards, how they felt about childhood, family, work, close friends and life in general at the time of beginning the love relationship; what they expected love to be like; what kind of lover they were looking for (their ideal image, if any); what they thought they had to offer a lover; how they came to meet; their first reactions on meeting; their thoughts while apart from the partner; their hopes and worries (if any); what happened to their other, regular life-activities as the love progressed; what they did with their times together; their sexual intimacy; how the respondent felt about the partner, and his estimate of the partner's feelings about him; whether there were manifestations of jealousy (and to what extent); the respondent's disappointments in the partner, if any; their frequency of contact; frequency and content of letters, if any; the number and nature of conflicts or arguments, and any temporary break-up or cooling-off period.

From Set 96 on, respondents answer those sets which unfold the remainder of the story.

Set 96
GREEN CARD: In the rest of this story what happens is . . .
WHITE CARDS: a. X and I fell in love with each other about the same time, and we have been in love ever since. b.

X and I fell in love with each other about the same time, but things did not work out and we finally broke up. c. X fell in love with me but I never fell in love with X; we finally broke off. d. I fell in love with X but X never fell in love with me. We finally broke off. e. X fell in love with me first, and hung on for a while, and I finally fell in love with X too. f. I fell in love with X first, and after I hung on for a while, X finally fell in love with me too [or other situations, for which cards were selected].

As you can see, these choices cover just about all the possible outcomes. Subsequent sets depend, of course, on which outcome you report. For example, if you chose 96 d, follow-up sets would include 'I felt X did not love me because. . . .' The longest set in the Card Sort asks you to detail some of the ways you showed your love. Obviously these vary to some extent between the sexes. Here are a *few* of the possible selections for a female respondent to choose from:

GREEN CARD: During the time I was most deeply in love, some of the things I did [or go on doing] . . .
SOME WHITE CARDS: d. I listened hopefully for the sound of his coming (or for the phone to ring). e. I hung on to any little sign of affection he gave me and tried to ignore the pain he gave me. f. I felt a pain deep inside whenever he paid attention to other women. g. I went out with other men just to prove to myself that X wasn't the only one I could attract. h. I got very upset when he withdrew from my touching him. k. I made love with him even when I didn't feel like it. o. I changed my style (clothes, hair, etc.) and my tastes (in art, films, etc.) just to please him. p. I used to wear the clothes he gave me, or liked best, until they fell apart. q. I composed poetry for him. r. I got anxious and worried if he was late, or displeased with me. w. I forgot to keep my diary up to date. x. I sent him funny cards. aa. I asked my husband to let me have a divorce. bb. I showed my love by being dependable and faithful to X. cc. I went on living more or less as usual.

Respondents whose relationships ended in a break-up described their recovery. Set 139 reads, for example, 'Now that it's over, and I look back I feel . . .', and the replies range from gratitude to bitterness to confusion. The stories leading to engagement and marriage arc continued right up to Set 170, which reads 'Looking back, I think our life together . . .'; and the replies range from 'has worked out perfectly;

it's almost too good to be true' to 'has not worked out well; I shouldn't have married X after all'.

The Samples

Interviews of lovers were first conducted in four cities: Brighton and London in England, and Peterborough and Toronto in Canada. An equal number of men and women and English and Canadians were interviewed. When 112 suitable interviews had been accumulated, these were analysed, and a tentative typology of love relationships was produced. Then this typology was tested on further samples, now totalling more than a hundred additional persons, including lovers in Toronto, Montreal, New York and San Francisco. In order to control for possible unknown variables in cultural background, all respondents thus far have been white and English-speaking (though not all have English as their native language). Further testing of the typology of lovestyles continues, including a project in South America, to study cultural variation in lovestyles. Obviously the results thus far have limited application. You will have to decide for yourself whether the theory of lovestyles helps interpret your experience of love.

The lovers I have interviewed are not a random selection from the population, nor do they need to be. It is not necessary to make a random selection of all dogs, in order to develop a systematic description of the various species of dogs. All that is necessary is that there be a good representation of those characteristics which are likely to vary. In the case of lovers, I began with nationality, sex, social class and age. Education, family size and religion were considered later. From early samples which were limited to the age range of 16 to 35 years, I expanded to include lovers up to the age of 71.

The first sample consisted only of heterosexual love relationships, but subsequent interviews have included homosexuals, though mostly males. Thus far, the lovestyles have proved as useful with homosexual love relationships as with heterosexual love.

Since the samples are not based on random selection from the general population, no conclusions can be reached about the distribution of lovestyles among types of people. For

258

example, it is not possible yet to know whether manic experience occurs more often among women than men, or storgic experience more often among working class people than in the middle classes.

However, it is interesting that in the limited samples studied thus far, there are fewer differences in lovestyles according to sex and social class than much expert writing on love would lead us to expect. Working class people are not necessarily confined to an 'inarticulate sex urge', as some sociologists have suggested. The insights of novelists such as D. H. Lawrence, John Steinbeck, Alberto Moravia, Stan Barstow, and Edna O'Brien, all of whom have described working class romantic love, are more in keeping with the results of my studies.

As for sex, there are few differences between men and women in preferences for various lovestyles, among the lovers I have interviewed. Neither men nor women seem more likely to be manic (obsessive, jealous, anxious). In their attitudes about love, women seem capable of as much playfulness and permissiveness as men. At least, I have interviewed some very ludic women. If there is more ludus among men than women in the whole population, it may well have more to do with social values and training, and with the lack of opportunities for women to be playful until recently, than with any inherent difference in the sexes – Byron and Disraeli notwithstanding!

Validity

How could I know if respondents were telling the truth? One method of assessing validity would be to interview both parties to each love relationship. This was largely precluded for many respondents by the fact that I assured them of anonymity. They were not about to 'tell all' if any other person was to become involved. Some respondents arranged to send along 'the other half', but the partner declined. Even when I was able to interview both parties, the question of validity was no nearer solution. When the stories agreed, it was interesting, but when they disagreed, how was I to prove which was correct without consulting some third party?

The fundamental problem of validity in the reconstruction of emotional experiences is not so much whether respondents deliberately lied to me – they had little motive for doing so – but whether they knew the truth to tell. How many of us are able to observe and recollect our emotional experiences objectively and dispassionately?

There are two schools of thought about methods of assuring greater validity when asking people for information about themselves. One school argues that the methods used should be as 'objective' and 'Standardised' as possible, so as to eliminate all 'interviewer variables'. The other school argues that you can't expect valid self-disclosure when you treat the respondent like a bundle of data. R. D. Laing, Sidney Jourard and others have argued for sensitive rapport and even mutual disclosure as methods for obtaining a truer picture of the respondent's experience. I lean towards this approach.

The capacity of the respondent to report details of a love experience is likely to vary with the lovestyle itself. Mania imprints on the memory those words, moods, cues, which the casual ludic lover never notices in the first place, or else ignores. Since there are different moral attitudes in our society towards the different lovestyles (ludus is often deplored as promiscuity, for example), a respondent may be more likely to suppress and 'forget' certain behaviour.

The systematic but amoral stimulation of the Love Story cards helps to resolve these problems. There is no moral order implicit in the selections themselves. Both a report of sex on the night of first encounter, and a report of an asexual or 'Platonic' relationship, can be made merely by pulling a card from a set and dropping it into the response box. The interviewer naturally makes no comments on any respondent's selection. At the same time, the memory is prompted by seeing a wide variety of events and ideas presented on the cards.

Reliability

Social scientists are always and rightly dubious of each other's findings. They want verification, by repeating the same study elsewhere and obtaining similar results. The trouble with much of the existing literature on love is that its reliability cannot be tested. A therapist reporting the analysis of experiences of love disclosed by patients, may well present a reasonable argument. But the patients and their experiences, as well as the particular methods of observation of the therapist, are inaccessible to other observers.

One advantage of the Love Story Card Sort as a method of observing experiences of love is that it can be replicated. The fifty printed pages of questions in the 170 sets will not be of much interest to the ordinary reader, who would not be in a position to process the results anyway. However, they are available to any researcher seriously interested in testing the theory of lovestyles.[1]

Professor Thomas Lasswell, a sociologist at the University of Southern California, has already devised a simple test of fifty questions, on six major types (storage, agape, mania, pragma, ludus and eros – which he calls the SAMPLE profile). He has verified the usefulness of these types in tests of large samples of respondents, as well as in clinical practice in marriage counselling.

Processing the Data

'How do I love thee? Let me count the ways,' wrote Elizabeth Barrett Browning; but I doubt that she had mathematical data processing in mind. Since calculation of a specific lovestyle out of the hundreds of items of data reported by even one single respondent in the Love Story Card Sort proved to be a tedious and complex business, I doubt that many readers will want more than a cursory explanation.

All the cards selected by respondents – or the special answers they supplied – were coded. These codes were sorted, and reduced to a little more than 200 basic factors in love relationships. These factors were reduced in turn to 32 'key' factors. These factors are listed in Table 3. A key factor consisted of a prescribed selection of a combination of more general data. For example, factor 6 in Table 3 reports that the respondent 'frequently felt unhappy feelings of jealous possessiveness'. This factor was considered present in a given relationship only if there was repeated evidence of a defined minimum intensity of jealous feelings.

Naturally the male pronoun is used in the table merely for

1. Write care of the publisher.

Table 3. Key factors in the description of love relationships

1. Respondent believed his childhood was happy compared to that of his peers.
2. His life and work were satisfying at time of falling in love.
3. He believed being in love would be primarily an unhappy experience.
4. He felt a loss of control over his own feelings during love.
5. He attempted to compel the beloved to show more feeling, more response.
6. He frequently felt unhappy feelings of jealous possessiveness.
7. He found his thoughts obsessively preoccupied with the beloved.
8. He wanted to see the beloved much of the time (at least daily).
9. He was consciously aware of being or falling in love.
10. He had great expectations of the beloved's favourable response.
11. He and the beloved spent much of their time together in direct personal interface – 'alone together'.
12. He felt strong approval of beloved's looks at first sight.
13. He felt strong physical, sexual attraction to beloved.
14. Sexual intercourse occurred very early in the relationship.
15. Respondent was quite optimistic from start that beloved felt reciprocal sexual attraction.
16. He rapidly and intensely disclosed himself to beloved.
17. Sexual intimacy continued at a frequent and intense level.
18. As relationship developed, respondent remained optimistic, attracted.
19. As relationship developed, respondent tried to 'cool out' beloved.
20. Respondent held back on self-disclosure and commitment to partner.
21. He carefully analysed and weighed the relationship.
22. He was aware, from early on, of warning signs of trouble ahead.
23. He consciously controlled his display of feelings towards partner.
24. He was increasingly aware of partner's flaws, shortcomings.
25. He consciously controlled verbal discussion of feelings with partner.
26. Arguments, fights, disagreements became commonplace between lovers.
27. Respondent was frequently anxious, worried; his jealousy increased.
28. Actual jealous scenes occurred between lovers, involving others.
29. Sexual hang-ups and misunderstandings hindered the relationship.
30. Respondent tried to foresee and plan future of relationship.
31. Respondent accepted partner's lack of intensity or holding back.
32. Respondent held back on own intensity so as to remain mutual with partner – but not out of disapproval of partner.

brevity and simplicity; the factors apply equally to both sexes, and to heterosexual and homosexual relationships.

As you might expect, not all factors are equally relevant to all relationships. Once a reasonable number of lovers had been interviewed it was possible to calculate the statistical probability of any two given factors occurring together in the same relationship. Sometimes this probability was very low. For example, it is unlikely that factors 4 and 23 (control and loss of control) will occur together. When they do, this is a signal that a specific lovestyle, called manic ludus, is probably involved.

By sorting out the key factors in Table 3 which were generally likely to occur together, or 'cluster' in love relationships, I was able to tease out from a jumble of data a few of the most distinctive patterns of loving, or lovestyles. I used much the same technique you would use to recognise the silhouettes of different animals, even if all you saw was a shadow cast by each animal on a wall. You would look for the cluster of size, type of legs, shape of head and long trunk that signals 'elephant', the rather different cluster of typical parts that says 'camel', and so forth.

The key factors were sorted into six classes: predisposing anxiety, mental preoccupation, sensual rapport, manipulative control, conflict and tension, and companionship. Then the individual respondents were arranged, first one way and then another, until the best 'fit' between their patterns of behaviour in different classes was achieved. For example, all those with high levels of predisposing anxiety were grouped together, then those with very low levels. Then both groups were sorted again according to sensual rapport. It was much the same process you would use to sort your library for shelving. Perhaps you would start by subjects (novels, art, history), then by size of book within each subject, then by author. The technical name for this process is scaling.

The result of one such scaling is shown as Table 4. These are the 'silhouettes' cast by ten different groups of respondents (numbered 1 to 10 across the top of the chart). As you will notice, the profile of group 1 is very different from that of group 10. There is no predisposing anxiety (worry before the relationship begins) in group 1, and a great deal in group 10. On the other hand, there is much companionship in group 1, and little in group 10. At the bottom of Table 4, the differences in profile are collected into solid columns. As you can see, no two are alike, but there are strong similarities between some neighbouring columns.

The summary portion at the bottom of Table 4 rather resembles a geologist's cutaway diagram of layers of rock. Perhaps many lovers have worn out their bits drilling for 'oil' in the wrong lovestyle!

In any event, it is clear that data processing and scaling have led to a rather different picture of the variations in lovestyle, in Table 4, than was first suspected at the time Table 1 was developed. There are ten groups or lovestyles in Table 4 and six in Table 1, but the number is not important. After all, how many distinct colours are there? It all depends on our purposes.

Table 4 represented a great step forward in the analysis of love, because it is independent of the particular details of any individual love relationship. Instead, its arrangement depends on overall patterns, represented by the 'key factors'. To use our geological analogy again, the diagram is one of *strata*, not of individual rocks. Moving one or two items here or there in the pattern will not make much difference in the overall picture.

But which lovestyles is Table 4 all about? What should we call group 1, for example? These are love experiences with little anxiety, but much companionship. Or those in group 10? These seem just the opposite to group 1 – there's a lot of anxiety, mental preoccupation, and tension.

The process of analysis is too detailed – and required too long a time – to be described in detail here. In the end, it became clear that group 1 best suited the description of *storge* as set out in Table 1. Group 5 suited *ludus*. Beyond that, however, the original types drawn from literature and defined in Table 1 had to be altered. Group 8 became eros, with less conflict than originally expected. Group 10 became mania – with more attempted control than Table 1 foresaw. Group 9, mid-way between 8 and 10 in each section of Table 4, became the transitional love, manic eros. In turn each of the other major lovestyles was identified.

More than the bold outline of distinctive lovestyles is available in Table 4. Each 'group' represents not merely a different approach to love, but also a different category of

Table 4. Profiles of ten lovestyles

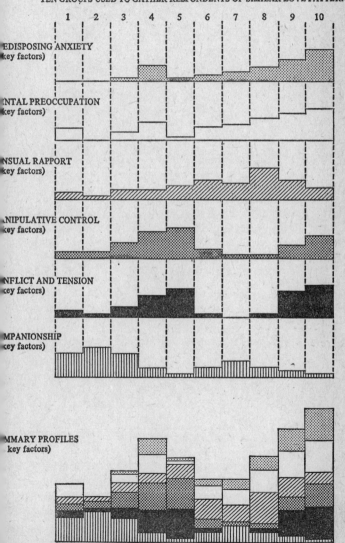

TEN GROUPS USED TO GATHER RESPONDENTS OF SIMILAR LOVE PATTERNS

1 2 3 4 5 6 7 8 9 10

PREDISPOSING ANXIETY
(key factors)

MENTAL PREOCCUPATION
(key factors)

SENSUAL RAPPORT
(key factors)

MANIPULATIVE CONTROL
(key factors)

CONFLICT AND TENSION
(key factors)

COMPANIONSHIP
(key factors)

SUMMARY PROFILES
(key factors)

STORGE   LUDUS   EROS   MANIA

Table 5. *The probability of various characteristics occurring in each of eight common lovestyles*

Probability of occurrence in:

Number	Characteristic	Eros	Ludus	Storge	Mania	Ludic eros	Storgic eros	Storgic ludus	Pragma
1.0	Lover considers his childhood less happy than average of peers	R			U				
1.1	Lover is discontented with life (work, etc.) at time of encounter			AN	U				
1.2	Lover has never been in love before (in his opinion)				U	R			
1.3	Lover wanted to be in love or have love as security	R	AN		AA		AN	AN	
2.0	Lover and beloved are at least five years apart in age		AN		AA		AN	AN	U
2.1	Social class background of lover and beloved is markedly different			R			U		R
2.2	Lover and beloved were total strangers before love relationship			AN		U			R
2.3	Lover has clearly defined ideal image of desired partner (*several)	AA	AN	AN	AN	U*	AN	R	AA
3.0	Lover felt strong gut attraction to beloved on first encounter	AA	R	AN	R	U	AN		
3.1	Lover soon preoccupied with thoughts about the beloved	AA	AN	AN	AA			R	
3.2	Lover believed partner's interest at least as great as his (hers)		U	R	AN		R		U

3.3 Lover eager to see beloved every day (or almost) from beginning	AA	AN	R	AA	R	AN	R
3.4 Lover soon believed this could become a permanent relationship	AA	AN	R	AN	AA	AA	AN	U
3.5 Lover worried, anticipated problems from start of relationship	AN	AN			AA	AN	AN
3.6 Lover saw 'warning signs' of trouble but ignored them at start	R	R	R	AA	R	AN	R
4.0 Lover deliberately restrained frequency of contact with partner	AN	AA	U	R	R	R	U
4.1 Lover restricted discussion of his feelings with beloved	R	AA	U	R	U	U	U
4.2 Lover restricted display of his feelings with beloved	R	AA	U	U	R	U	U
4.3 Lover discussed future plans with beloved	R	AA	R	U	R	U	U
4.4 Lover discussed wide range of topics, experiences with partner	AA	R	R	AA	AN	AN	AA
4.5 Lover tried to control relationship but feels he lost control	AA	R	AN	R	U	R	AA
4.6 Never lost ability to be first to terminate relationship	AN	AN	AN	AA	AN		
4.7 Lover tried to force beloved to show more feeling, commitment	AN	AN	R	AA	U	R	R
5.0 Lover tried to analyse relationship, weigh it in his mind	AN	U	AN	U	R	R	AA

AA = Almost always (90%+) AN = Almost never (10%−) U = Usually (75%−89%) R = Rarely (11%−25%)

Table 5. The probability of various characteristics occurring in each of eight common lovestyles —continued

Number	Characteristic	Probability of occurrence in:							
		Eros	Ludus	Storge	Mania	Ludic eros	Storgic eros	Storgic ludus	Pragma
5.1	Lover began to believe partner was holding back, really loved more	AN							
5.2	Lover believed in sincerity of partner	AA		U	AA	U	AA		
5.3	Lover blamed partner for difficulties of relationship	R	U	R	U	R	AN		
5.4	Lover jealous and possessive but not to point of angry conflict	U	AN	R		R	AN		
5.5	Lover jealous to point of conflict scenes, threats, etc.	AN	AN	AN	AA	R	AN	AN	AN
6.0	Tactile, sensual contact very important to lover	AA		AN		U	AN		R
6.1	Sexual intimacy achieved early, rapidly in relationship	AA	U	AN	AN	U	R	U	
6.2	Quality of sexual rapport taken as test of love by lover	AA	U	AN		U	AN	U	R
6.3	Lover willing to work out sex problems, improve technique	U	R		R	U		R	U
6.4	Continued high rate of sex, tactile contact, later in relationship			R	R	U	R		R
7.0	Lover declared love first, well ahead of partner	U	AN	R	AA		AA		R

7.1	Lover considers love life most important activity, even essential	AA	AN	R	AA	AA	R	R
7.2	Lover prepared to 'give all' for love once under way	U	AN	U	AA	AA	R	R
7.3	Lover willing to suffer abuse, even ridicule of partner		AN	R	AA	R	R	AN
7.4	Relationship marked by frequent differences of opinion, anxiety	R	AA	R	AA	R	R	R
8.0	Relationship ends with lasting bitterness, trauma for lover	AN	R	R	AA	AN	R	R

AA = Almost always (90%+)   AN = Almost never (10%—)   U = Usually (75%–89%)   R = Rarely (11%–25%)

specific, real-life experiences reported by actual lovers. By going back to the detailed reports of these lovers, more information could be culled and correlated with each lovestyle. For instance, the curious combination of anxiety, manipulation and tension in mania (group 10) could be explained by closer study of the individuals who experienced this lovestyle. Table 4, after all, deals with only 32 key factors; there was much more data than that in the interviews.

For instance, it was possible to sort out all the lovers who reported erotic experiences, and look at their reports on ideal images of the beloved. It was possible to tease apart the otherwise similar reports of pragmatic and storgic-ludic experiences, by noting the emphasis, in the latter, on discretion.

A summary of some of the most characteristic differences between lovestyles is shown in Table 5. It starts with the predisposition of the lover (section 1.0 to 1.3), deals with topics such as control and expression of feelings (section 4), and ends with a break-up (where this applies). Table 5 is a sort of scoreboard of lovestyles. When a given characteristic (stated on the left side) is relevant to a certain lovestyle, this is indicated by an entry in the appropriate column. A blank indicates that a characteristic neither confirms nor denies the existence of a certain lovestyle. For example, there is no association between unhappy memories of childhood (1.0) and the ludic lovestyle, among my respondents. On the other hand, it is rare for such memories to occur in conjunction with an erotic experience of love. As the note indicates, R means 'rarely' – that is, occurs less than 25% of the time among respondents studied thus far.

It will now be apparent that the descriptions of the various lovestyles in Chapters Two to Ten of this book are actually elaborations of the data contained in Tables 3, 4 and 5. For example, Table 5 indicates that a relationship is most likely to be erotic (rather than, say, ludic or storgic) when there is a strong ideal image, strong approval on first sight, preoccupation with the beloved, and so on. These factors, numbered 2.3, 3.0 and 3.1 in Table 5, are 'almost always' found in eros, as indicated by the AA entry in the eros column. That is, each characteristic was found in at least 90% of the respondents whose overall pattern of ideas, behaviour, and attitudes to love more closely resembled the profile of eros in Tables 3 and 4 than it resembled any other lovestyle.

Most readers will prefer to use the verbal profiles of each lovestyle, together with Tests One and Two, to identify their favourite lovestyle(s). But to demonstrate how Table 5 works as an analysis of lovestyles, let us apply it to an example we have already discussed, that of Philip to Mildred in *Of Human Bondage* (see Chapter Thirteen).

Table 5 tells us that if the lover is discontented with life he is more likely to be manic (U in this column) than storgic (AN, or almost never, in this column). Of course this one fact is no more conclusive as proof of mania in Philip and Mildred's relationship than legs are proof that an animal is a dog. On the other hand, we can begin to suspect that it is not a bird if there are no wings, and not storge if the lover is discontent with life.

When we add Philip's unhappy childhood memories (1.0), the fact that Mildred is a total stranger (2.2), and so forth, then this relationship begins to take on more and more of the appearance of mania. In all, we find that 32 of the characteristics in Table 5 point towards mania as 'usually' or 'almost always' a reasonable diagnosis, while only one characteristic points away from mania. (This is 1.2, which suggests that mania is more likely when the lover has never been in love before; Philip has had previous love experience.)

There are ten characteristics which suggest a probability of eros (a few overlap mania), while twenty-five argue against eros. The remainder, of course, are blanks, not indicative either way. There are seven indicators for ludic eros, nineteen against; eight for storge, eighteen against. Obviously, the most likely diagnosis so far is mania. However, it is interesting to note that ludus is a close second, with eighteen against, but thirteen for. There are numerous hints in Maugham's story that Philip is not quite so madly in love as he seems, hints which originate, of course, in the autobiographical nature of the story and Maugham's own hindsight.

Of Human Bondage is a deservedly famous love story because it implies a realisation many of us encounter only after a personal bout of mania: namely, that there is a certain quality of acting or performing in this mad love which is not quite sincere. This calculating or self-manipulative quality, typical of ludus, may be what has led some analysts of mania to argue that it arises merely from 'love of love' rather than love of a person. That part of our psyche which remains the detached, rational observer, while the rest of our being pines, suffers and dotes on the beloved, keeps reminding us that we are behaving rather foolishly – but we answer 'I can't help it'. 'Pure' mania would presumably imply the complete silencing of that rational observer in the self, and full immersion in the furies and follies of this obsessive and jealous type of love. But the result would probably be a serious commitment to the manic belief that life without the beloved is not worth living, and the lover would have either to end his life (thus removing himself from the category of possible interview respondents!) or transcend and transform himself.

In the more calculated, 'performed' mania of Philip, as portrayed by Maugham, an aftermath of cynicism or of exhaustion into the resigned quietude of storge is more likely. Maugham ends Philip's story with a storgic aftermath, but in the author's own life, the outcome was cynicism.

But just a moment! I'm drifting into an analysis of the literature of love again. There seems to be no end to the possible and interesting applications of the theory of love-styles. You can continue this pursuit of love on your own. What is important here, is that a systematic theory of love-styles is available, which does not depend solely on impressionistic observation. The lovestyles which emerge from the data processing of interviews of actual lovers are not the same as those which I found in the literature. The agape of Table 1 is gone in Table 5. But what remains is a clear definition of those species of love whose descriptions have some counterpart in experience. No unicorns or centaurs here: these are the kinds of loving that ordinary people are really living.

Bibliography

Since this is as much a record of the author's sources as a list of recommended 'further reading' for those interested, a number of works have been included which are either out of print or only available in the United States. Wherever possible, however, date and place of publication have been given of the most recent English edition.

Anshen, Ruth, *The Family, Its Function and Destiny*. New York, 1959.

Argyle, Michael, *The Psychology of Interpersonal Behaviour*. London, 1967.

Ashley, Maurice, *The Stuarts in Love*. London, 1963.

Aubert, Wilhelm, *The Hidden Society*. London, 1965.

Baber, R. E., *Marriage and the Family*. New York, 1953.

Barbu, Zevedei, *Problems of Historical Psychology*. London, 1960.

Barzun, Jacques, *Romanticism and the Modern Ego*. Boston, Mass., 1947.

Bates, A., 'Parental Roles in Courtship'. *Social Forces*, Vol. 20 (1942).

Bauer, B. A., *Woman and Love*. New York, 1971.

Beard, Mary R., *Woman as a Force in History*. New York, 1962.

Beauvoir, Simone de, *The Second Sex*. London, 1972.

Becker, Howard, and Reuben, H., *Family, Marriage and Parenthood*. New York, 1955.

Bell, S., 'A Preliminary Study of the Emotion of Love Between the Sexes'. *American Journal of Psychology*, Vol. 13 (1902).

Belperron, Pierre, *La Joie d'Amour*. Paris, 1948.

Benoit, Hubert, *The Many Faces of Love*. London, 1955.

Bergler, Edmund, *Unhappy Marriage and Divorce*. New York, 1946.

Berl, E., *The Nature of Love*. New York, 1924.

Berne, Eric, *Games People Play*. London, 1970.

Berteaut, Simone, *Piaf*. London, 1973.

Besterman, T., *Men Against Women*. London, 1934.

Bianquis, Genevieve, *Love in Germany*. London, 1921.

Biegel, H. G., 'Romantic Love'. *American Sociological Review*, Vol. 16 (1951).

Blau, Peter M., *Exchange and Power in Social Life*. London, 1964.

Bloch, I., *Sexual Life in England, Past and Present*. London, 1938.

Blood, Robert O., *Love Match and Arranged Marriage*. Glencoe, Illinois, 1967.

Blood, Robert O., *Marriage*. Glencoe, Illinois, 1969.

Blood, Robert O., 'Romance and Premarital Intercourse Incompatibles?' *Marriage and Family Living*, Vol. 14 (1952).

Blood, Robert O., 'Universities and Diversities in Campus Dating Preferences'. *Marriage and Family Living*, Vol. 18 (1956).

Bolton, Charles, 'The Development Process in Love Relationships'. Unpublished Ph.D. thesis, University of Chicago, 1959.

Boroff, David, 'Sex, the Quiet Revolution', in H. K. Girvetz (ed.), *Contemporary Moral Issues*. Belmont, California, 1968.

Bowerman, C. E. and Ray, B. R., 'A test of the theory of complementary needs'. *American Sociological Review*, Vol. 21 (1956).

Briffault, Robert, *The Mothers*. London, 1960.

Broderick, C., and Fowler, S., 'New Patterns of Relationship between the Sexes among Pre-adolescents'. *Marriage and Family Living*, Vol. 23 (1961).

Buerkle, J., 'Analysis of marital adjustment'. *Marriage and Family Living*, Vol. 23 (1961).

Burkhardt, J., *The Civilization of the Renaissance in Italy*. London, 1958.

Burgess, E. W., *The Family, from institution to companionship*. London, 1971.

Burgess, E. W., 'The Romantic Impulse and Family Disorganization.' *Survey*, Vol. 57 (1927).

Burgess, E. W., 'Women's Status and the forms of Marriage'. *American Sociological Review*, Vol. 48 (1943).

Burgess, E. W., and Cottrell, L. S., *Predicting Success or Failure in Marriage*. New York, 1939.

Burgess, E. W., and Wallin, Paul, *Engagement and Marriage*. New York, 1953.

Burgess, E. W., and Wallin, Paul, 'Homogamy in Social Characteristics'. *American Journal of Sociology*, Vol. 49 (1943).

Burton, A. (ed.), *Encounter: Theory and Practice of Encounter Groups*. London, 1969.

Calverton, V. F., and Schmalhausen, S. D., (eds), *Sex in Civilization*. London, 1929.

Cattell, Raymond B., *The Scientific Analysis of Personality*. London, 1965.

Cavan, Ruth, *The American Family*. New York, 1953.

Chardonne, Jacques, *L'Amour c'est beaucoup plus que l'amour*. Paris, 1957.

Chaytor, H. J., *The Troubadours and England*. Cambridge, 1923.

Chesser, Eustace, *The Sexual-Marital and Family Relations of the English Woman*. London, 1956.

Childs, J. R., *A Biography of Casanova*. London, 1961.

Christensen, H. T., 'Cultural Relativism and Premarital Sex Norms'. *American Sociological Review*, Vol. 25 (February, 1960).

Christensen, H. T., *Marriage Analysis*. New York, 1950.

Cleugh, James, *Love Locked Out, a survey of love, licence and restriction in the Middle Ages*. London, 1963.

Comfort, Alex, *Sexual Behaviour in Society*. London, 1950.

Coombs, R. H., 'Reinforcement of values in the parental home as a factor in mate selection'. *Marriage and Family Living*, Vol. 24 (1962).

Coser, Ruth L., *The Family, its Structure and Functions* [edited readings]. New York, 1964.

Coulton, G. C., *Social Life in England from the Conquest to the Reformation*. Cambridge, 1918.

Crew, Louie, and Norton, Rictor, 'The Homophobic Imagination, an Editorial'. *College English*, Vol. 36, No. 3 (November, 1974).

Cruse, A., *The Englishman and his Books in the Early Nineteenth Century*. London, 1930.

Cuber, J. F., 'Romance and Marriage'. *Marriage and Family Living*, Vol. 11 (1949).

Cuber, J. F., and Harroff, P. G., *Sex and the Significant Americans*, London, 1965.

Dalziel, M., *Popular Fiction a Hundred Years Ago*. London, 1958.

Danielsson, B., *Love in the South Seas*. New York, 1956.

Danville, G., *La Psychologie de l'Amour*. Paris, 1895.

D'Arcy, M. C., *The Mind and Heart of Love*. London, 1945.

Davis, Kingsley, *Human Society*. London, 1970.

Davis, Kingsley, 'The Sociology of Parent-Youth Conflict'. *American Sociological Review*, Vol. 5 (1940).

Davis, Kingsley, 'Statistical Perspective on Divorce'. *Annals of the American Academy of Political and Social Sciences*, Vol. 272 (1950).

Davis, M. R., 'Propinquity of Residence before Marriage'. *American Journal of Sociology*, Vol. 44 (1930).

Dean, Dwight G., 'Romanticism and Emotional Maturity'. *Marriage and Family Living*, Vol. 23 (February, 1961).

Dell, Floyd, *Love in the Machine Age*. New York, 1926.

Denomy, A. J., 'An Enquiry into the Origin of Courtly Love'. *Medieval Studies*, Vol. 6 (University of Toronto, 1944).

Denomy, A. J., 'Fin Amors, the Pure Love of the Troubadours'. *Medieval Studies*, Vol. 7 (University of Toronto, 1945).

Ditzion, S., *Marriage, Morals, and Sex in America*. New York, 1953.

Dodd, W. G., *Courtly Love in Chaucer and Gower*. New York, 1913.

Dronke, Peter, *Medieval Latin and the Rise of the European Love Lyric*. Oxford, 1969.

Duvall, E. M., 'Adolescent love and the search for identity'. *Marriage and Family Living*, Vol. 26 (1964).

Ehrmann, Winston, *Premarital Dating Behaviour*. New York, 1959.

Ellis, Albert, *The American Sexual Tragedy*. New York, 1954.

Ellis, Albert, *The Intelligent Woman's Guide to Man-Hunting*. New York, 1963.

Ellis, Albert, 'A study of human love relationships'. *Journal of Genetic Psychology* (1949).

Ellis, Havelock, *Little Essays on Love and Virtue*. New York, 1930.

Ellis, Havelock, *The Psychology of Sex*. London, 1937.

Ellis, Havelock, *Sex in Relation to Society*. London, 1937.

England, R. W., 'Images of love and courtship in family-magazine fiction'. *Marriage and Family Living*, Vol. 22 (1960).

Epton, Nina, *Love and the English*. London, 1960.

Epton, Nina, *Love and the French*. London, 1964.

Epton, Nina, *Love and the Spanish*. London, 1964.

Fiedler, Leslie A., *Love and Death in the American Novel*. London, 1970.

Fielding, W. J., *Love and the Sex Emotions*. New York, 1933.

Finck, H. T., *Primitive Love and Love Stories*. New York, 1889.

Finck, H. T., *Romantic Love and Personal Beauty*. London, 1887.

Flaceliere, Robert, *Love in Ancient Greece*. London, 1960.

Fletcher, Ronald, *The Family and Marriage in Britain*. London, 1969.

Folsom, Joseph K., 'Love and Courtship', In Howard Becker and Reuben Hill. (eds), op. cit.

Foote, Nelson, 'Love'. *Psychiatry*, Vol. 16 (1953).

Foote, Nelson, 'Sex as Play', in Ruth L. Coser. (ed.), op. cit.

Ford, C. S., and Beach, F. A., *Patterns of Sexual Behaviour*. New York, 1951.

Fowlie, Wallace, *Love in Literature*. Bloomington, Indiana, 1948.

Foxon, David, *Libertine Literature in England*, 1660–1745. (Reprinted from *The Book Collector*. London, 1963).

Freud, Sigmund, *Civilization and its Discontents*. London, 1963.

Freud, Sigmund, *Contributions to the Psychology of Love*, Collected Papers, Vol. IV. London, 1957.

Freud, Sigmund, *Group Psychology and Analysis of the Ego*. London, 1940.

Freud, Sigmund, *The Standard Edition of the Complete Psychological Works*. London, 1957.

Fried, Enrita, *On Love and Sexuality*. New York, 1960.

Friedan, Betty, *The Feminine Mystique*. London, 1971.

Friedenberg, Edgar, *The Vanishing Adolescent*. Boston, Mass., 1959.

Friedlander, Ludwig, *Roman Life and Manners under the Early Empire*.

Fromm, Erich, *The Art of Loving*. London, 1957.

Fromm, Erich, *The Sane Society*. London, 1956.

Fromme, Allan, *The Ability to Love*. New York, 1965.

Geraldy, Paul, *L'Homme et L'Amour*. Paris, 1960.

Giffen, L. A., *The Theory of Profane Love Among the Arabs*. New York, 1971.

Gill, F. C., *The Romantic Movement and Methodism*. London, 1937.

Gilson, E., *The Mystical Theology of Saint Bernard*. London, 1940.

Gist, M. A., *Love and War in the Middle English Romances*. Philadelphia, Pa., 1947.

Goffman, Erving, *Encounters*. London, 1973.

Goffman, Erving, *The Presentation of Self in Everyday Life*. London 1971.

Goode, W. J., 'The Theoretical Importance of Love'. *American Sociological Review*, Vol. 24 (February, 1959).

Goode, W. J., *Women in Divorce* (also published as *After Divorce*). Glencoe, Illinois, 1956.

Gorer, Geoffrey, *The Americans*. London, 1948.

Gorer, Geoffrey, *Exploring English Character*. London, 1955.

Gould, Thomas, *Platonic Love*. Glencoe, Illinois, 1963.

Gouldner, Alvin W., 'The norm of reciprocity'. *American Sociological Review*, Vol. 25 (April, 1960).

Grant, Vernon W., *The Psychology of Sexual Emotion*. London, 1957.

Gray, Charles, 'Scale Analysis with Gradgram'. *General Research Analysis Methods*, mimeographed paper. (1059 Hilyard St., Eugene, Oregon 97401, 1967).

Greenfield, Sidney M., 'Love and Marriage in Modern America, a Functional Analysis'. *Sociological Quarterly*, Vol. 6.

Gross, Llewelyn, 'A Belief Pattern Scale for Measuring Attitudes Toward Romanticism'. *American Sociological Review*, Vol. 9 (1944).

Grunwald, Henry A., 'The Disappearance of Don Juan', in *The Light of the Past*, collected articles from *Horizon*. New York, 1965.

Grunwald, Henry A., *Sex in America*. New York, 1964.

Guyon, René, *The Ethics of Sexual Acts*. New York, 1941.

Haller, William, 'The Puritan Art of Love'. *Huntingdon Library Quarterly*, Vol. 5 (January, 1942).

Hamilton, M., 'What is Love?'. *Hibbert Journal*, Vol. 25 (1927).

Hayakawa, S. I., 'Popular songs and the facts of life', in S. I. Hayakawa (ed.), *The Use and Misuse of Language*. New York, 1962.

Hays, H. R., *The Dangerous Sex – The myth of feminine evil*. New York, 1952.

Hazo, Robert G. *The Idea of Love*. New York, 1967.

Henriques, Fernando, *Love in Action*. London, 1970.

Henriques, Fernando, *Modern Sexuality*. London, 1968.

Henriques, Fernando, *The Pretence of Love*. London, 1962.

Henriques, Fernando, *Prostitution in Europe and the New World*. London, 1963.

Herman, R. D., 'The going-steady complex'. *Marriage and Family Living*, Vol. 17 (1955).

Hobart, Charles W., 'Attitude changes during marriage and courtship'. *Marriage and Family Living*, Vol. 22 (November, 1960).

Hobart, Charles W., 'Incidence of Romanticism in Courtship'. *Social Forces* (May, 1958).

Holbrooke, David, *The Quest for Love*. Tuscaloosa, Alabama, 1965.

Hollingshead, A. B., 'Cultural factors in the selection of marriage mates'. *American Sociological Review*, Vol. 15 (1950).

Horne, H. H., *Shakespeare's Philosophy of Love*. New York, 1945.

Horton, David, 'The dialogue of courtship in popular songs'. *American Journal of Sociology* (1957).

Houghton, W. E., *The Victorian Frame of Mind*. New Haven, Conn., 1957.

Huizinga, John, *Homo Ludens*. London, 1970.

Huizinga, John, *The Waning of the Middle Ages*. London, 1972.

Humphreys, Laud, *Out of the Closets: the Sociology of Homosexual Liberation*. New York, 1972.

Hunt, Morton M., *The Affair*. New York, 1971.

Hunt, Morton M., *The Natural History of Love*. New York, 1959.

Hunt, Morton M., *The World of the Formerly Married*. New York, 1966.

Hyde, H. Montgomery, *A History of Pornography*. London, 1964.

Hyde, H. Montgomery, *The Other Love*. London, 1971.

Ibert, J. C., and Charles, J., *Love the French Way*. London, 1964.

Iovetz-Tereschenko, N. M., *Friendship-love in adolescence*. London, 1936.

Isenke, N., *Sex and Love Today*. London, 1961.

Jourard, Sidney, 'The Body Taboo'. *New Society*, No. 627 (November 9, 1967).

Jourard, Sidney, *Disclosing Man to Himself*. New York, 1968.

Jourard, Sidney, *The Transparent Self*. New York, 1972.

Kardiner, A., *Sex and Morality*. New York, 1954.

Katz, Alvin M., and Hill, Reuben, 'Residential propinquity and marital selection'. *Marriage and Family Living*, Vol. 20 (February, 1958).

Kelly, G. A., *The Psychology of Personal Constructs*. New York, 1956.

Kelso, Ruth, *Doctrine for the Lady of the Renaissance*. Urbana, Illinois, 1956.

Kenmare, Dallas, *Love the Unknown*. London, 1965.

Key, Ellen, *Love and Marriage*. London, 1911.

Kiefer, O., *Sexual Life in Ancient Rome*. London, 1934.

Kierkegaard, Sören, *Anthology*. New York, 1947 (*The Diary of a Seducer, The Aesthetic Validity of Marriage*).

Kierkegaard, Sören, *Purity of Heart Is to Will One Thing*. New York, 1957.

Kierkegaard, Sören, *Works of Love*. London, 1972.

Kirkpatrick, Clifford, 'A statistical investigation of the psychoanalytical theory of mate selection'. *Journal of Abnormal and Social Psychology*, Vol. 32 (1937).

Kirkpatrick, C., and Caplow, T., 'Courtship in a group of Minnesota students'. *American Journal of Sociology*, Vol. 51 (1945).

Kirkpatrick, C., and Caplow, T., 'Emotional trends in the courtship experience of college students'. *American Sociological Review*, Vol. 10 (1945).

Knight, T. S., '*In Defence of Romance*'. *Marriage and Family Living*, Vol. 21 (May, 1959).

Köhn-Behrens, Charlotte, *Eros at Bay*. London, 1962.

Kolb, Wilson L., 'Family Sociology, Marriage Education and the Romantic Complex: A critique'. *Social Forces*, Vol. 29.

Koller, Marvin R., 'Residential and Occupational Propinquity'. *American Sociological Review*, Vol. 13 (1948).

Koller, Marvin R., 'Some Changes in Courtship Patterns in Three Generations of Ohio Women'. *American Sociological Review*, Vol. 16 (1951).

Komarovsky, Mirra, *Women in the Modern World*. Boston, Mass., 1953.

Krich, A. M., (ed.), *Anatomy of Love*. New York, 1960.

Laing, R. D., *Interpersonal Perception*. London, 1966.

Landis, J. T., 'Length of time required to achieve adjustment in marriage'. *American Sociological Review*, Vol. 11 (1946).

Landis, J. T., and Landis, M. G., *Building a Successful Marriage*. New York, 1948.

Landis, Paul H., 'Control of the Romantic Impulse through Education'. *School and Society*, Vol. 34 (1936).

Latourette, Kenneth, *A History of Christianity*. New York, 1953.

Lawrence, D. H., *A Propos of Lady Chatterley's Lover and Other Essays*. London, 1967.

Leavis, Q. D., *Fiction and the Reading Public*. London, 1965.

Lecky, W. E. H., *History of European Morals*. London, 1869.

Leger, Pierre, *La Canadienne Francais et l'Amour*. Montreal, 1965.

Lemert, Edwin M., *Social Pathology*. New York, 1951.

Lepp, Ignace, *The Psychology of Loving*. New York, 1963.

Lewis, C. S., *The Allegory of Love*. London, 1936.

Lewis, C. S., *The Four Loves*. London, 1963.

Lewis, Robt. W., *Hemingway on Love*. Austin, Texas, 1965.

Licht, Hans, *Sexual Life in Ancient Greece*. London, 1931.

Lilar, Suzanne, *Aspects of Love in Western Society*. London, 1965.

Linton, Ralph, *The Study of Man*. New York, 1936.

Lobell, John and Mimi, *John and Mimi: a Free Marriage*. New York, 1972.

Locke, H. J., 'Marital adjustment'. *American Sociological Review*, Vol. 23 (1958).

Longworth, T. C., *The Worship of Love*. London, 1954.

Lowrie, S. H., 'Dating theories and student responses'. *American Sociological Review*, Vol. 16 (1951).

Lowrie, S. H., 'Early and late dating'. *Marriage and Family Living*, Vol. 23 (1961).

Lowrie, S. H., 'Factors involved in frequency of dating'. *Marriage and Family Living*, Vol. 18 (1956).

Lucka, E., *The Evolution of Love*. London, 1923.

Lynch, Hillquit, 'The Romantic Complex of the Adolescent'. Unpublished Ph.D. thesis, University of Texas (University Microfilms, 63–5248).

Mace, David and Vera, *Marriage East and West*. New York, 1959.

Mace, David and Vera, *The Soviet Family*. New York, 1964.

Madariaga, S. de, *Englishmen, Frenchmen, Spaniards, an Essay in Comparative Psychology*. London, 1929.

Magoun, F. A., *Love and Marriage*. New York, 1948.

Malinowski, Bronislaw, *The Sexual Life of Savages in North-western Melanesia*. London, 1969.

Mann, Peter H., *The Romantic Novel, A Survey*. London, 1969.

Mannheim, Karl, *Ideology and Utopia*. London, 1966.

Marcus, Steven, *The Other Victorians*. London, 1969.

Marcuse, Herbert, *Eros and Civilization*. London, 1969.

Marrou, Henri I., *Les Troubadours*. Paris, 1963.

Martin, Del, and Lyon, Phyllis, *Lesbian Woman*. New York, 1972.

Martinson, F. L., *Marriage and the American Ideal*. New York, 1960.

Maurois, André, *Seven Faces of Love*. New York, 1944.

May, Rollo, *Love and Will*. London, 1972.

Mayer, John E., *Jewish-Gentile Courtship*. Glencoe, Illinois, 1965.

McCaffrey, Joseph A. (ed.), *The Homosexual Dialectic*. New York, 1972.

McCall, G. J., and Simmons, J. L., *Identities and Interactions*. Glencoe, Illinois, 1966.

McGregor, O. R., *Divorce in England*. London, 1957.

McKinney, John, 'Constructive Typology', in John T. Doby (ed.), *An Introduction to Social Research*. New York, 1967.

Meister, Robert, (ed.), *A Literary Guide to Seduction*. London, 1963.

Moller, Herbert, 'The Social Causation of the Courtly Love Complex'. *Comparative Studies in Society and History*, Vol. 1 (1959).

Montagu, M. F. Ashley, *Marriage Past and Present: A debate between Robert Briffault and Bronislaw Malinowski*. Boston, Mass., 1956.

Montague, J. B., 'Adolescent Anxiety'. *American Sociological Review*, Vol. 20 (1955).

Mordell, Albert, *The Erotic Motive in Literature*. New York, 1962.

Morgan, E. S., 'The Puritan and Sex'. *New England Quarterly*, Vol. 15 (1942).

Muret, C. T., *Marriage as a Career*. New York, 1936.

Newcomb, Theodore M., 'The Prediction of Interpersonal Attraction'. *American Psychologist*, Vol. 11 (1956).

Niebuhr, Reinhold, *Faith and History*. New York, 1949.

Niebuhr, Reinhold, *The Nature and Destiny of Man*. New York, 1949.

Nimkoff, M., and Wood, A. L., 'Courtship and Personality'. *American Journal of Sociology*, Vol. 53 (1948).

Noonan, John T., *Contraception*. Cambridge, Mass., 1965.

Norton, David, and Kille, Mary, *Philosophies of Love*. San Francisco, California, 1972.

Nygren, Anders, *Agape and Eros*. London, 1953.

O'Neill, Nena and George, *Open Marriage*. London, 1973.

Ortega y Gasset, Jose, *On Love*. London, 1967.

Parca, Gabriella, *Italian Women Confess*. London, 1963.

Perutz, Kathrin, *Liberated Marriage*. New York, 1973.

Pike, E. Royston, *Love in Ancient Rome*. London, 1965.

Pineo, Peter C., 'Disenchantment in Later Years of Marriage'. *Marriage and Family Living*, Vol. 23 (1961).

Praz, M., *The Romantic Agony*. London, 1970.

Pursell, W. van Loenen, *Love and Marriage in Three English Authors*. Stanford, California, 1963.

Quinlan, M. J., *Victorian Prelude*. London, 1966.

Raymond, W. O., 'Browning's Conception of Love as represented in Paracelsus'. *Papers of the Michigan Academy of Science, Arts and Letters*, Vol. 4 (1924).

Reich, Wilhelm, *The Sexual Revolution*. London, 1972.

Reik, Theodor, *Of Love and Lust*. London, 1949.

Reisman, David, 'Listening to Popular Music' in *Individualism Reconsidered*. Glencoe, Illinois, 1954.

Reiss, Ira L., *Premarital Sexual Standards in the United States*. Glencoe, Illinois, 1960.

Reiss, Ira L., *Social Context of Premarital Sexual Permissiveness*. New York, 1967.

Reiss, Ira L., 'Toward a Sociology of Heterosexual Love Relationships'. *Marriage and Family Living*, Vol. 22 (1960).

Rham, Edith de, *The Love Fraud*. New York, 1965.

Rieff, Philip, *Freud, the Mind of the Moralist*. New York, 1961.

Rimmer, Robert H., *Adventures in Loving*. New York, 1973.

Rosenfels, Paul, *Homosexuality: The Psychology of the Creative Process*. New York, 1971.

Roszak, Theodore, *The Making of a Counter Culture*. London, 1971.

Rougemont, Denis de, *Love in the Western World*. New York, 1956.

Rougemont, Denis de, *The Myths of Love*. London, 1963.

Rougemont, Denis de, 'The Romantic Route to Divorce'. *Saturday Review of Literature*, Vol. 31 (November 13, 1948).

Russell, Bertrand, *Autobiography*. London, 1975.

Salerno, N. A., *Romantic Love in Victorian Poetry*. Unpublished Ph.D. thesis, Stanford University, 1962 (University Microfilms).

Santayana, G., *The Sense of Beauty*. New York.

Scaglione, A. D., *Love and Nature in the late Middle Ages*. Berkeley, California, 1963.

Schachter, Stanley, *The Psychology of Affiliation*. Stanford, California, 1972.

Schellenberg, J. A., and Bee, L., 'A re-examination of the theory of complementary needs'. *Marriage and Family Life*, Vol. 22 (1960).

Schneider, I., (ed.), *The World of Love* (2 vols). New York, 1964.

Schoepperle, G., *Tristan and Iseult, a Study in the Origins of Romance*. London, 1913.

Schofield, Michael, *The Sexual Behaviour of Young People*. London, 1970.

Seltman, Charles, *Women in Antiquity*. London, 1956.

Sherif, M., and Cantril, H., *The Psychology of Ego-involvement*. New York, 1947.

Shideler, Mary M., *The Theology of Romantic Love*. New York, 1962.

Simenson, W., 'Courtship Patterns of Norwegian and American University Students'. *Marriage and Family Living*, Vol. 18 (1956).

Simmel, Georg, 'The social role of the stranger', in E. A. Shuler *et al.*, *Outside Readings in Sociology*. New York, 1953.

Singer, Irving, *The Nature of Love*. New York, 1965.

Slater, E., and Woodside, M., *Patterns of Marriage: A study of marriage relationship in the urban working classes*. London, 1951.

Slater, Philip, 'Social Limitations on Libidinal Withdrawal'. *American Sociological Review*, Vol. 28 (1963).

Smith, E., 'Courtship Values in a Youth Sample'. *American Sociological Review*, Vol. 18 (1953).

Smith, William, 'Rating and Dating'. *Marriage and Family Living*, Vol. 14 (1952).

Sorokin, Pitirim, *The Ways and Power of Love*. Chicago, Illinois, 1967.

Spilka, Mark, *The Love Ethic of D. H. Lawrence*. Bloomington, Indiana, 1966.

Stark, Werner, 'Peasant Society and the Origins of Romantic Love'. *Sociological Review*, Vol. 1, New Series (December, 1953).

Stephens, W. N., *The Family in Cross-Cultural Perspective*. New York, 1963.

Stern, Karl, *The Flight from Woman*. New York, 1965.

Stevenson, David L., *The Love-game Comedy*. New York, 1966.

Strauss, Anselm, *Mirrors and Masks*. Glencoe, Illinois, 1959.

Strauss, Anselm, 'The ideal and chosen mate'. *American Journal of Sociology*, Vol. 52 (1946).

Sussman, Marvin (ed.), *Sourcebook in Marriage and the Family*. New York, 1955.

Sussman, Marvin, 'Parental Participation in Mate Selection and its Effects on Family Continuity'. *Social Forces*, Vol. 32 (1953).

Suttie, I. D., *The Origins of Love and Hate*. London, 1935.

Taylor, D. L., 'Courtship as Social Institution in the United States'. *Social Forces*, Vol. 25 (1946).

Terman, L. M., *Psychological Factors in Marital Happiness*. New York, 1938.

Theodorson, George A., 'Romanticism and Motivation to Marry in The United States, Singapore, Burma and India'. *Social Forces*, Vol. 44 (1965).

Thibaut, John, and Kelley, Harold, *The Social Psychology of Groups*. New York, 1959.

Tillich, Paul, *Love, Power and Justice*. London, 1960.

Toby, Jack, 'The Case against Romance' in Toby and H. C. Bredemier, *Social Problems in America*. New York, 1961.

Toffler, Alvin, *Future Shock*. London, 1973.

Trainer, Russell, *Sex and Love among the Poor*. New York, 1968.

Udry, Richard, *The Social Context of Marriage*. New York, 1966.

Valency, Maurice, *In Praise of Love*. London, 1958.

Van Deusen, Edmund L., *Contract Cohabitation: An Alternative to Marriage*. New York, 1974.

Vyvyan, John, *Shakespeare and the Rose of Love*. London, 1960.

Walker, Alexander, *Sex in the Movies*. London, 1968.

Waller, Willard, *The Family*. New York, 1951.

Ward, Maisie, *Robert Browning, The Private Life*. London, 1968.

Watt, Ian, *The Rise of the Novel*. London, 1972.

Watts, Alan W., *Nature, Man and Woman*. London, 1973.

Westermarck, E. A., *The Future of Marriage in Western Civilization*. London, 1936.

Westermarck, E. A., *Three Essays on Sex and Marriage*. London, 1934.

Whyte, Wm. F., 'A slum sex code'. *American Journal of Sociology*, Vol. 49 (1943).

Williams, Charles, *The Figure of Beatrice*. London, 1943.

Winch, R. F., 'Mate Selection', in R. F. Winch, (ed.), *Selected Studies in Marriage and the Family*. New York, 1962.

Winch, R. F., *The Modern Family*. New York, 1952.

Winch, R. F., 'The Theory of Complementary Needs in Mate Selection'. *American Sociological Review*, Vol. 20 (1955).

Wolff, Kent H., 'On Surrender', in Bennis and Schein (eds), *Interpersonal Dynamics*. Chicago, Illinois, 1964.

Yablonsky, Louis, *The Hippie Trip*. New York, 1968.

Young, Virginia, 'Love and Compulsion'. *Peace Research*. Toronto (January, 1974).

Young, Michael, and Willmott, Peter, *Family and Kinship in East London*. London, 1969.

Young, Wayland, *Eros Denied*. New York, 1964.

Zakuta, Leo, 'Equality in North American Marriages'. *Social Research*, Vol. 30, No. 2 (1963).

Zweig, Paul, *The Heresy of Self-Love*. New York, 1968.

More Fascinating Reading from Abacus:

PRIMAL MAN: THE NEW CONSCIOUSNESS
DR. ARTHUR JANOV AND DR. E. MICHAEL HOLDEN   £2·50

THE PRIMAL REVOLUTION
DR. ARTHUR JANOV   £1·75

THE PRIMAL SCREAM
DR. ARTHUR JANOV   £1·50

SEXUAL SIGNATURES
JOHN MONEY AND PATRICIA TUCKER   £1·50

PARAPSYCHOLOGY AND THE NATURE OF LIFE
JOHN L. RANDALL   £1·75

THE BOOK OF EST
LUKE RHINEHART   £1·75

THE AGE OF CAPITAL
E. J. HOBSBAWM   £3·50

THE AGE OF REVOLUTION: EUROPE 1789–1848
E. J. HOBSBAWN   £1·75

SMALL IS BEAUTIFUL
DR. E. F. SCHUMACHER   £1·75

INVENTING TOMORROW
MICHAEL ALLABY   £1·75

THE DEVIL'S PICTUREBOOK
PAUL HUSON   £1·75

AN ANATOMY OF DRAMA

MARTIN ESSLIN

An Anatomy of Drama begins by defining drama and showing how deeply rooted it is in society. Because drama is a
collective experience, of which the audience's reaction is a
vital part, it can be used not only to spread, but also to test
out objectively certain truths about ourselves.

Later chapters explore the connection between drama and
society, the nature of dramatic illusion, the relation between
the dramatist's style and the actor's performance, and the
place of theatre among the other media.

Martin Esslin is one of the few theatre critics who combine a wide and deep knowledge of international drama
with a close involvement in the day-to-day production of
plays. This conjunction of experiences enables him to provide, in this book, a highly stimulating view of drama both
as an art and as a function of the society in which we live.

0 349 111731   *Arts*   95p

LOVE AND ADDICTION

BY STANTON PEELE WITH ARCHIE BRODSKY

Revealing insights into the way many lovers are bound in a 'Protection Racket' based on their mutual needs.

Love and addiction: the juxtaposition is startling but perceptive. The Western world's favourite panaceas, love and drugs, are often resorted to from similar motivations of psychological insecurity. The other person in a 'love' relationship often serves simply as a 'fix' for the more dependent partner.

This provocative and challenging book, the work of a prominent social psychologist, focuses on personal relationships to explore what addiction really is – psychologically, socially and culturally. It presents lucid guidelines for analyzing existing relationships in terms of their potential for mutual growth, and it will help individuals to strengthen their own sense of identity. The ultimate goal is a stronger, independent self, and a capacity to love out of a positive desire to share oneself.

'A rare book, like "Future Shock", that is destined to become a classic!'

Psychology Today

0 349 12703 4   *Psychology*   £1·50   *Illustrated*

All Sphere Books are available at your bookshop or
newsagent, or can be ordered from the following address:
Sphere Books, Cash Sales Department,
P.O. Box 11, Falmouth, Cornwall.

Please send cheque or postal order (no currency), and allow
19p for postage and packing for the first book plus 9p per
copy for each additional book ordered up
to a maximum charge of 73p in U.K.

Customers in Eire and B.F.P.O. please allow 19p for
postage and packing for the first book plus 9p per copy
for the next 6 books, thereafter 3p per book.

Overseas customers please allow 20p for postage and packing
for the first book and 10p per copy for each additional book.